Trading Without Gambling

Develop a Game Plan for Ultimate Trading Success

MARCEL LINK

WILEY

John Wiley & Sons, Inc.

Published by John Wiley & Sons, Inc., Hoboken, New Jersey.
Published simultaneously in Canada.

For general information on our other products and services or for technical support, please
contact our Customer Care Department within the United States at (800) 762-2974, outside the
United States at (317) 572-3993 or fax (317) 572-4002.

Wiley also publishes its books in a variety of electronic formats. Some content that appears in
print may not be available in electronic books. For more information about Wiley products,
visit our web site at www.wiley.com.

Library of Congress Cataloging-in-Publication Data:

Link, Marcel.
    Trading without gambling : develop a game plan for ultimate trading success /
Marcel Link.
        p. cm. – (Wiley trading series)
    Includes index.
    ISBN 978-0-470-11874-0 (cloth)
    1. Speculation. 2. Futures. 3. Stocks. I. Title.
    HG6041.L564 2009
    332.64–dc22

                                                                2008022104

Printed in the United States of America.

10 9 8 7 6 5 4 3 2 1

Dedicated to all the people who bought my first book,
giving me the opportunity to write another, and,
to all the people I ignored and didn't have time for
while I wrote this book.

Contents

Acknowledgments

I'd like to thank the following people:

Stephen Isaacs of then McGraw-Hill for giving me a shot with my first book;

Dr. Alexander Elder, for assisting me in getting an agent for this book;

Ted Bonanno, that agent who helped me land a deal for this book with John Wiley & Sons;

Kevin Commins, Laura Walsh, and Emilie Herman of John Wiley & Sons for working with me on this book, for giving me free rein, and for putting up with my requests for extensions;

Those unfortunate copyeditors at Wiley who had to fix my grammar;

And last, my family for letting me ignore them while I finished up the book.

Introduction

So here I am again, writing another book. After the incredible runaway success of my debut smash book *High Probability Trading*, there was interest in another, so here I am. If you haven't read my first book you should instantly go out and buy a few copies of it now.

Anyway, *High Probability Trading* realistically took a trader through the steps of becoming a better trader showing him how to succeed and how to avoid pitfalls. It covered many aspects of trading including entering and exiting trades, money management, making and back testing systems and fighting many of the personal demons traders have.

NO GAMBLE TRADING

If you took everything from the first book, put it into a funnel and strained out the fluff, the key things would all boil down to one basic concept and that is the importance of making a trading and game plan to trade with, and following it, of course. This new book will take that concept and expand on it as I believe it to be the key to successful trading.

Many people look at trading as a gamble, and yes there is risk involved, but a well-prepared trader, with a solid game plan and discipline can learn to trade without gambling, the same way the professional gamblers do.

Though I'll show examples of my trading and talk about technical analysis, this book is not about how to pick market bottoms or giving you great trading systems, instead it will focus on how you can become a better trader. They key to winning in the markets is planning for it and knowing in advance how to react to certain situations, and this is what a game plan will do for you. Trading is not simply about buying and selling, but about the knowing when, and why to do so.

WHY THIS BOOK

I have found over the years that there are many ways to make and lose money in the market. For those who read my first book you'll know I have a very down to earth way of looking at the markets and my writing style is how I talk. I never say I'm trading the Standard and Poor's 500 futures, I say the S&Ps and that's how you will see it in this book. I try to write as if I'm talking to you as a friendly mentor, not some arrogant know-it-all lecturer. I'm not trying to make you believe I have the holy grail of trading or that I'm the best trader out there. I've been trading 20 years now and I've had my share of mistakes, but I learned from my mistakes, and believe me there were many. It is this learning process that I'll try to pass on to you. I got a call today from a trader in Hawaii, saying that he learned more from reading my first book than from his two years in grad school. I actually have gotten many e-mails and calls over the last few years thanking me for helping people become better traders. It's little things like that that make writing a book worthwhile, because as my first editor said to me, most people do not write books for the money.

Throughout the book I'll give examples of trades and positions I put on the day I'm writing. Lately, I've been mostly trading the Dow Jones electronic futures and the S&P E-mini, which I just refer to as the S&Ps most of the time, some crude and a few select stocks. So I'll probably be giving examples using those. You won't find charts from five years ago that show the perfect textbook head-and-shoulders pattern that an author researched for weeks trying to find to make a point. Instead, I'll give you patterns from the day I was writing. I tend to talk about my many mistakes over the years, and you'll gain a lot of knowledge if you learn from them like I have. Making mistakes and learning from them is the most powerful tool you could have. You learn a lot more from mistakes than from good trades, as you likely take good trades for granted and never realized why they are good. Many of the positive reviews I got about *High Probability Trading* said something like, "I wish I had read this book when I first starting trading, I would have saved a lot of money." "Mr. Link seems to have been looking over my shoulder as he wrote this book. I can clearly see so many things I have done wrong."

In setting out to write this book I realized I do not need to write a 700-page tome on trading. There really is not that much to say about creating a trading and game plan. What I will give you though is a concise, straight to the point idea on how to trade better by having these plans. I will do my best to not throw in a useless overflow of information. Though I do add a bit of humor and some interesting facts here and there that hopefully doesn't offend anyone. The goal of the book is to apply every subject to just one thing and that's how it relates to your trading plans. Whether I'm talking about stops, discipline, risk, entering a trade or anything else, it will relate to the trading and game plan.

Though I do talk about both trading and game plans, this book will be more about using a game plan than about making a basic trading plan. You'll understand what I'm talking about after the first few chapters.

I could detail what a game plan is here but my first couple of chapters won't be nearly as riveting if I do. What I can tell you are the basic benefits of a game plan:

- It will force you to select a trading style.
- It will encourage you to study the markets.
- It will help you pick the best trades.
- It will prepare you for what the market has to offer.
- It will help you monitor and exit trades.
- It will keep you from overtrading.
- It will keep you financially in line.
- It will keep you focused.
- It will take the gamble out of your trading.

And it will make you a better trader.

A LITTLE BIT ABOUT ME

When I started out I always thought trading was easy and fun. I was a little lackadaisical in preparing for the markets and was undisciplined. Yes, trading was easy, making money, however, wasn't as easy. I did so many things a trader should not do, that not surprisingly I lost a good amount of money trading. Even when I started I was really good at technical analyses and picking markets levels, however, I suffered in areas like discipline, overtrading, and not being prepared. What would happen is I'd do great for a while and then blow out. Granted, I was definitely undercapitalized at the beginning, but I still could have done okay if I had been disciplined. Having had the luxury of being in constant contact for 15 years with both successful, professional traders and those who didn't have a prayer, I've been able to see one key difference they possess. Winning traders worked hard at being knowledgeable and had a definite plan and trading strategy they consistently followed, and most of all they were disciplined about adhering to their plans. Once I was able to adopt those things, I was able to turn it around and become successful.

To side track for a second, I went to a seminar recently and the speaker was talking about what success means to different people. To some it means having the most dollars, houses, and toys. To me it means being able to do what I want. I can take six months off and do nothing and not worry. Three years ago I bought an upscale bar/lounge in Manhattan that did quite well and I was offered three times my investment after six months. Then I rented a ski house in Park City, Utah, and skied for 78 consecutive days. I traded in the morning until about noon (2 P.M. New York time), then walked the 30 seconds to catch the shuttle for the one-minute ride to the base of the mountain and skied for the next five hours. Two years ago I spent quite a bit of the fall in Provence and Tuscany doing absolutely nothing. And the last two years I have stayed home raising my kids. Now I'm about to opening up a new bar/restaurant. I may not make as much money as some big-time traders, but I believe I am more successful than most as I get to do a lot of things people envy.

A BRIEF PROFESSIONAL HISTORY

After a short stint as a stockbroker in 1987, I worked as a crude oil options clerk on the floor of the New York Mercantile Exchange. A few years later, I scraped together and borrowed $30,000 and began trading NYFE and U.S. Dollar Index futures on the floor of the New York Financial Exchange and Cotton Exchange. With the popularization of the E-minis in the late nineties, the NYFE has become practically obsolete. When I started, it was the poor man's version of the S&P futures, moving about half as fast and with smaller margin requirements. Being undercapitalized, I only lasted about three months before I lost half my capital on one mistake. Not having enough money to trade from the pit anymore, I joined forces with another trader and formed a trading partnership. We began to trade a few more markets, as well. While he stayed in the ring, I had a booth where I could look through charts, managing our positions and worked on system writing. Eventually we went our separate ways. I left the floor to trade out of a brokerage office, with several other experienced ex-floor traders.

Between 1995 and 1997, I took a break from trading full-time to go to graduate school. When I finished, I decided to start a discount brokerage firm called Link Futures. Online trading had just started creeping into the futures industry at that time, with relatively few firms having an Internet presence. We offered deep discount brokerage and had a trading room where traders could trade from. Unfortunately, as the Internet caught on, larger firms and clearinghouses started undercutting each other in price and once again I was undercapitalized to compete and make it thrive. The bright side of this was that my trading started to get consistently better as I watched what my clients did wrong.

In March 2000, when I was offered a position to trade equities, it didn't take much thought to decide to go for it. My potential as a trader was much greater than with the brokerage firm, so I made the move to concentrate on being a proprietary equity trader.

In 2002, I set out to write *High Probability Trading* and got fired because it was against the company's policy for employees to write anything or talk to the media. So I decided to just trade futures from home. The book ended up doing fairly well and I was amazed at its success and the reviews from people who read it and said they wished they had read it years ago. And though I recall how time-consuming and tedious it was writing that book, here I am again.

Good luck. Enjoy the book and feel free to e-mail me at Marcel_Link@yahoo.com, or visit my web site MarcelLink.com.

CHAPTER 1

Everyone Needs a Plan

A new wide-eyed, aspiring trader asks a learned, wealthy, success-ful trader, "How can I end up with a million dollars in the stock market?" The old trader scratches his head and after some thought says, "Start with $2 million."

I was having trouble figuring out how to start this chapter and therefore this book, until I was listening to a New York Mets game in my car last week. During a rain delay the announcer, Steve Somers, was talking about Pedro Martinez, a three time Cy Young award winner, and for those non-baseball people, that means he was the best pitcher in baseball for the year. Somers was talking about how good a pitcher Pedro is and how he has been able to adjust due to injuries and age, as well as how he can adjust to batters in a game. He was saying Pedro has many different game plans, and he can easily switch them once he is in a game. This ability to know what is and isn't working is what makes him one of the most dominant pitchers in baseball.

THE HANGING CURVEBALL

And I was thinking, "Hey, this is a great analogy for what I'm trying to say." So here is how I would describe it. Pedro Martinez has a main plan (which is like a trader's trading plan); that plan is to do everything possible to win. It includes mastering his pitches, knowing the opposition, and stay-ing healthy by eating right, resting, and working out. He has worked hard to develop his pitch selection arsenal, his pinpoint control, and his ability to throw from different arm angles and speeds. These are all things that were done prior to his pitching on any given day. Part of his main (trading) plan is to know when he is getting tired and when to come out of a game. His main plan doesn't change often, but he will be constantly reevaluating it to make sure it is working and for ways to improve it. For example, in recent years he's added a cut fastball to his regular fastball and his speed has dropped from the low 90s to the mid to upper 80s, though he can reach back and still throw a little faster when needed. Once he is happy with his main plan it pretty much stays the same until the next evaluation.

However, each individual game and situation brings something new to the plate, and Pedro has different game plans he will use depending on the situation. As part of the game plan he will study opposing batters to learn what does or doesn't work. He will have an overall game plan for the game as well as adjustable plans for each batter. He doesn't just rely on throwing a fastball for strikes. He knows there are times he can rest his arm and try to get groundball outs instead. Some items in this game plan could be, if the curve is working, keep throwing it. If Barry Bonds is swinging at pitches in the dirt, keep throwing them there. If another batter is not going for them then throw it closer to the strike zone for him. If the count is 0–2 throw a changeup or a curve, unless Jeter is batting and keeps hitting those. If his fastball up and inside is not working, throw it low and away. If so and so hitter has been hitting curves away lately, pitch him inside. When something is not working, he figures out what it is and fixes it. A lot of this mental work is done between innings and with the help of a coach, not in between pitches, when his emotions could get the best of him.

With injuries and age slowing down his fastball in the last few years, Pedro relies more on control these days and he is able to adjust in a game. What makes him an outstanding pitcher is his ability to adjust. Similarly, a trader needs to review his game plan and adjust his positions all the time. The best pitchers will do this, while the poor ones keep throwing hanging curves and never learn to adjust. They get sent back to minors and then end up selling used cars a couple of years later.

Sorry to those readers who haven't a clue what I just wrote. I'm sure someone in France is saying, "Merde, what eez zeez 'hanging curve?' Zeelly Americaans wizz zeer zeelly games. Now futbol—zat eez a game."

So to clarify, a hanging curve is a bad pitch that often leads to a home run. A curveball is a pitch that is slower then a fastball and is supposed to curve away from the batter, making it hard to hit. However, a hanging curveball fails to curve and just hangs like a big fat grapefruit, making it quite easy to hit. A pitcher who does this often will not be a pro very long.

A TYPICAL BAD TRADER

So how does this relate to trading? Let's say John, the really bad trader, has been long crude oil for two days now, and is up $2.00 on the trade. He got long because all he hears about on TV is how crude is going to the moon and because he just paid $3.00 a gallon at the pump last week. Now two days later, it opens 20 cents lower and sells off a bit, and he fears the worst and sells it at the market. By the end of the day however, it has rallied up a dollar and a few days later it's up four bucks from there with barely a down move. Not only did he never get back in, in fact he shorted it, because he thought it would retrace a bit giving him a chance to get back in on the long side. By the end of the week he's lost $4,000 on a trade that should have made him $4,000.

Why? Because he never had a trading plan for the trade or a game plan for what to do with it after he got in. He threw a bad pitch because he didn't do his homework and then threw a few more as he wasn't prepared and let his emotions get the better of him. His reasons for getting into the trade were not thought out. High gas prices alone are not a good reason to buy oil impetuously. You need to thoroughly think out a trade before jumping in. And then, once in the trade, John had no idea what he wanted out of it. You cannot trade this way and expect to make money. You should always have a plan for your trades if you want to make it as a trader, as trading on impulses will not get you very far.

A TYPICAL GOOD TRADER PREPARED WITH A PLAN

On the other hand, a good trader will make a thorough analysis of the situation before jumping in. He might take a look to see where crude oil is on a chart, considering: Is it overbought? How much risk is involved? How much can he hope to make on the trade, and so on? After meeting any criteria he may have, he will next look to time an entry if he has decided to get in. One of the things that make this trader better is that after deciding to buy, but before getting in, he will start to make an exit strategy for the trade. After getting in he will evaluate the trade on a regular basis.

Basically, he would have a both a plan of attack and a defensive strategy for the trade, or more precisely he would have a game plan for the trade from start to finish.

If you look at Figure 1.1, you can see the situation where these scenarios could have happened. Crude oil was in the news a lot these days as

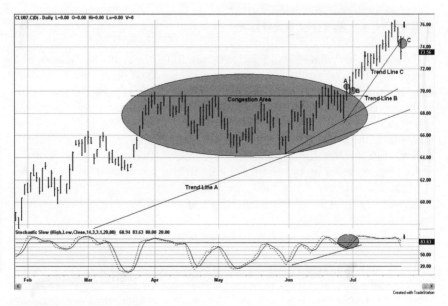

FIGURE 1.1 Crude Oil
Source: © TradeStation Technologies 1999. All rights reserved.

gas prices were at record highs, and it looked like the market was going for another record high after being in a congestion stage for a short while in the strong uptrend. Though a prudent trader wouldn't jump into a trade based on it being in the news, let's just say Harry, from here on in, the good trader, looked at the chart the day of the shaded circle A, drew a couple of trend lines and said, "You know what, this looks like a good situation. It meets all my criteria [his trading plan]: It's in a major uptrend [not seen in its entirety in this chart but shown with Trend Line A]. It is fairly close to the trend line; it just broke out of a small congestion area at $70, retraced a bit and now has broken out again; it is near all-time highs; and the risk measured by Trend Line B is acceptable, given the potential for it to take off. A good place to have a stop would be just below that trend line so the risk is about two points. The stochastics are high, but not yet crossing over, and the upward trend line in them is a bullish signal. Should the stochastics turn below the overbought area I'll get out, as if the market breaks the trend line."

Now Harry has made a trade that fits his trading style and the criteria set out in his trading plan. Plus, he has made a game plan as to what to do with it. He doesn't get shaken out two days later at circle B like John does, but instead holds for another week and sells at circle C when both the trend line C is broken and the stochastics cross below the overbought territory. Harry likes to draw trend lines and since the market got pretty steep, he adjusted the angle to come up with trend line C. The bottom line is that Harry, having a game plan, makes close to $4,000 per contract while John, the yo-yo, lost $4,000 on the same trade.

By the way, I'm editing the book now and wrote the above more than a year ago. Crude oil has since hit $135 dollars a barrel. Good thing I didn't start shorting when I thought it was overpriced at $70. And Pedro Martinez since has torn his calf muscle, spent most of last year on the disabled list with a torn rotator cuff, and followed that up at the beginning of this year with a strained hamstring; so much for that staying-healthy theory I had earlier. It just goes to show how things can change.

THE TRADING PLAN AND THE GAME PLAN

What this book is all about is how to reduce the gambling aspect of trading. Many people perceive trading as nothing more than a gamble. And to many traders it is. But there are many traders, who year after year and month after month make money trading. They have learned how to separate gambling from trading and their results show that it is possible to do. I believe anyone can do it as well if they are willing to do the work it takes. For me, that hard work is developing and trading with a plan. There is probably no greater tool you can have then a proper, well thought out plan.

When I talk about plans I refer to two types, the trading plan and the game plan. Though they work together, they are two different creatures that rely on each other to work. A good trading plan with no game plan won't work. That's like Pedro having the best fastball and curveball in world but not knowing when to throw them or who to throw them at. On the other hand, without a trading plan, a game plan is not nearly as strong. It's like Pedro deciding he needs to throw a knuckleball in a tough situation, but realizing too late he never learned how to throw one. But once he gets both of these plans working together, he can win a lot of games and be the superb pitcher he is.

This holds for traders as well. The main reasons for having these plans are to ensure you make smart trading decisions all the time, to help you exit a trade and to make sure you know what you are risking and how much you stand to gain prior to making a trade. Without the aide of plans, you are starting behind the eight ball. Your chances of succeeding are so much smaller if you are trading haphazardly, as opposed to when you have a proper plan to guide you. Throughout this book you will see just how important a trading and game plan will be in making you a better trader. I've traded with and without a trading and game plan, and I know for sure, my results are exponentially better when I have the guidance of a proper plan behind me.

If you have read my first book, *High Probability Trading*, you will know that I stress that having a plan is a very important ingredient in becoming a top trader. In that book, I had a chapter devoted to trading and game plans. And it is from there that I got the idea for this book.

The Trading Plan

The trading plan comes first, and it is the board based trading strategy each trader should have. It should reflect a trader's trading style, trading strategies, and risk aversion. A trading plan doesn't have to have a system set in stone, but it can have known-to-work strategies like "buy dips in an uptrend and don't risk more then 5 percent of equity on any given trade." A trading plan won't change much from day to day, as it consists of a trader's systems and money management plans. It does need to be reviewed on a regular basis, but overall it usually stays the same. Though this book is not about how to make a trading plan, I'll expand on the basics of doing so in the next chapter.

The Game Plan

Once a trading plan is in place, a trader needs a plan to be able to attack the markets on a day-to-day basis. This will be the game plan and it will change constantly as it reflects new market conditions. Markets have something new to offer all the time and a well-prepared trader can take advantage of this by preparing how to react in advance. This may include moving stops, knowing what you will do after an unemployment number is released, or waiting for a market to reach a trend line before getting in. The game plan will include finding trades, timing, knowing how much to trade, where to exit, and how to adjust risk. You should reevaluate your positions on a regular basis and come up with new scenarios so that you can alter your game plan as the market changes. This book will focus more than anything on how to use a game plan to your advantage. And if you learn how to make and use one, you will become a trader who leaves very little to gambling.

A DISCLOSURE OR TWO BEFORE WE CONTINUE

Now, before I continue, I just want to make it clear that these are just my ideas and should not be taken as gospel or the holy grail of what a trading and game plan are. These are just outlines on which you should expand. This book is not for the lazy trader. You will not find any get-rich-quick strategies or systems to make you a million dollars. This book will make you a better, more alert trader, but you will have to work to improve your trading. Hopefully though, after reading it you will have a couple more tools in your arsenal that will lead you in the right direction. I know you are trying to be a better trader because you bought this book and that's a start. If you are glancing through this book in a bookstore, just take the plunge and buy it. Anyway, I hope I can help you.

CHAPTER 2

The Trading Plan

A trader and God are speaking. The trader asks God, "What is a million years like to you?" "Like one second," answers God. The trader then asks, "What is a million dollars like to you?" God answers, "Like one penny." The trader then asks, "Can you spare a penny?" "Sure," says God, "give me a second."

As I get started with the basis of the book I need to spend the next two chapters distinguishing in more detail between a trading plan and a game plan. I also need to lay out the foundations of how to make and use each of these plans. This chapter deals with the trading plan, and you can probably guess what the next one is about.

WHAT IS A TRADING PLAN?

So what is a trading plan? In its simplest form a trading plan is a basic guideline a trader uses giving him a reason for any trade he makes. It doesn't have to be elaborate or complex, though the more detailed it is, the better. A trading plan encompasses all your trading thoughts and is a combination of a few things. First, it's a combination of a trading system or trading methodology that generates both entry and exit signals. This doesn't have to be a mechanical system that automatically generates signals, but it can be a simple trading strategy you follow with discretion. Regardless of which it is, the strategy points you in the right direction. Without a strategy a trader would have no method of knowing when to buy and sell, in which case he'd be trading randomly.

The second main part of the trading plan consists of money management parameters. This is where amongst other things a trader figures out how much he is willing to risk in general, at any given time, and per trade. An example would be to risk no more than 4 percent of total capital on any given trade or to not have more than $10,000 at risk at any given time. Money management should not be taken lightly; in my opinion it's more important than trade selection. No matter how good you are, you will be wrong often and it only takes one uncontrolled trade to wipe you out. It's money management alone that will make the difference between blowing out and being around for the next trade. Make sure you spend the time to have a solid money management approach as it may save you one day.

A trading plan doesn't have to be written on paper, but it does help immensely to actually write one out and then periodically review it. If you don't have one written out, start thinking about doing it. Read through this chapter once to get the gist of what I'm talking about and then reread it to get you started on making your trading plan. Even a simple plan is better than no plan. If at the very least you know how much to risk per trade and what market scenarios to trade, you will improve your trading.

A SIMPLE TRADING PLAN

A trading plan could be as simple as:

> *Buy two contracts whenever the market (for the rest of this book market can mean stock, index, futures, or anything you trade) is in an uptrend and it has been down for two days and on the third day it opens positive and stays positive after 30 minutes. Exit with a stop loss if the market goes below the low of the previous day, exit with a profit if the market has moved up five points or after three days. This trade may only be done if the risk is less than two points.*

This is a trading plan I just made up, and I have no idea if it works. Though simple, it includes a trading strategy both for entry and exits, and a money management parameter in the sense of a stop, position size, and total risk. Someone could follow this every day and not have to think very hard about what he is doing. However, before one does follow it, he should take the time to check and see if it has been successful in the past. Later in this chapter I'll discuss how to make a more professional trading plan. For now I just want to show the basics.

WHY A TRADING PLAN?

The most inclusive answer would be: to make money. A trading plan will include trading strategies that you should have tested that give you the best chance of winning, in other words, the high probability ones with a back tested positive expectancy. Without a plan, traders are trading on whims and could go long one day and short the next, given the same the market conditions and scenarios. They have nothing to judge their trades on and therefore may act differently one day from the next based on their bias. This turns trading into a crapshoot, which as you may infer from the title of this book we are hoping to avoid. With a proper plan you will have a real reason to be in a trade and will reduce emotional and spur of the moment decisions, as these types of trading decisions will not normally lead to a positive bankroll. If all your decisions were made during nonmarket hours with timing and execution being your main concern during market hours, you will dramatically increase your chances of success. An example of this would be the crude trade in the previous chapter. It was a spur of the moment trade by John, with little thought process as he had no plan to base his trade on. Meanwhile, when Harry made the trade it was because it fit into his trading plan, and he was able to profit from it because it was planned out.

By having a trading plan you will not be chasing the markets or making trades due to a news flash or some other silly reason. You will also reduce the number of trades made, which will save you a ton of money on commissions. Plus, you will always know when to exit every trade, which is as important as getting in. By not sticking to a plan, you can easily fall into the trap of throwing hanging curve after hanging curve when losing in hopes of recouping losses. A trading plan will keep you focused throughout the day and hopefully limit your foolishness. Another reason for having a trading plan is so you know just how much to risk and where you should set stops to take a loss. If you have a maximum loss level and it gets hit, it shouldn't freak you out because you would have been prepared for it, however, if you never set a maximum loss level, you could watch your whole account disappear as you hope for a rebound.

The trading plan will give you a predetermined reason for every trade, which in turn will lower the gambling aspect of your trading. Good traders do not rely on luck. Yes, luck is great to have, just like when playing poker, but like a good poker player, a good trader doesn't rely on luck in the long run, instead he has his skills, strategy, and rules that, when followed, allow him to act and react to all conditions and come up on top. And this is all made possible through successful planning, not by accident or luck.

POKER EXAMPLE

I like to compare good traders to good poker players. By "good" I mean those who can make a living playing the game. A good poker player becomes good not by playing hand after hand, but by learning the game as he plays those hands. He takes the time to learn the odds of getting cards and knowing how much to risk on a hand in order to have favorable odds. For example, if he has an 8 to 1 chance of making a card and there is $200 in the pot then by betting $10 he is getting 20 to 1 odds, making this a nice bet. If the pot had only 40 bucks in it then he is making a foolish bet as he is only getting 4 to 1 odds while taking an 8 to 1 chance of hitting his card. Part of his plan is to only make bets when he has favorable odds versus pot odds. He doesn't chase inside straights when the pot odds are against it, like an amateur would. Another part of his plan would be to know his bankroll and to know what dollar size game he can play and how much he can afford to lose on any given night, so that he can keep playing the next day. A player can't have a chance of winning at a table where hands start at $100 if he only has $500 to play with. However, he has more then enough to win at a $5 table. Also, if a player has been playing for a while he makes notes of opponents, so he knows who is aggressive and who is tight, who bluffs and when, who he can bluff, and who never goes out. Bluffing is an acquired skill and a good player knows when he can and cannot get away with it. He starts to pick up signs (tells) other players give when they have good or bad hands. Part of his plan is knowing that Fred plays with his chips when he has a good hand, so it would be wise to fold. Little factors such as this are what a good poker player sits down to the table with, and in the long run he will outplay the average schmo who sits down and bets hand after hand without a clue as to what he is doing.

A BUSINESS PLAN FOR TRADERS

Putting together a proper plan will force a trader to focus on his strengths while letting him avoid conditions that are unfavorable. In High Probability Trading, I refer to a trading plan as a trader's business plan. Very few businesses succeed without a business plan, so why should a trader think he's above it? Trading is a business and don't ever forget it or take it as less than that. Business plans are made either before going into business or when trying to raise more capital once in business. This should hold true as well for traders. Before you get serious about trading full-time, you should take some time and put together your business plan.

Make believe you are going to raise money from people to trade with. When a CTA (commodity trading advisor) or hedge fund manager makes a disclosure document, he is in effect making an elaborate trading plan, as everything that should be in a trading plan is in his disclosure document. Basically it includes his objective, strategy, risk, costs, and expected returns. Your goal should be to know the same and you should do it before you risk a dime.

You won't just say, "Hey Harry, I have an idea that will make us a lot money in crude futures. Give me $250,000 and I'll do my best, I think we can make $2 million, with almost no risk." Well Harry may have some colorful and somewhat painful suggestions as to what you can do with your idea. Instead you should give him a detailed plan of what you are going to do, how you plan to do it, how much is at risk, and what are the chances of losing his investment. Then let him make an intelligent decision based on the information you gave him. Now, if this plan was important for Harry to make a decision, it should be even more so for you as it's your freaking money on the line when you are trading.

MAKING A TRADING PLAN

Now that hopefully you see the importance of a trading plan, it's time to start making one. Though a proper trading plan can have anything you feel should go in it, it should account for the following parameters:

- Entering a trade.
- Exiting a trade.
- Stop placement.
- Position sizing.
- Money management parameters.
- What to trade.
- Trading time frames.
- Back testing.
- Performance review.
- Risk vs. reward.

Each one of these things is a critical part of trading, but when combined they become an invaluable and powerful trading tool. Other things that are not so easy to pinpoint but should be taken into account are a trader's emotional makeup and his trading style. Each trader will have a unique trading and risk style, which is why it is impossible to have a canned trading plan that anyone can use. If a trading plan doesn't fit your trading style and thoughts, you will have trouble following it no matter how good it is, which means each trader should custom build his own. A good book really can't give you a trading plan that will work for you, but it can give you guidelines to help make one that fits your trading style and risk tolerance. Sure, many books will give you systems that work, but a system is only part of a trading plan. And without money management it is useless. Though this book leans more to trading with a game plan than a trading plan, my first book will give you enough ideas to put together a solid trading plan. But you still have to make it yourself.

As you start making a more elaborate and professional looking trading plan you should go back to the idea of trying to convince someone to give you money. In that case, people would want to know some basics like what kind of returns are reasonable to expect? Does this include the trading costs? How much can they lose at worst? Are there any unexpected variables that can wipe you out? They'll ask about your trading strategy, which includes entry and exits; which markets, stocks, or sectors you will trade; what will be your hold times; how will you use stops; did you back test this system, and so on. They will also want to know about your money management plan, which will tell them how much you will risk at once, how you will prevent yourself from losing all of the money, how many markets you will be trading, and so on. If you can answer these questions you will be a much better trader than someone who can't.

BREAKING DOWN THE TRADING PLAN

The Trading Methodology or System

For starters, a trading plan will include a system or trading methodology you will use to trade with. A trading system is basically a set of rules and conditions that will get you in and out of the market. You can have several systems, if you like, that differ with different market conditions. Some people hear the words "trading system" and think it must have computer generated signals. That's not true; systems do not have to be mechanical. They can be totally discretionary as long as they follow the same rules all the time. A signal in a system can simply be buy on Tuesday if Monday is an up day. Or it could be a discretionary methodology you use to make trades. You may look at several indicators and then make a decision based on them in combination with a news story. It doesn't matter as long as you're consistent and have rules you follow. But regardless of whether it's computer generated or not, make sure you back test the system over historical data. The main drawback with nonmechanical systems is that it's much harder to back test discretionary systems. You can learn the hard way to see if your ideas work, which is by losing money in the market, or you can back test. You want to make sure your ideas have a history of working, because if they didn't work in the past, they probably won't work tomorrow.

By having a system or methodology, you will know how and what you will trade; nothing should come as a surprise and you will reduce the number of bad trades you make. Oh, I'm certain you will still make lots of bad trades. But you'll probably make fewer. Bad trades are different from losing trades. Many good trades will not work out and you may lose on them, however, bad trades are stupid mistakes that a system can prevent. With a system, you'll know that if a certain condition is met you will be in the market, and win or lose this has proven to be a good trade in the past. However, no matter how bored you are or how much extra margin you have, if these conditions or criteria are not met you shouldn't do anything.

Don't Forget about Getting Out   One thing I need to stress is that entering a trade is only half a trade. You need to get out of them as well. Too many people come up with great buy signals but then forget they have to exit a trade. Even more important than getting you into a trade, a system must have rules for getting you out of the trade as well. Don't ignore this part of trading, the exit really is the difference between what makes a winning or losing trader. Look back at the crude trade, an exit strategy is what makes one a better trade than the other. A good system will have options for getting you out of winning, losing, or break-even trades. I would say that before you even enter a trade, you should know where or why you would get out, both with a winning and a losing trade. I didn't use the word "stops," but it is implied in this paragraph. Though a game plan will monitor the stops, the trading plan sets the parameters for them. What's good about having predetermined exit rules is that once in a trade, a trader can relax a bit and not have to look at the market tick by tick.

Money Management   Though a trading system is important, money management and risk parameters are an even more important part of the trading plan than the actual buy and sell signals. You need to know how much to risk, how many contracts or shares to trade, when to increase position size, and which stocks or markets you can afford to trade. A money management plan will let you know how many total trades you can have on at once and how much you should risk in each and/or in total. Knowing how to use the proper position size is a large part of money management and also of determining how well you do. Trading more than you can afford to lose can easily get you into trouble, even if you are right on a trade. If you trade above your means, you may not be able to hold the position when there is a little blip against you. So even though you were correct in the long run, you may end up exiting with a loser.

If you work on a good risk plan you will reduce the chances of blowing out. I know that anytime I took a really big hit it wasn't because I was wrong in the market (yes I was wrong, but the reason I blew out was I used poor money management and traded too large a position or allowed myself to risk too much on a trade). Hell, I even blew out once being right in the market direction. But I tried so large a position that I panicked when it immediately went against me, and I reversed my position trying to make up the loss.

Do yourself a favor and take the time before you trade to come up with a good risk plan as it will make having and following a game plan so much easier. If you have been trading for years, take an hour and evaluate what you think is your risk strategy. Later in the book I'll go over money management plans in detail. I'm not sure which chapter it is yet. Just look in the table of contents if you can't wait to get to it.

Knowing Your Trading Mentality

When making a trading plan you should figure out which stocks, sectors, or commodities you will trade. Markets move differently from each other, some trend more often, while others are choppier, some are wilder than others with wider ranges, and therefore you have to trade less size and use wider stops. People have preferences for some markets over others and this is all part of their trading mentality. Unless you are using a software program that scans everything and tells you which stocks/markets meet your criteria, your trading plan should be tailored to the stocks or commodities you will be looking to trade.

For some people it's fairly easy, they just trade the S&Ps, others may only trade oil driller stocks, while others may include any stock over $20 with at least a million shares a day traded. It's not important what you plan on trading, just know it in advance so that during market hours you can focus on trading and not have to worry about finding markets.

Another part of the trading mentality is determining your trading time frames when you are making a system. Some people can hold stuff for years while others get fidgety after 12 seconds. The shorter the term you hold, the more you will trade and the smaller your stops and targets will be. I'm definitely not a quick in and out guy, so I can't follow a system that my friend Bruce, who makes 200 trades a day, would use. I prefer holding for a few days to a couple of weeks. So I have larger targets and therefore bigger equity swings. When he holds stuff overnight he will call me and everyone else he knows who trades 15 times to see what we think. He then sleeps like a baby, waking up every hour or two crying. Again, everyone is different and this difference should be incorporated into the trading plan.

Back Testing

I touched upon this already, but if you want to succeed take the time to make sure your ideas work. Back testing your systems is so critical it can't be overstated. Though there are software programs like TradeStation that will do it for you, if you are computer illiterate, take a chart and do it by hand. And when you do back test, keep in mind trading costs. Do not make the stupid mistake of back testing a system and forgetting to include how much commissions, fees, slippage, software, live feeds, exchange fees, and so forth will take out of your account. Make sure these are accounted for or you will be in for a surprise. Bruce, who is a very active day trader, has days when his commission costs are over $5,000. Tack that onto losing days and your account will go deep into the red faster than you'd like.

CLOSING THOUGHTS

The main reason for the lack of trading plans is that they can be time-consuming and difficult to make. Most people want to get right to trading and don't want to spend the time and energy needed to write out a trading plan, so they ignore it. This is one of the biggest mistakes a person will make, because the lack of guidance from a main plan will just lead to many, many more mistakes. Having a plan on paper will help you establish and keep to concrete rules, while helping you avoid emotional decisions made when the market is heated up or you are losing. People are irrational and can become horrible traders when under the gun and losing. If you have set rules hopefully you will follow them and keep on track. Finally, I want to say that you should keep reviewing your performance and plan. You can't improve unless you learn from mistakes. Reviewing is an important aspect of trading as you'll see throughout this book.

CHAPTER 3

The Game Plan

Harry and John are talking. John says to Harry he recently lost big in the market. Harry asks, "Were you a bull or a bear?" "Neither," says John, "just a plain simple ass."

After developing a trading plan, a trader should then come up with a game plan that will help him to implement that trading plan. The game plan regulates the day to day decisions one makes when trading and is what is used to execute the trading plan. The difference between a game plan and a trading plan is that a trading plan may specify buying X number of contracts when the market is within half a point from a trend line and risk two points on the other side of it should it break through. The X is determined by a formula in the money management plan part of the trading plan. The game plan will then be used to identify when the criteria is met, to time entry into the trade, to determine how many contracts to actually trade, to prepare the exit strategies, to monitor the risk, and do anything else vital to the success of that trade. The importance of the game plan is that it prepares you for the trade while making trading a little bit easier.

ALWAYS BE PREPARED

Trading decisions are best done when the market is closed, giving the trader something to work with when the market opens. When I used to day-trade stocks I'd go home every night and review the market. I make a list of which stocks I'd want to buy and which I'd want to short. I already had trading strategies, now I just needed to find trades and setups. I'd look for trend lines and areas of support and resistance or breakout levels, where I wanted to be involved. Plus, I also planned where I wanted to get out or reverse my positions. The next day when trading, I'd already have a list of what I wanted to trade and at what levels and both targets and stop areas; this was my game plan for the day. My trading plan told me what my stock criteria was, for example, stocks trading above $20 a share with average daily volume over 500,000 shares and an average trading range of over $1.00. It told me how much I could risk and what technical indicators I would use to confirm these trades. But on a day-to-day basis the game plan was what I used to trade with. I always reevaluated my game plan at lunchtime and made any adjustments to it should the market have changed. I tried to identify new opportunities to trade in the afternoon and reevaluated my risk levels and stops on open positions so that I was always prepared. I now trade mostly the Dow Jones and S&P 500 futures indexes but the idea is the same. The market has been in a strong uptrend the last four months as I write this in November 2006, so I don't do much in and out trading during the day; instead, I hold and monitor my trades, moving stops and adjusting risk and trying to figure out when the market may top and what I will do when it does. But as part of my game plan, I look for additional buying opportunities when the market opens lower, and I'll make a day-trade after 3 P.M. if the market is strong.

WHY A GAME PLAN

The main reason for a game plan is to keep you focused on the market while helping you to make the best possible trading decisions you can. Without a game plan you can be compelled to trade on whims, out of boredom, because of a news event, to recoup losses, or because some other trader liked it. These types of trades are the result of either not having or not following a game plan. With a good game plan, a trader can have different strategies for different scenarios and will know how to react regardless of what the market does. The market is unpredictable and a trader needs to be flexible when trading. If something happens, he'll hopefully be prepared for it, making only anticipated trades instead of trades made for the excitement of trading. Sure, by being more selective, there will be times when, in hindsight, you will wish you'd made a big trade. But unless the trade is part of your plan, it's okay to miss it. So what if you miss a few trades, there will be many more trading opportunities, so don't worry about capturing every move of the market. Instead, focus on making the best trades.

THE BASICS OF THE GAME PLAN

I'm not going to get too detailed in the rest of this chapter as that's what the rest of the book is about, and then I'd have a big fat book that repeats itself. So for now, let's just say the bottom-line basics are knowing *what you will trade, how much you will trade, where you will enter,* and *where you will exit.* Everything else including money management is to support and establish these points. I'll briefly go through a few of the important aspects that will help to make the basics easier. These will all be covered in greater depth throughout the book.

KNOW YOURSELF

This applies to the trading plan as well. In order to have any chance of succeeding and following a plan, you must cater it to fit your style. Simply put, you will have trouble trading if you are going against your basic tendencies. And no matter how good a plan it is, it will be hard to stick to if it is not your own. What works for some just won't work for others. People have different time frames, risk parameters, disciplines, and styles. Some like to go long all the time, some like going short, some like trading with the trend and some look for reversals, and so on. If traders didn't have different styles, no one would ever be able to buy a stock as everyone else would be trying to do so at the same time with no sellers in sight. Different styles and thoughts are what make liquidity in trading possible. People can make money regardless of what their style of trading is, just make sure you find one that fits your makeup, if you want to succeed. As I write this book I'll do so in the style that works best for my character. Your job is to take my concepts out of the book and then develop your own plans. Do not expect to find the holy grail of trading in my words. Instead, you'll find what I feel comfortable with and what works for me, but keep in mind I may have a higher risk tolerance than you do.

DRAWING UP SCENARIOS

The thing I found to work best for me is to draw up every possible scenario that could happen. Do this both before you get in and then once you are in the trade to really help you. Most novice traders only dream about the big profits they are going to make and forget to consider that the market may go against them. They then have no strategy for what to do if it does, becoming like deer in headlights. But if you had predetermined that you'd get out at some set point, you begin to make trading so much easier and more profitable.

I'm a firm believer in letting your profits ride. If you are an investor you can hold on for years, but as a trader you need to be realistic about when to get out. If you are day-trading a stock with an average trading range of $1.20 a day and it's up $1.10 on the day, and there is no special news to make it move more, it may be a good idea to get out or even short if that is your style. You can accomplish this by drawing up scenarios and knowing that if the stock moves over $1.00 you will look to time an exit. Though I like to draw up my scenarios during off market hours, I do review the market throughout the day to see if I have to make any adjustments to my plan.

WORST-CASE SCENARIOS

As with everything in life you should always be prepared for the worst that can happen. As part of a game plan try to think of everything that could go wrong with your trades, whether you can control them or not. At least by knowing the risk factors involved, you could be prepared to do something about them. If you haven't thought them through, then should the worst happen, you will be in for a shocker and may freeze up not knowing what to do. You can have everything planned so nice and perfect and then a rumor of a terrorist attack drops the Dow 200 points in a heartbeat and the whole market dynamics change, not to mention your P&L. There is little you can do about it; just know that anything can happen in trading. When I was a foolish know-it-all 22-year-old trading on the floor, I took a big hit when the market nosed-dived one Friday. My game plan at the time was solely to try and make $1,000 a day. I had no real plan for what to do should my trading go haywire. And there was one day when I got off to a horrendous start and it kept escalating and I kept increasing my size hoping to make it up on the first correction. Being on the wrong side of a really bad trade and over-margined, I didn't want to take the loss, so my solution was to take the position home and then hide from the clearinghouse on Monday morning, hoping the market would bounce back. My $8,000 loss from Friday escalated on Monday as I did nothing, and it eventually grew to $13,000 when the clearing-house liquidated me at the market lows on Tuesday and wiped out half my account and barred me from trading on the floor until I came up with more money.

I've seen some really incredible things over the years and though it may not happen often, you should always be prepared for the worst. Stuff like unexpected rate cuts whilst you are taking a poop and stocks go $13 against you, terrorist acts, a CEO dying in a plane crash and a stock crashes with the news. A computer geek puts out a phony report about a CEO quitting, which makes the stock drop 50 points and gets halted. The power goes out in your office and you can't exit trades, the Dow is down 150 points at 3 P.M. only to close up 150 after an incredible late day rally and you go from a $10,000 profit to a margin call. Lumber goes limited up for 15 days then reverses and goes limited down for the next 10 days, while you are stuck in the position.

In the back of your mind you should have a worst-case scenario strategy prepared if anything extraordinary does happen. This doesn't mean you should constantly fret about the worst that could happen, but do know what you will do if you are ever on the wrong side of an unexpectedly bad trade without a stop.

MAKING YOUR PLAN WORK

More than just having a plan to trade with, you have to know that it works and how to make it work. A plan is not worth anything if you do not know how to use it or you simply do not follow it. You should never assume your plan is great either. Some people have a trading plan that they use all the time but never make any money with. Well, maybe this plan just outright sucks and needs revamping until it makes money or needs to be forgotten and a new one made. Following are some steps you can take to ensure that your plan works.

Constant Reviewing

Part of your trading plan should be how and when you will review your trades, game plan, and performance. It doesn't need to be a written journal (though I recommend it), but you should have a method of monitoring positions as well as going over trades to figure out what you did right or wrong. I like to start with open positions keeping focused on whether the trade is still within the parameters of which it was originally made. If it is not, or the reasons the trade was made have changed, you may have to watch the position more closely or get out. Reviewing is an ongoing event that will make you a better trader. How often you review depends on the time frame you trade. A long-term trader may only need to look once a day or week, while a scalper has to be doing it nonstop.

Some Things that Should Be Reviewed on Open Trades
- Has it reached the target area?
- Is it close to the target area and should it be watched more closely?
- Should you add to it or cut back?
- Is it simply not working as planned?

- Is your money better spent elsewhere?
- Should a trade be closed now or held longer?
- Is it approaching a stop level?
- Did you ignore stop levels?
- Has volatility changed?

After you have reviewed the open trades, go over your losers. I like to review losing trades that I exited correctly with a small loss. To me these are the most important trades of all and it is a behavior I want to reinforce. I am more proud of getting out of something with a small loss that would have turned out to be a huge loss, than I am about having a winning trade. I consider these to be good trades because I did the right thing. I'll try to remember what I saw to make me get out quickly and if I see that setup again, I hope to act correctly again. Having had a weakness for letting losers get too big, I like to see I've improved in this area. If I let a trade get really bad, I try to understand why I did so, so I don't do it again. Next I go on to ones that I let get away or just acted stupidly on, regardless of whether I made money or not. I'll try not to repeat the same mistake in the future, (easier written than done). The last thing I review is my winning trades, and again, I'll try to learn from them. This whole process really doesn't take long to do at all, just a few minutes after the close and it is worth much more than the effort one puts into it. Those who never review their trades will never learn what they do right and wrong, so don't ignore this simple homework.

Don't just review the trades but constantly check the plan itself for validity. You may be losing money and the reason may be that your game or trading plan is faulty so keep making sure that it is sound. You also want to review to see if you followed your plan. There is nothing worse than on paper having planned out a great trade, the market did exactly what you thought it would, and yet you screwed it up and lost money. You need to follow your plans if you want to succeed; if you can't, then trading is not going to make you rich.

Discipline

Discipline is not actually part of a game plan. But in order to succeed you better have it, as it is the glue that makes it everything come together. First of all, you need the discipline to make a trading and game plan and more important is that you need the discipline to stick to your plan. Once you start deviating from a plan, it's easy to start losing and making emotional trading decisions. You'll start making trades you shouldn't, you'll overtrade, you'll risk too much, hold too long, and overall make poor trades.

It is easy to lose discipline whether you are on a winning or losing streak. When winning, you may think you are better than the market and don't have to follow a plan. When losing, you may try anything in desperation. Both cases are asking for disaster. You really should never allow losses to change your trading plan. If you've had a few losses, continue following your plan (as long as you know it's sound). Don't change your trading style, become more aggressive, or stubborn. You need to understand that a loss is just a cost of doing business, ignore it and move on to the next opportunity. The worst thing that you can do is to start trading heavier to make back losses. If you are continuously losing, stop trading until you've examined your trading plan, as it may be the cause. On the other hand, don't lose discipline and ignore your trading/game plan after a winning streak. Many traders get too cocky after a good streak thinking they are invincible and will make carelessly thought out trades with too much size, then one or two losses can quickly wipe that smirk off their faces. If you have been trading well it might just be the plan that got you there; don't ignore it.

One last thing I wanted to mention is that similar to discipline, staying focused is crucial to making the trading and game plans work. You can have a great trading plan, but if your mind is scattered throughout the day, you will not be able to carry out your game plan. If you are busy changing diapers, writing a book, planning a 700-person New Year's Eve party, opening up a bar/restaurant, remodeling your apartment, or accidentally stumbling upon the abundance of free porn on the Internet for three hours a day, your trading will suffer. If you don't have the proper time to dedicate to the market, you will need to change your trading and game plans to trade less and hold positions longer or take a break from trading as I had to at several times in the year and a half it took to write this book.

I actually finished writing the book last week, and I'm editing it and piecing it together now. It did take a while to write this book, but mostly because I didn't do much on it for about a year of that time, as I was too busy with other aspects of my life. As I've become busier especially while writing, I had to cut back on trading and have pretty much stopped day-trading. As I did this I had to revamp my trading plans to accommodate my new style, and that meant trading longer term. Becoming a stay-at-home father to a six–month-old and a two-year-old along with opening a bar/restaurant doesn't give you much time to concentrate on day-trading, though it's much more rewarding (the being a stay-at-home dad part at least). Now, 18 months later, one kid is in preschool and the other is taking classes and, as you'll discover later, there is now someone home to watch them, and the bar is up and running, and the book is pretty much done. So I do plan to step up my trading in the next month as soon as the final touches on the book are complete. But first I will make sure I have the proper trading and game plan.

CLOSING THOUGHTS

As I continue this book, I'll try to reinforce all the things a winning trader will do and compare them with how a losing trader would act in the same situation. I believe you can learn a lot from watching bad traders and learning from their mistakes. Don't take the losing traders' examples in this book lightly. Try to find any of their qualities in yourself and think about what you could do to change them. If you see you have any of these traits make a note of it and then work hard on fixing it. You could become a much better trader simply by making fewer bad trades. When I give winning examples, see how they differ from what you would do, and then see what you can take away from it to make your trading better.

You'll also notice that most of this book is not about actual trading but about things to do during nonmarket hours to make your trading better. I believe more money can be made by being properly prepared for the market than by actually trading it. This means doing your homework before and after the market closes.

CHAPTER 4

Get to Know Yourself

A minister and a stockbroker are waiting in line at the Pearly Gates. Saint Peter comes up to the broker and says, "Hello Joe, you've done great work, we'd like to welcome you to heaven. Take this silken robe and golden staff and enter the gates. As the stockbroker goes into heaven with his beautiful robe and golden staff, the minister walks up to the gates, and Saint Peter hands him a cotton robe and wooden staff and opens the gate, with nary an acknowledgment to the minister. "Just a minute," says the minister. "That man was a stockbroker, he gets a silken robe, a golden staff, and a wonderful welcome, but I, a loyal pastor for the last 37 years, a minister who has preached the ways of the Bible, gets somewhat of a cold shoulder? How can this be?" "Up here, we work by results," says Saint Peter. "While you preached, people slept; his clients, they prayed nonstop."

T his chapter, though important, is one that can be easily said in a few pages, which makes it my favorite chapter in the book. It's straight to the point, and anything else would be sugarcoating it.

In order to become a successful trader you need to have a plan and a strategy that is catered to your trading style and personal characteristics. And before you can have that plan, you need to figure out what works and feels best for you. It is very hard to try and use a strategy if it goes against some of your basic trading principles. Someone can have the best system in the world that works amazingly well for him, but if a different person tried to use it, it might not work at all. A different person may sometimes try to overrule or second guess a system or strategy; he may not take every signal it produces, thinking he can do better. He may feel like if he held longer he might make more, or worse he may feel a loser could turn into winner if he holds on just a little bit longer. It's because of these things that if a trader wants to be able to follow a trading and a game plan, they need to fit his style of trading. As you will see, there are many types of traders and traits people have and very few are alike. Hey, if everyone thought the same the markets would not be efficient.

DIFFERENT TYPES OF TRADERS

I've been stressing how important it is to know your style of trading. I've seen hundreds of traders over the years and most have their own nuances that make them special or not so special. Traders and people differ in so many ways that if I were to write a page on every type of trader I knew, I could fill this book quite easily. There are people who like to short and those who like to go long, there are traders who trade only based on news and others who only look at charts. There are some who trade off the news but confirm their decisions with charts and there are others who trade off of charts and use the news to make their final decisions. Some traders scalp for a few ticks, others hold on forever. Some look for trends, some for reversals, and others for range bound markets. Some use Moving Average Convergence/Divergence (MACD) or Relative Strength Index (RSI); others may use Bollinger bands and stochastics. Even among those who use the same indicators, many traders look at them in many different ways.

Traders also differ in risk aversions; some are not afraid to risk more per trade while others are too scared to trade, and risk very little, not giving themselves time to let a trade work. Some have lots of money, while others barely have enough to open an account. Some traders work for Goldman Sachs and can move a market, while others do one contract at time. Some people like to have no position at the end of the day and others like to trade overnight. Some have holding times of two minutes, others two weeks. Some have egos while others are modest. Some like green eggs and ham and some do not. And then there are unlimited combinations of all the above, which when put together make very few traders similar.

As you can see I can go on and on about the different types of traders and trading styles there are. Your concern is figuring out which type of trader you are.

A COMMON THREAD

Even though there are many different types of traders, there is one thing all the good ones have in common and that is that they all have great discipline. They may go about it different ways but in the long run they have to have discipline to succeed. Their styles of trading can be totally different, but without discipline nobody is going to be making money. Discipline is important in so many aspects of trading that I'll devote a chapter to it later.

FIGURING OUT WHO YOU ARE

If you've been trading for while figuring out what type of trader you are will be easier. If you're a novice trader, then you may have no idea what will work best for you. Above I mentioned different characteristics that traders may possess. There are way too many to list, so figuring out who you are is something you have to learn on your own through trial and error. The more you trade, the more you will realize what you like and do not like as well as what seems to work best for you. This is where the "tuition of trading" comes into play.

The tuition of trading is what I call the first couple of years of trading, when you would normally be losing money. Though you may be losing money during this time, these losses are invaluable as you should be learning from every mistake you make. Because there are no classes at Harvard to teach you how to trade, the only way to learn is by risking money (tuition) and going through the school of hard knocks. After a couple of years you should be ready to graduate and hopefully you will still have some money left. Paper trading is a way to get started but it won't help you nearly as much for two reasons. First is that you won't have the patience to paper trade for three years to gain the proper experience and second is that you will learn a lot more about who you are with real money on the line. Though this book may not help you discover who you are, it will help you acquire some of that education you need to do so.

TRYING A DIFFERENT STYLE

The other day I was speaking to my friend Bruce who has been a successful trader over the years. He started trading in a new office with a guy (Mr. X) who has been a real moneymaking machine for quite a while. However, their styles differ. Bruce's new trading "mentor" is a notorious shorter, while Bruce could trade from either side but likes going with the trend. Since Mr. X has made a ton of money in the markets, Bruce thought he would try following his trading style. So while the market has been "strong as a bull" lately, Bruce has been shorting almost nonstop and losing money all the while. Now he is pissed off at himself because if he had kept to his trading style he would have cleaned up during this time period. Mr. X is unfazed by a little losing streak, because he'll make it up by trading more aggressively once the market does turn. But this is not Bruce's style. He doesn't like big equity swings and needs constant winners and reinforcement all the time. Needless to say, after a little losing streak he started to press just a bit and traded beyond his normal risk parameters, hoping to recoup some losses. Even when going back to his own style of trading he deviated from his normal trading plan in that he traded a bit too aggressively. This all stemmed from his trying to use a trading style that was someone else's, no matter how good that person was.

THE IMPORTANCE OF KNOWING YOUR STYLE

In order to be a winning trader, you are going to have to start trading with a set of rules and strategies you can follow all the time. In order to be able to follow those rules and strategies, you'll need to be totally comfortable with them. If you start doubting or second-guessing them, you put yourself at risk. For example, you may like trading with the trend and are looking at a trade in a strongly trending stock. Others are telling you it's about to reverse and that you should short it. They may give you several reasons and show you indicators why it will happen. You may soon start rationalizing why it may go down as you weigh all the information, even if it's against your style.

So let's say you listened and went short, but then it doesn't reverse immediately. Now your gut may start telling you what a fool you were to listen, and you start panicking because this is not your type of trading and the stock is still strong, so you get out quickly. However, the market soon peters out and takes a nosedive. You lose money on the trade, yet the people who convinced you to short all did well on it. Why? Because they traded their style and you traded against your style. You can see how this could happen in Figure 4.1. The shaded oval in this chart is where the action is taking place. I've added a blown up picture of the chart in Figure 4.2, which will help you to see it better.

Let's say Harry (the good trader) looking for the market to reverse saw a sign at spot A. He saw the large spread between his two moving

FIGURE 4.1 Daily Chart of SLB
Source: © TradeStation Technologies 1999. All rights reserved.

averages, which led him to believe the market might retrace a bit to narrow that spread. He also saw that both the stochastics indicator and RSI were overbought, giving the market a good chance to come off. He saw that the market closed on its high the day before and failed to follow through the next day. He rationalized that if we had just a little bit of a sell-off, the indicators could all turn, making for a great short. So he decided he would short on the next morning if the market opened weaker. He shorted at a level indicated by oval A. He would use a stop two points above the high made the day before (indicated by the line marked Stop). John (who never makes money) on the other hand went against his gut to short the stock on Harry's suggestion. He looks at the chart and sees a strong uptrend and deep inside feels funny shorting. Though John decided to make the trade based on a little peer pressure, he couldn't handle the strong opening a few days later (oval B) and got out. Harry, however, had his stop in so he did nothing. He noticed the divergence between the market and the indicators, which led him to believe that this might be a false rally, so he let his trade ride. The divergence between the slope of indicators and market is a little hard to see in the blown-up chart. But the market peaked while the indicators did not, making for a great indication that this uptrend could be dying out. The

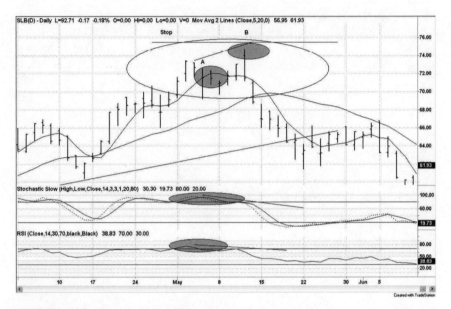

FIGURE 4.2 Close Up of the SLB
Source: © TradeStation Technologies 1999. All rights reserved.

market opened strong but then sold off the rest of the day, week, and month, making a nice trade for Harry. This is a great example of why it is hard to trade against your style of trading. As soon as something doesn't go your way you will be double guessing yourself and will have trouble allowing a trade to develop.

TWO SIDES TO EVERY STORY

If you trade against your nature of going with the market direction you will have trouble when markets are getting ready to reverse. You may look at a chart and an indicator and see one thing, while another person who likes to look for reversals may see something totally different. You will look for every little excuse to get you out of a trade, you may get anxious and not be able to hold as long as you should, and so on. However, if you are a trader who likes reversals and makes a trade in a stock that is turning, you will have different opinions as to what the market is trying to say. You will come up with reasons why it will go down when someone else looking at the same chart will see the opposite.

So who is right? Well, only the future will tell, but if you both have strategies you are confident in, it doesn't matter if you win or lose on a particular trade. However, once you start getting wishy-washy on a decision then you have a good chance of being wrong. After that comes one of the deadly sins of trading and that is making subsequent bad trades to recoup a bad trade. It's quite common with new traders who haven't learned to take losses yet. Losses are part of the game, let them go and move on to a new trade and forget about a previous bad one. Do not let losses eat you up inside or lose sleep over them; just try and keep them small and learn from them.

CLOSING THOUGHTS

There's not much more I can add to this chapter without getting into the next chapter. In order to be a great trader you are going to need a sound trading strategy that you can only develop once you have figured out a trading style that you feel comfortable with. If you are somewhat new to trading, you will go back and forth between coming up with a strategy and figuring out what type of trader you are. It will be trial and error for a while. If you can find other traders who are successful and you can sponge some information from them, it will be invaluable. If you don't have the luxury of other traders at your disposal, then you will have to read a lot of books and try different things until you figure it all out. Don't get discouraged though, it takes time to learn how to trade to your utmost potential. It took me several years. I was lucky. When I started as a clerk on the floor of the New York Mercantile Exchange and then got my own seat on the Cotton and New York Futures exchanges, I was surrounded by great traders who taught me a lot. I was able to gather information from many people and slowly develop my own style from all those different profiles I was privy to.

CHAPTER 5

Trading Strategies

Some Market Definitions:

Bear: What your trading account will be when you take hot stock tips based on your barber's advice.

Bull: What your broker uses to explain why the stock you bought went down.

Bull Market: A random market movement causing an investor to mistake himself for a financial genius.

I've touched upon this subject already, but a tested strategy is the cornerstone of successful trading. It forces you to make predetermined trades, thereby reducing your chances of making stupid mistakes. What I refer to as a strategy is the part of the trading plan that produces your entry and exit points. It's either the system you use or the process you use to come up with your trades. If you prefer to think of it as a trading system, go right ahead. It is just one part of the more elaborate trading plan, which also contains risk and money management, but for now let's just focus on the actual strategy.

TRADING STRATEGIES

In order to be able to implement a game plan you need to have a repeatable process you use to make trades. Whether it's systematic or discretionary you should still have a set of procedures you follow to make trade after trade. You need not be limited to one strategy. You may have a different strategy for trending markets than you do for a choppy market. However, you then need another strategy to help you figure out when a market is choppy or trending. You can also have a strategy you use when news makes a market move that overrides your normal trading strategy. You could even have strategies that are unique per individual market.

As you already saw there are many different styles of trading. Well, the same holds true for strategies, though developing one is much more difficult than figuring out your style of trading. Your style and habits will come naturally to you. You just need to be aware of them as they do. In the long run it's your style of trading that will determine your strategies. The strategy however is something you have to work at and develop and back test over and over again until you get it right.

YOUR STRATEGY NEEDS TO FIT YOUR STYLE

The previous chapter was about knowing your style of trading. And though it was short, it is oh so important, because you need to develop a strategy that complements your trading style. If not, you will not be able to follow it as well as you should. Your trading strategies should fit both your unique risk adverseness and your trading preferences. If you are a low-risk person then you will not be able to mentally trade, like a high-risk taker would, and will get scared out too often, possibly breaking the rules of the strategies should they call for holding through large drawdowns.

Coming up with the right strategy is something that is not so straightforward at the beginning. You need to actually trade for a while and gain experience, while at the same time experimenting with different —and possibly bad—ideas and strategies, some of which may work and some may not. It is not until after you have done this that you can decide on the style and strategy that you are most comfortable with and that works best for you. It is natural to trade confused at the beginning, and you may not be profitable during this learning period, but chalk it up to the tuition of trading, which you are paying to learn how to trade. It's in this period that you are developing trading styles, strategies, money management skills, and of course your overall trading plan.

TECHNICAL STRATEGIES

If you are a technical trader, you will most likely use indicators in your strategies. Before you put them into a strategy you will need to figure out which indicators will work the best for you, and you will need to learn how to use them. There are countless indicators you can use when trading, many of which will tell you the same thing. Using them together may be overkill, so I find it best to keep it simple. Indicators can also be used differently by different people. A breakout trader can use the RSI one way, while a reversal trader can use it to confirm a market is overbought, and a third person can look to see if there is divergence between the indicator and the market. Like everything else, finding out which indicators you like will take time and a lot of trial and error. Toy around with the indicators you think you like until you figure out what works for you. You will learn a lot about trading when you really start getting into how indicators work and respond to the market. Though I devoted a few chapters to it in *High Probability Trading*, you may want to pick up a good technical analysis book (I like John Murphy's *Technical Analysis of the the Futures Markets*; he also has one for financial markets) to have as a reference guide when learning to trade using indicators.

Fundamental Strategies

Not all strategies are based on technical analysis. Some are purely based on fundamentals and news. Others can be a combination of both technical analysis and fundamentals. An example of a fundamental strategy is you purchase a stock when an earnings report comes out that is better than the previous quarter's earnings, and you hold onto the trades until net earnings per share decreases for a quarter. This would be a long-term system with no technical analysis involved at all, but it's still a trading system. To be safe you should include a stop that may be derived using some technical analysis, too. But you can put in a monetary stop that doesn't.

There are many ways to trade using purely nontechnical strategies. You could trade off of the unemployment numbers, or the American Petroleum Institute (API) reports if you trade the energies. Some people use the weather to trade markets like corn or orange juice. Some use earnings for stocks, or the Consumer Price Index (CPI) or Producer Price Index (PPI) numbers. Whatever the case may be, if you are going to trade off of the news you should have a preplanned strategy for it. You should test your ideas and put them in a trading plan, and then you should be prepared for the trading day by including them in your game plan. Your strategy could say something like if the API numbers show a lower than expected stockpile in crude inventories and the market rallies, buy on the first dip. However, if the market does not rally then short. I definitely would recommend combining this with technical analysis so you can determine exit points, stops, and how much to risk. Without charts it becomes a much more difficult task to determine these things. I like to have a clear picture in front of me, so I don't have to guess when to exit. It's because of this that many traders don't even bother with the news. They look at the charts and believe that the news is reflected in the market, so why bother with more clutter in their heads? I used to be that way, but now I like to know why things happen.

Discretionary Strategies versus Systematic Strategies

There are two main types of strategies, well actually three, when you combine the two. First, you can have a totally systematic strategy, which generates pure buy and sell signals that you follow to the letter. The ultimate example of a systematic strategy would be a black box programmed trading system. These are systems that are bought and generate signals without you even knowing how the system was made. The system can even be set up to automatically enter trade orders in the market so that the trader doesn't even have to be in front of a machine. The traders have little say in what happens as the orders go in despite what they think or feel. The average trader with a program like TradeStation can do the same thing. If he has a system on his computer, he can have it send orders directly to the brokerage firm while he is out golfing.

The other type of strategy is discretionary, where your trading decisions are hopefully based on a formula/strategy/system you have developed but aren't automatically entered into the market and you have some say as to what you want to do. Discretion has a very wide base spectrum. In the worst case, discretionary trading can mean you have no rules and your trades are made off the cuff and you never know what they may be. But this approach is not going to make anyone a great trader. A trader can be discretionary, yet still follow a system. He may have several indicators he looks at, and when he gets two of three giving the go-ahead he takes the trade. Or he can have a solid system but then use discretion as to when to enter the trade. He may get a go-ahead signal from some news item but then use a technical analysis strategy to correlate it and plan the trade.

You do not need to have a computerized system to have a system, as long as you have buy and sell rules you will have a system/strategy. Then you can use discretion as to when to take the trades and how many contracts to trade depending on the risk. I think most traders fall into this category. The ones who turn out to be successful, though, are the ones who have proven strategies that generate the signals, whether they are automatically entered or the trader uses some discretion. The problem with discretion comes when traders have little discipline. These are people who constantly jump the gun or let trades go by because they overanalyze them. But more importantly they have no discipline when it comes to getting out of trades. It's always hard for a person with poor discipline to exit a trade with a small loser. Even if the system tells him otherwise, he can always find an excuse for staying in. I would recommend a person start out by never breaking the rules. If you have a system that generates signals on your computer, take every trade with no thought process at all until you learn discipline. Once you gain that discipline then you can start thinking a bit.

If you can't do it, hire someone to sit at your computer and do it for you. There was one time when I had to run an errand, so I had a nanny come and watch my son who was sleeping (he always napped from 2:30 P.M. to 4:30 P.M. letting me trade in the afternoon). I was long the S&P with a stop in but no exit order. I told her to sit at my computer, and I drew her a target area where I wanted to get out and said if the market goes to here press this button (I had already set up my order), then cancel this other order (my stop). Though she was terrified, she followed my system signals to a tee, and I could not have done any better myself.

As you develop into a better trader, I would say it is okay to use some discretion because you will start to see things in the market that can help you avoid bad trades or getting out at the worst time. I like to use discretion to time my trades, especially in strong trending markets. If I get a signal in a strong market, I'll look to see if I can get a pullback before diving in. This is actually part of my strategy, so it's not like I'm breaking any rules.

Look at the five-minute chart in Figure 5.1 for an example of this. The market has been in a strong uptrend then had a small five-day dip and now looks like it is ready to go back up as seen in Figure 5.2 (I'm looking at the last day of the chart.) I'm going to skip a few steps and go to the five-minute chart to show how I'd wait for a pullback before getting in.

I get my signal at the first oval as the market breaks out of a little congestion in the upward sloping triangle. I don't want to jump the gun or get filled two points away, so now I sit and wait for the pullback. For me, that signal comes when the stochastic indicator hits oversold and turns upward. We are in a strong market, so I'm content with getting in as soon as it turns upward and not waiting for it to leave the oversold area. I draw a trend line and place a stop and I'm good. Just for fun let's say I missed this trade and got a different signal later on. I could use the sell-off just before Entry 2 as a place to get in. The divergence between the stochastics and the market would be an entry signal. I'd then make a new trend line and place an appropriate stop.

BUILDING SYSTEMS

In order to be able to write a strategy you need to have some trading experience, an experienced trader to help you, or some reference from which

FIGURE 5.1 5-Minute S&P
Source: © TradeStation Technologies 1999. All rights reserved.

to start. Books, trading magazines, and the Web are a good way for the beginning trader to start. Though these resources should just be regarded as reference and starting points, they can head you in the right direction. Go through a few books until you find a few systems that you think you could follow, then study them. Learn why the author is using the indictors he is using and how he is using them. Back test the system yourself to see how it actually works. Authors are not above giving you a system, back testing it on perfect data, and showing you optimized results. Sometimes they only back test it for the amount of time needed to get ideal results. They will cut out a bad period at the end or start of the system if it gives them better results, so do the work yourself and do not rely on an author. Next, play around with it, changing some parameters or adding an indicator so it suits you better. Keep testing it. Make notes as to what a change does to its overall profit and loss.

You can also buy systems if you want to try that approach. If you read any trading magazine or go to a trading web site, you will see systems for sale all over the place. However, I don't believe you'll be successful trading a purchased system. First of all, it will be hard to follow it in the manner the creator intended it to be used. You will always be better able to

FIGURE 5.2 Daily S&P
Source: © TradeStation Technologies 1999. All rights reserved.

follow a system you came up with yourself. Even if your system is inferior, it may yield better results than one you cannot follow. Second, when you use someone else's system, you are not learning anything about trading, you are simply placing buy and sell signals. This may be fine for some people. But because you are reading this book I expect you want more than that.

The best method of creating a strategy is by being around other traders and watch what they do. You will be able to pick up features of their trading that you like and soon you'll be able to devise your strategies. By having mentors you can ask questions and have them guide you when you are struggling. But make sure you are listening to people who know what they are doing. I've found that it's usually the losers and beginners who like to give the most advice. Not everyone has the luxury of being surrounded by great traders, so those who don't will need to work harder.

Be Patient

Developing a strategy is not something you will do overnight. It takes time do get this right. I believe that until you have been trading about two years you won't have all the tools you need to do it properly. During those first two years you will be learning the different indicators, how they work, and how the market reacts to them, as well as how it reacts to the news. Don't get discouraged, you cannot start trading and a week later expect to know everything. You will get to know your style of trading as well as some of the nuances of the market, but it will take some time. My first strategies came from reading *Technical Analysis of Stocks and Commodities* magazine and my limited knowledge of technical analysis plus stuff people told me would work. Armed with these tools, I put together some basic rules and started to trade with very little back testing. I didn't last too long. For one thing, I didn't have a clue about risk, but more on that later in the book. I was trading using strategies that I thought would work but in reality they were not positive trading scenarios. Though some of these systems generate purely systematic signals, I only expected them to work because the magazine said they'd be positive. I didn't know any better at the time. I thought if I just followed a good system, it would work for me.

MY BEGINNINGS WITH SYSTEMS

I remember one of the first systems I used to trade. It was a system that a friend told me he got from a friend in Chicago, whose friend traded with Ed Seykota. Ed Seykota was one of the traders mentioned In Jack Schwager's *Market Wizards*, which was one of the most popular trading books back when I started trading. Anyway, this system was just hearsay handed down through a chain of people. It now reminds me of playing a game of telephone as a kid where one person starts by saying, "My mother has very nice hair," and by the 50th person it comes out as, "Your father's feet smell like a chair."

Maybe at one point it was a valid system if it actually did come from Ed Seykota, but I have no idea if it did. And even if it did, how many alterations did it go through before it got to me? Maybe I only got part of the system and something was left out. The system was a reversal system that did have merits, but I never really bothered to test it over an extended period of time. I thought if it came from a market wizard it must be good. I didn't make money trading this system, but at least I had something to work with when I started making my own systems. I was still a novice trader and had few tools, but this system helped me a lot—not in my actual trading, but it helped me learn what a system should be. It took over a year for me to adapt it with tools I learned to use and to make it my own and back test it over a decent period of time. There is no way I could have done it during my first year of trading; I just didn't know enough to have done so. But once I learned how markets react and how to manage my money and how to use trend lines and moving averages and stochastics and read hundreds of different trading strategies, I was able to put some solid rules together to make this and a few other systems work for me. I'm sure that if Ed Seykota had gotten hold of my system he probably couldn't have made money with it--unless of course he dissected it and made some changes to it and reverted it back to his system.

So relax. Don't go crazy all at once. Trading is a lot of trial and error. It will take you time to get things right, so be patient and don't blow your wad all too quickly. It really is important to get past the first year or two and still have money to trade with as you get better.

The Importance of Back Testing

I'm not going to spend too much time in this book talking about how to back test, but you need to know how important it is. Whenever you buy, borrow, or make a system or have a trading idea you think may work, back test it before you risk your money. No matter what you may think the results will be, check it for yourself. If you have one of the better charting software programs, like TradeStation, you can easily test your systems with it. Even though the TradeStation programming language is called Easy Language it will take you a bit of time to learn how to write your systems, but once you get the hang of it, it's not too hard at all. I recommend taking a few systems out of trading magazines and entering them into TradeStation to get the hang of how to write and program a system. Take the time to learn it, as it will definitely pay off later.

TRADESTATION CHANGES

One quick note, many people have e-mailed me saying they cannot get some of the systems I wrote about in *High Probability Trading* to work for them. There is a reason for this. I wrote them using TradeStation 4.0, currently they are on Version 8.3, and somewhere along the line they changed the way you enter systems. Before, you would write one long system with all the signals in it. Now it's broken up into different segments for entries and exits, making it a little different.

If you don't have a fancy program to analyze your trading ideas you can always do it by hand. You can pretty much get free charts of anything on the Internet, even intraday charts. Print out what you need and then manually go through it and write down your entry and exits and how you would have done. Your goal is to come up with a strategy that has worked in the past. Because if it didn't, odds are you will not make any money trading it in the future.

When you do back test, make sure you take into account two sometimes forgotten elements. One is commissions and fees and the other is slippage. Commissions can quickly turn a winning system into a breakeven one, because not only do you have to make a little extra on your winning trades to cover costs, you also have to cover the commissions on your losers. Slippage also can be deceiving. Slippage is the cost associated with trading that is the difference between where you think you will purchase or sell something and where you actually do get it. For example, if your system gives you a signal to buy at the market when the price reaches above 93, your system may show 93.05 as the entry point, but in real life you will probably get 93.10 or worse if the market is moving fast. Here is an example of the power that commissions and slippage have to hurt you:

You get a signal to buy at 93.00, at the time the market is 93.00 bid, offered at 93.05, so you pay 93.05. An hour later it's still trading at around 93.00 and you want to exit. However, this time the market is 92.95 bid at 93.00, so you get filled at 92.95. Your commission on the trade was $8.00 for 1,000 shares. So you end up losing $100 on the trade itself plus another $8 on the commission for a total of $108 in a stock that was virtually unchanged. Your system would have it as a wash, getting in and out at 93 even, but in reality you took a loss. So don't take these costs for granted and learn to incorporate them into your back testing if you want to stay realistic.

Another important reason for back testing is to find out the biggest drawback and longest losing streak of the system. You may think you have a great system because it is positive, but what you may not realize is that it normally has 10 losses in a row and can lose as much as $10,000 during a bad streak. This is something you would want to know before trading it. Maybe these losses are too much for you to handle and, as such, you would not be able to trade this system successfully as you would second-guess it once a losing streak occurred. Remember, you need to be comfortable with a system in order to trade it properly.

DON'T BE STUBBORN

One thing to keep in mind when using trading strategies is that they may be bad, even though you think you are trading a winning system. In reality, maybe you tested it wrong using insufficient data, or maybe you didn't test it at all. Regardless of why, don't fall in love with a strategy because you think it's great. If it is not working, reevaluate it and don't be afraid to throw it out and start again. Try retesting over a longer period with more data or over different market conditions. Maybe you only tested it in a trending market and now you are in a choppy market, and the system just will not work well under these conditions.

One good reason you want to know the biggest drawback and longest losing streak is that it will help you evaluate if and when to toss out a strategy. Maybe you think it's time to toss out the system because of four losing trades in row, but in reality this may be normal for this system, as may be an $8,000 losing streak at any given time. If this is the case and the positive streaks outweigh the losing ones and you have the risk adversity to handle these types of streaks, then you do not have to throw out the system.

You need to examine your strategies on a regular basis, so you can determine if they are still valid. If you are losing money trading a system and you test it over and over again and it seems like it should be positive, then maybe you are doing something wrong in following it. You can find this out by testing it over the period in which you traded and comparing the results. A system is only as good as the person following it. Once you start using discretion and ignoring signals, you will alter the results of the system. Maybe the system is just fine, and it's just you that needs tweaking and discipline.

WHY SHOULD YOU HAVE A STRATEGY?

This is simple: to give you an edge. The main purpose of the strategy is to make you trade with rules that you have determined will work. It will keep you from trading foolishly and from overtrading—at least from the part of overtrading that comes from putting on too many trades. Though some strategies call for a lot of trades, a strategy will at least keep your trades focused on what you think are the best trades. When you do not have a strategy each trade you make has no rhyme or reason behind it and could be totally the opposite from one similar situation to the next. With a strategy you should trade the same way, time after time after time, and hopefully you will be right more often then not, or else it's time to toss out or tweak the strategy.

Having trading strategies will help you focus on the good trades. Think of it like having on blinders that keep you from seeing all the garbage out there. These blinders will only let you see situations which you know have a good chance of working out and will keep you from acting on impulse on others you haven't prepared for. In my opinion trading is all about making the highest probability trades and ignoring all the others, and without proven strategies you cannot get that edge.

WHAT GOES INTO A STRATEGY?

Regardless of how you get your signals, a trading strategy is made up of a few things. I am going to separate money management from this part of a strategy and deal with it on its own in a later chapter. But keep in mind that the best trading strategies and a great system will not help you one bit without a proper money management strategy. So ignoring money management for now, the first thing that you will need is an entry signal, which is then followed by an exit signal. The exit is composed of two parts. One tells you when to get out with a profit and the other tells you when to get out with a loss. The exit signals are partially derived from your money management strategy, but we'll discuss that later. Other things that you may have in your system are the time frames you will trade and the holding period of your trades. You may have different systems for different markets or types of markets. You may have different systems to trade long-term and short-term. This may call for you to look at different time frames and holding periods when making your trading decisions. Regardless of these things you still need the basics: a buy, a sell, and a protective signal to have a proper strategy.

THE ENTRY

The first part of your system will be a signal to get you into the market. For example:

Short if the market dips below the trend line for two periods.

Though not as important as exiting a trade, you cannot trade if you never enter the market. The goal of the trading plan is to have a strategy that gives you trades that will have a good chance of making money. By having a system that gives you entry signals you will be making better trades than if you just winged it, which, in turn, starts you off on the right foot. If you want to succeed you need to have a valid reason for every trade you enter. Having a strategy that gives you a reason for getting in will make your trading so much easier. However, as you'll see in a second, getting into a trade is the easy part. It's the getting out where you'll determine if you make or lose money.

EXITS

Anyone can get into a trade, it's pretty easy. You just buy or sell anything at any time for any reason and you are in a trade. However, in order to make money you need to know when to get out. I could give the same trade to two traders, John and Harry, and Harry will be most likely to make money on that trade because he knows how to plan an exit. Even if he loses on it, he will probably get out with a smaller loss and restrict his damage. This, in my eyes, is long-term winning.

I'm not going to spend too much time writing about exiting now as I'll delve into it later in the book, but I'll go over the basics of it to give you an idea of what goes into the trading plan. First of all, you will want a signal that will get you out with a profit. This signal can also get you out with a loss even though it isn't meant to act as a stop. You can see how this may happen in Figure 5.3. Here, I'm using a simple moving average crossover system that only takes trades in the direction of the major trend. It buys at the close of the day when the faster moving average line crosses over the slower one. I got a buy signal at the circle E1 and sold it at circle X1 for a great trade. The next trade happened at circle E2 when the averages crossed again. I would have placed a stop just below the lows of the previous move indicated by stop line S1. Now, even though the market had not reached the stop line at the time, the trade was liquated because I got an exit signal telling me the reason I entered the trade has changed.

After the exit signal you will need a stop signal to give you a safety net. Stops are complicated, because of the many ways you can use them; again,

FIGURE 5.3 Daily Dow Jones
Source: © TradeStation Technologies 1999. All rights reserved.

more on them later in the book. But overall they are just there to protect you. One thing to keep in mind is that your loss target should always be less than your profit target. If you are risking three points to make two points then you are making a poor trade. When I trade, I look at my exit before my entry and determine the risk involved and the potential earnings I can make. If the ratio is good then I start looking for an entry. If you are writing a system, look for this in your back testing. Is the proper place to put a stop versus the amount you can make reasonable? If not your system won't work. Knowing where to place stops will make you a winning trader on its own, so don't ignore them like many traders do. Even in the previous example where I do not have a set profit target, I know that in an uptrend the market has potential to move up 5 to 10 times what I was risking with my stop on a good trade. This is the start of a winning formula, you just need to be right enough times to make it tradable.

One other note, some systems will always keep you in the market. These don't use stops but use the exit signals to not only get you out of the market but to get you in the other way. The theory behind these is if I don't want to be long I should be short. These strategies are normally used by overtraders, who always have to be in something and need the action. Even if you have this type of system, I recommend using an emergency stop to protect you should the system fail to give you a signal quickly enough if you are losing big on a trade. If you go back to the chart in Figure 5.3 and remove the rule of only taking trades in the direction of the major trend, you have a system that is always in the market. Instead of getting out at point X1, you would be exiting and getting short at the same time.

TIMES FRAMES AND HOLDING TIMES

It's not enough to just have buy and sell signals, you need to determine the time frame you will be looking at and how long you will be holding trades. Here is a time where knowing yourself comes into play. Some people can hold forever and others need to get in and out all the time. As you develop your strategies, you need to take this into consideration. You need to know what time frame charts you will look at when you make your trade. Are you going to be basing your trades off of a one-minute chart or a weekly chart? I recommend looking at a range of time frames to get a true market picture and to time your trades. However, you should have a base time frame somewhere in between to actually make your trading decisions. I also recommend that when you choose your stops you look at a time frame above what you are trading to base them on.

One of the things that worked for me was looking at an even smaller time frame to actually pull the trigger. I have found that in the past I had of habit of rushing into trades. My signals would get me into the market at the highest point of a move. I was not very patient about getting in and I would get in at horrible places. One of the most helpful things I have implemented into my strategies are conditions that make me wait for pullbacks before getting into a trade, the same held for exits. I'd panic and get out at the worst levels possible. The way I do this is by overlapping two strategies. One is the basic get in signal using a daily and/or 60-minute time frame and the other is a timing signal that is usually a 1- or 5-minute time frame. I also use a weekly or daily time frame to figure out the long-term situation and give me more fodder for planning my exits. However, when it comes to actually pulling the trigger, I'm usually looking at a short time frame to time the exit if I'm not stopped out. I'll get into more detail later in the book on how to use different time frames to make trades.

STICK TO YOUR TRADING STRATEGY

This shouldn't need to be said, but once you have a strategy, use it. If you have back tested it and it works, don't deviate from it or second-guess it. If you put on a trade, make sure it is part of your strategy. Don't just randomly put on trades because you feel like it. Make sure they are in your strategy and in your game plan. Once you have your trading and game plan set, you'd be wise to follow it.

CLOSING THOUGHTS

I know I've been a little contradictory about following a system and being discretionary. I do believe you need a core system to point you in the right direction, but you can actually make the trades using discretion as long as you follow your rules, are consistent, and your trades are premeditated. This may not apply to active day traders as they have to react quickly, but even then, they should have recognizable patterns they see all the time that they act upon. As I write this book, it will be geared more toward the trader who uses discretion in his trades, as the purely systematic trader doesn't really need to follow a game plan as much because he is on autopilot. The person who uses discretion in his trading really needs the guidance of a game plan to keep him on track.

Once again, if you want to succeed, you will learn to make a game plan everyday that employs your trading strategies and you will follow it.

CHAPTER 6

Know Your Markets

A guy new to trading has been paper trading for a year now and is still afraid to make a real trade. He just watches the markets all day long making mental trades. Last week, he lost his mind.

Just like you need to know yourself, you also need to know what you are trading. This includes the individual stocks or commodities you may trade, as well as the overall markets in general. It means knowing everything you can learn about them to make you a more efficient trader in those markets. You should get to know every little nuance of what makes a stock tick, how much it could move, how liquid it is, the risks involved trading it, and so on. These are just a few things that can affect a stock, there are a lot more factors I'll discuss later. These are things you should know before entering into a position, so that you can control your risk. You also should know the macro picture of what you are trading. You should be aware of what type of market you're in; is it choppy, trending, near a reversal or support point, and so on? If a market is on a good run, find out why, it can help you determine how to trade it and when to maybe ease up. Just looking at a five-minute chart of a stock will not help you much, but if you know the overall picture of the market you'll fare much better.

MARKETS DIFFER

In the same way that every trader is different, well, every market or stock has its own uniqueness about itself. Markets have different liquidity, different spreads, different high to low intraday moves, even different hours. The costs to trade them are different, the way they trend or how they react intraday are different. Some stocks are market leaders, some are followers. Some will move one way when interest rates drop and others a different way. Some are in all the hedge funds and are prone to huge swings if the funds get involved. Some markets react differently to news than do others. Some are largely dependent on news and weather, while others are more technical. Some are very active at night and others don't even trade after hours. I could keep going on and on but you get the picture.

THE MEGA TRADER

One reason for the uniqueness of markets is that each market tends to have the same group of players trading them day in and day out. It's the summation of all these traders' uniqueness that moves a market the way it does. To make it clearer, think of all the people who regularly trade cocoa as one mega person. He will have a different uniqueness than the mega trader of cotton. It is this style of the mega trader that gives each market its own feel. If all the traders who trade cocoa started trading cotton instead, I bet cotton would soon start having the same patterns as cocoa. It's just a theory of mine.

I know from experience that markets have different ways of moving along a trend. When trading the stock indices (Figure 6.1) for example, if the market is having a strong day, it tends to have quick run-ups, takes a breather by dipping a bit and then continues on its way, only to have another small fast dip as it overextends itself once again and the pattern keeps repeating. In crude oil (Figure 6.2), I've noticed a slightly different pattern on a strong trending day, and that is that instead of dipping when it stops going up the market tends to trade sideways until the trend line catches up to the market, and then it will rally again. Yes, there are many times when it dips, but compared to the S&Ps, it has been more common to see these sideways retracements.

Both these patterns happen as the day traders take their profits after a quick gain and look for a better buying opportunity. After a quick dip or sideways move, they come back in for more and drive the market up again. They make their few ticks, are happy, and then sell. I'm not sure why one market shows a different pattern than another, but I'm aware it happens. You only learn this by watching the market move day in and day out. Once you are an experienced trader, you will get a feel for when it's ready for its dip and advancement. When I worked on the floor, I was usually able to tell just by the sound of the crowd what was about to happen.

FIGURE 6.1 5-Minute S&P
Source: © TradeStation Technologies 1999. All rights reserved.

FIGURE 6.2 5-Minute Crude Oil
Source: © TradeStation Technologies 1999. All rights reserved.

KNOW WHAT YOU ARE TRADING

If you are going to trade, you should take the time to learn the essence of a market or stock. Some things can be learned quickly but others you will only learn over time and by trading. The longer you have been trading a particular market, the better you will know how it reacts. Trading is a learning process and if you are attentive you will always be able to learn something new.

Start by getting to know the basics. If you are trading a futures contract, make sure you know its margin, the hours it trades, and when the contract expires, rolls over, or goes into delivery. I remember once trading the front month in crude and not realizing it was last day of trading, and I got stuck with taking delivery of 5,000 barrels of oil. I panicked a bit because I lived in Manhattan and space in a Manhattan studio apartment is quite tight. I was concerned about what I was going to do with all that oil. I figured maybe I could make an end table or two but that still left me with a lot of barrels of oil and I didn't even have a car back then. Luckily my clearinghouse took care of it (at a cost, of course). These things are not uncommon and I have had a customer do it once as well. It is also not uncommon to not realize when a market closes. Because futures markets all have different hours, people who trade a lot of them can get caught taking positions home they don't really want, simply because they are careless and were so caught up trading crude oil that they forgot to get out of their soybean position at 2:15 when it closed. Yes, they can get out after hours, but they may not get as good a price and they may get a margin call if they are undercapitalized. It's not that difficult to know what opens and closes at what times, and it is something you ought to know. Another simple thing you should know (and again, I've been guilty of this) is what a tick is worth in a commodity. The first time I traded coffee I had no idea that a penny move was worth \$37.50, (I actually thought it was worth \$3.75), nor did I take the time to notice that on average it moved about \$1,500 a day. I made a trade based on someone's recommendation without really studying it. This was a lot more action than I was used to getting in crude, which at the time was trading at \$18/barrel and had about a \$300 swing on a good day. It was both scary and exciting trading coffee. But I soon realized I wasn't capitalized properly for it.

The same holds for stocks, there are some stocks that move with a one-penny spread and others have a dollar spread. You need to know this before getting involved. The larger the spread is the more you are risking if you are wrong. When you trade Microsoft at \$28 a share you know that if you change your mind and get out right away you will only lose maybe a penny or two, but if you trade Google at \$628 a share then you may be out a dollar a share before it has even begun to move.

This leads to the importance of knowing the volatility and liquidity of a market. The best indicator for knowing liquidity is to look at volume. A stock that trades 24 million shares a day will take a convoy of Mack trucks to make it budge. You can trade it all day long and get the bid and the ask for it if you are patient instead of paying for it. On the other hand, if you are trading a goofy stock like AKF (Ambac Financial Group), that has an average trading volume of less than 80,000 shares a day, and you try to buy 5,000 shares you could actually make the stock move a little, at least temporarily until you are filled. Then it will most likely go back where it was before you bought it. It's harder to trade thin markets as you have to pick your spots much better just to get a fair price. Look at Figure 6.3 and you'll see that it's hard to find any support from a thinly traded stock. I have never looked at this stock and just found it randomly searching for a thin stock. Commodities can be quite dangerous when trading thin markets. Unless you are on the floor yourself, you can get taken for a ride in a thin market. Your stops may get filled even if the market is not in the area. Mysteriously at lunchtime when there are three guys in the pit the market could make a quick move to hit the stops and come right back. I've seen it happen and I've been a part of it when I traded on the floor, so yes, it does

FIGURE 6.3 1-Minute AKF
Source: © TradeStation Technologies 1999. All rights reserved.

happen. Just remember the thinner the market, the better you have to pick your stop locations or the more likely they are to get filled.

WHAT'S THE REAL RISK?

As part of their uniqueness markets have different risks involved, which you should be aware of when trading them. You may think you can only lose up to your stop levels, but this is not always true. How much you could actually lose when trading a stock or commodity is not always controllable and you should be aware of this. Some stops can easily be blown through especially in thin markets, and you may get filled at levels much worse than you thought. Commodity markets can also lock limit and then your stop level is meaningless. This could cause you to get stopped out at a price you were never even expecting to be possible. The wider the spread in a stock is, the bigger the risk is, as you saw above. Markets or stocks that are news sensitive are much riskier. For example, $50 biotech companies that have a new cancer drug waiting to get approval by the Federal Drug Administration can become penny stocks in less than a day if they do not get that approval. A stop in this instance would do you no good.

In commodities you may want to be aware of how often the market has a habit of locking its limit. If you don't know what that means, some commodity markets have a limit they are allowed to move in one day (say two points), if they hit that limit they can't trade in the direction of the limit any more for the rest of the day. (So if a market is plummeting and hits its down limit, it will not trade below that price, it can, however, trade above it.) This can be quite costly, when you are on the wrong side of the trade and can't get out. Some markets, especially the thin ones, have a greater tendency than others to lock their limits for the day or for several days. Managing your risk when this happens is tough, so make sure you know how likely a market is to lock its limit before you jump into a trade. There are options to help you when you are in a locked position and one of those options is options. Options will keep trading even when a market is locked. So if you are stuck you can trade the options on a commodity to help you protect yourself, but this is usually costly as they become quite overpriced.

Another factor determining how great the real risk can be, is what happens overnight. Some markets can have wild moves overnight and open past where your stop loss level may have been. You then get stopped out at the open without a say, and this could be a few to a lot of points from where you thought your worst-case scenario was. As you get to know stocks and commodities better you will get a sense of which markets can hurt you the most overnight, and you then can trade accordingly.

TIME FRAMES AND CHARTING

Another factor associated with the liquidity and volatility of a market is
which time frame best suits that market. Some people like to look at different time period charts depending on the market they trade. With a thin
stock, a one- or five-minute chart may look spotty, while in IBM you can
comfortably get good entry and exit spots using a one-minute chart. Compare a one-minute chart (Figure 6.4) of AKF and IBM to see the difference.
There is no way you could make a reasonably smart trade based on a one-
minute chart of AKF but you could from the IBM chart.

If you are trading the thin AKF then you'll need to up the time frame to
maybe 10 minutes or 30 minutes to get a decent picture that may actually
tell you something. That means you may have to have a longer hold period
for that stock than you would for one where you can more easily get in and
out of a trade. I've added a 30-minute chart of AKF in Figure 6.5 and even
here it is a little spotty, but at least you can see some resemblance to a real
chart in it and you could use it to get into and out of the stock. I would only
trade this kind of stock if I was planning on holding it for quite a while, like
weeks or years. I have bought a few of them over the years, and they were
always long-term plays.

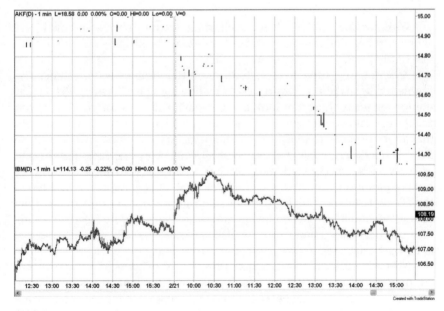

FIGURE 6.4 1-Minute AKF vs. IBM
Source: © TradeStation Technologies 1999. All rights reserved.

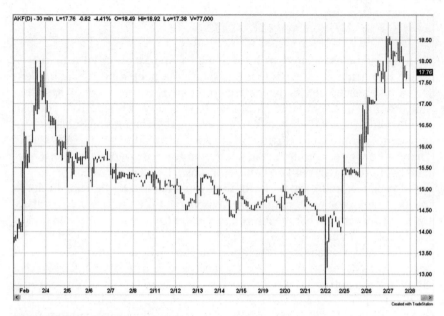

FIGURE 6.5 30-Minute AKF
Source: © TradeStation Technologies 1999. All rights reserved.

While we are on the subject of charting, I want to bring up how I look at charts when I'm trading the index futures, as it will apply throughout the rest of the book.

As you know, I like to look at different time frames when I trade. The problem when trading a futures contract like the Dow Jones or S&P is that the longer term chart you look at, the smaller amount of good data you get. As you can see in Figure 6.6, there are only a few months worth of data that are reasonable to look at; the rest are just useless dots. This is because the futures do not trade very much at all when they are back months and are only shown as the settlement price. This limited charting makes it very hard to plot indicators and get a full idea of what is going on. I've included the 50- and 200-day moving averages in Figure 6.6, but you can see they are only useful in the last couple of months because before December they factor in 0 as data points. You can also see there is really nothing to grasp at if you were trying to plot a long-term trend line.

Now if you look at the actual Dow Index (Figure 6.7) you will see a much nicer, fuller chart on which you can draw your trend lines, have proper long-term moving averages, and make your trading decisions from. If I were to condense this chart you could even see five years of solid data on the screen to give you a longer term picture, with the futures contract

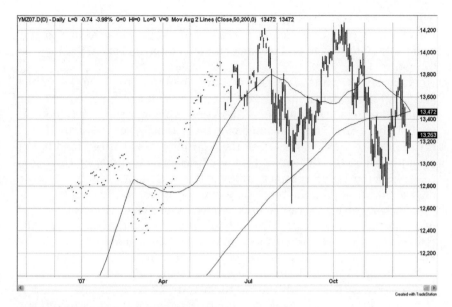

FIGURE 6.6 Daily Dow Mini Futures
Source: © TradeStation Technologies 1999. All rights reserved.

FIGURE 6.7 Daily Dow Index
Source: © TradeStation Technologies 1999. All rights reserved.

what you saw above is all you get. You can, however, get a fuller picture with futures using continuous charts. There are people who like to stay true to the futures and will use a continuous futures chart to get their information.

Continuous charts are where the front month of the futures contract gets charted and the contracts get rolled over as they expire to make one smooth flowing long-term chart. There are two common ways to do this, but both have problems associated with them. Usually there is some spread in the price of contracts between the expiring and new front month. For example, when the December Dow contract expires it can be trading at 13,526 and the March contract, which is the next month, will be trading a little at 13,592, due to the time value, interest rates, and traders' expectations. When you try to combine two contracts on a chart, you can do so by using the real prices, which will result in a gap appearing on the chart at the time of rollover. But this will mess up your technical analysis, as old trend lines, supports, resistance levels, and so forth will be not be helpful anymore, and new ones will have to be redrawn with each new contract. Yet it may not be easy to properly redraw them as data has just changed and levels move as a result of when a new contract becomes the front month and has a 70-point gap from the old one. The change in the data may lead you to believe that a market has broken a support level when in reality it did not.

The other way you can chart continuous data is without gaps. You just plot the new contract at the point where the other left off and then adjust the price of back months to coincide with the current front month. The December contract now looks like it was trading 13,590 when it rolled over and not 13,526 as it actually did. The problem with this method is you can sometimes get very strange pricing as you go back in time. It is not uncommon to see markets with negative values if the data gaps are large enough between front and back months.

The problem with both methods is that you lose some accuracy when making the adjustments. If you compare the charts in Figure 6.7 (the actual Dow index) with that of Figure 6.8, which is a back adjusted continuous futures chart, you'll see how some of the technical points have changed.

For example, point A in Figure 6.8 is only a few points lower than the previous low made about two weeks prior. In Figure 6.7 it's quite a bit lower, which in this case may have given you a signal to short or a stop that Figure 6.8 wouldn't have, albeit a signal you probably wouldn't have wanted anyway. But in another example, the low made by point C in Figure 6.8 is below the low made at point B, however in Figure 6.7 it is above point B. Though it may not have indicated a trading signal on the chart in Figure 6.7, it would have in Figure 6.8. Nevertheless, you can see how the two charts are a little different and how at some time or other you may make a trade based on one chart that you wouldn't have made using

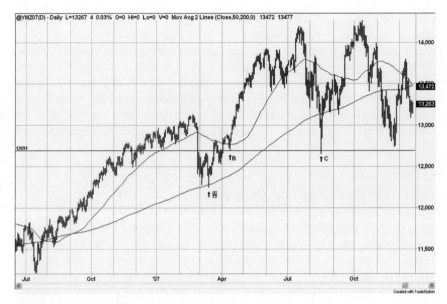

FIGURE 6.8 Continuous Dow Mini Chart
Source: © TradeStation Technologies 1999. All rights reserved.

another. Because the futures market can be a little more erratic, I prefer to just base my decisions on the actual indices in order to get a truer picture. Once I have that picture, then I make my trades with help of the smaller time framed futures charts.

A RANDOM RANT

One thing I find funny about trading books is that they give you an idea and then find the perfect scenario to show you a chart of. What the authors fail to tell you is that they probably looked at another 20 different spots where the strategy failed on the chart. But because they found one good one, it's good enough to be in a book. It's like a sports handicapper sending 50 people a free pick saying the New York Giants will beat the spread over the Dallas Cowboys this Sunday and then sending a different free pick to 50 other people stating the Dallas Cowboys will win. If the Giants win, he then e-mails 25 of the 50 people whom he told the Giants would win and tells them the Miami Dolphins will beat the spread over the Buffalo Bills the next weekend. Meanwhile, he tells the other 25 people that the Bills will win. After the Bills win, he tells 12 of those people that the New York Jets will beat the spread over the Chicago Bears on week 3, and 13 people get told that the Bears will win. He keeps doing this for another week or two until he has given a few people 5 consecutive winning bets. He then sends them an e-mail and says if you would like to receive more great picks, sign up for my service at $500 a week. These remaining people should be quite impressed with his picks so they may sign up, even though in reality he was wrong at least once to 97 other people. So just take what you see in books with a grain of salt. You may see the perfect scenario in a chart to prove a point and make it look great, when in reality it may have taken quite a bit of time looking for the right chart to prove that point.

WHO MOVES THE MARKETS?

Amongst the things you should know if you want to be a complete trader, is who moves the market. If it's a NASDAQ stock, you should know which market makers are the most active in it, and you should try and find out which position they are taking. Are they getting long or are they shorting? This is something you can get the hang of if you trade the stock all the time or you have a friend at Goldman Sachs you can call who knows everything.

You should know if the market or stock is included in any hedge fund and then know what the funds are doing. Are they buying or are they liquidating? Are they accumulating or shorting? These things can help you determine the possible direction of the market. If you know all the players and know what they are doing then you have a heads up. If you know all the hedge funds and major players are long then who is left to buy? No one—which is an indicator that the market may be running out of steam. You should also get to know the open interest in a futures market and understand what it means. Open interest when combined with volume can help you determine in which direction the market is most likely to go and it is a great tool to have.

OPEN INTEREST

Open interest is the total number of active or open contracts for any given commodity at the end of each day. It refers to the total number of contracts long or short in a delivery month that have been entered into and not yet liquidated by an offsetting trade or fulfilled by delivery. It measures the flow of money into and out of the market. For each seller of a futures contract there must be a buyer of that contract and they combine to create only one contract. Therefore, to determine the total open interest you only need to know the totals from one side or the other, buyers or sellers, not the sum of both. Open interest can change in three ways:

1. If one new buyer buys from one new seller, open interest will go up as there is a new contract being made.

2. If an old buyer sells to an old existing short. There will be one less open contract and open interest will drop by one.

3. If an old buyer sells to new buyer, it results in no change, as it's just the passing of an existing contract to someone new.

By keeping track of the changes in the open interest at the end of each trading day, you can get some information out of the market. Increasing open interest means that new money is flowing in and that the present trend will continue. Declining open interest means that the market is liquidating and implies that the trend is coming to an end. Watching open interest and combining it with volume and price direction can be a great method of preparing for the end of a trend or confirming a move. Using price, volume, and open interest together you can draw the following conclusions:

Price	Volume	Open Interest	Indication
Rising	Rising	Rising	Market is strong
Rising	Falling	Falling	Market may weaken
Falling	Rising	Rising	Market is weak
Falling	Falling	Falling	Market may strengthen

KNOW ANY CORRELATIONS

If you are trading stocks you should know if they are part of the major indices and how a move in the indices correlates to the stock. It need not be exact but you should know that if the Dow drops 100 points your stock would normally drop $1.50 or that a dollar move in your stock will move the Dow 11 points. Sometimes it's easier to look at the markets as a whole and get a determination of what a stock may do, instead of trying to figure out what a stock may do on its own. And if you knew the correlation between the two, you could time your trades a little better or know if a stock is stronger or weaker than the market.

You can look for correlations between stocks in a sector, or commodities and the price of gold, or oil, or the dollar, or between commodity groups like heating oil vs. crude oil. Many people trade the stock market based on what the bond market is doing. Many things affect different markets and there are correlations all over the place. The better you know them, the better you become as you may pick something up just a little faster if you are aware of them.

Are They Laggards or Leaders?

This leads me to another factor you should know when trading and that is whether the stock or market is a leader or a laggard. Within every sector there are the stocks that make the sector move first and there are others that move once the sector becomes active. Some stocks move in sympathy with other stocks, like if one bank has great earnings and rallies, the other banks will follow as well. It's good to know these things and which stocks do what as it will help you find opportunities to trade.

This isn't just true within sectors but in the market as a whole. There are some stocks that can move the market by themselves. Well, not by themselves, but so many other firms react with these stocks that it moves the market, and the one stock was the catalyst that made it happen. These are usually the big name stocks with huge volume. If a company like Bear Stearns has a bad earnings report every other bank may drop, as well as many other firms that depend on the banks, which can create a snowball effect and start an avalanche. I'm not telling you not to trade these stocks but be aware that sometimes the big safe stocks can be riskier to trade than the stocks that are laggards.

I used to trade at a firm that never liked it when people traded the leaders. They thought it was too difficult to compete with all the big players in those big stocks. Instead they preferred to find small and mid cap stocks with volume of 100,000 to 500,000 shares a day that would follow the moves. They had less competition and more time to react and felt they could trade better, and this is how they taught new traders. I never liked doing it, which is why I left, but it worked for them.

What Moves It?

Though I've always been a technical trader and barely looked at the news to trade, as I write this chapter I'm realizing how important being better educated can be. I still believe that everything is reflected in the price and that news may not help you react any quicker, but if you know why something did something, then you can be better prepared to exit a position when that condition is over. As a trader you should be aware of what moves the markets you trade. There are many factors that can cause a commodity or stock to move and you should be alert to them. Some of the things you should know are:

Which Reports Can Do What and When Do They Come Out?

There are so many reports that I'm not going to bother to list them, but an example or two are crop reports that will move the grain markets and the

Consumer Price Index report, which can move the whole stock market and different stocks in several ways.

When Do Earnings Come Out and What to Do with Them?

Not only should you know when earnings come out, but you should learn how to read a stock's reaction to them. Good or bad earnings is not important to me, it's how the stock reacts to that report that is key. Don't get caught with your pants down because you did not know the stock you shorted last night has earnings due today before the open.

How Do Markets React to Changes in Interest Rates and Foreign Exchange?

One of the most anticipated things in the market is the Federal Reserve's announcement on interest rates. A cut or hike greater or smaller than expected can trigger a huge move in a stock, future, sector, and whole market. But not all sectors and stocks react the same way, as some sectors react favorable to higher interest rates while other do not. You should know what a change in rates will do to the stuff you trade. And of course you should know when these announcements are due. Changes in foreign exchange can have more subtle effects on some markets, but nevertheless you should know if the stocks or commodities you trade are sensitive to them. As the U.S. dollar drops, gold will most likely go up. Cocoa is a market that can be affected by the British pound because London cocoa futures trading, which have a huge impact on worldwide prices, is conducted in British pounds. So, big fluctuations in the pound will impact the price of U.S. cocoa futures, due to the cross-currency fluctuations of the British pound vs. the U.S. dollar. There is constant arbitrage taking place between the New York and London cocoa markets so the rate between the pound and the dollar is very important. This is something the average person may not be aware of but it's good to know.

Is the Market Weather Sensitive?

Orange juice, oil, grains, the softs (coffee, sugar, cocoa, and cotton), cattle, and a few more, are very much weather-related products and a frost, drought, flood, or heat wave can send prices soaring in some markets. Or a slightly different weather pattern can send one market up while sending another down. Keeping abreast of the weather can help you determine which direction you want to be trading some markets. Hurricanes or threats of them, for example, can cause large moves in the oil markets and soft markets, but may not have any effect on cocoa, which is not made in the area affected by the hurricane.

ROUNDABOUT WAY WEATHER CAN AFFECT PRICES

I own a bar/restaurant and was just speaking to my produce vendor, who is a large nationwide company. We were talking about how ridiculous prices have gotten, and he said "you aint seen nuttin' yet." He was telling me how the recent flooding in the Midwest is going to drive prices through the roof and not just because the floods have made the grains hit record highs. It's because his cross-country truckers have to take alternate routes as the roads are impassable. He said it normally costs $4,200 to send one truck cross-country, and last week it was over $11,000 as they had to go through Canada. Between the extra manhours and extra gasoline, coupled with all-time record-high oil prices, the cost of a fajita at my place is going to go up.

Are There Any Seasonal Patterns?

You should be aware of any seasonal patterns present in what you are trading. For instance, heating oil being in more demand in the winter will cause it to be higher during the winter. Soybeans tend to have wilder swings the closer it is to harvest time. Harvest time for cocoa is September, and this typically lowers the market a little. There are many seasonal patterns out there, and if you know your market you can use them to your advantage.

Is the Market Sensitive to Foreign Events?

Some markets are very sensitive to what is going on in other countries. Cocoa can be moved by things happening in the Ivory Coast, coffee by Columbia or Brazil. Foreign exchange is obviously sensitive to other foreign markets, while others are less obvious. The huge rise in crude prices recently, amongst other things, has been attributed to the modernization of developing countries like China. If you want to be the best you can be, these are things you will need to know.

How Does It React to Different Times of Day?

Some markets move more in the morning, while others are more active closer to the end of the day. Some don't budge during lunchtimes and others tend to always rally. I have found that the S&Ps rally at 3:30 and tend to close gaps that were left in the morning. These are things you pick up over time the more you are familiar with a market.

Does It Move at Night?

Some markets barely move overnight and some make most of their moves overnight. You better know this before you start trading, or it can make you old fast. If a stock is going to make a big move overnight and gap lower in the morning, it can blow though any stop you may have. Though this is hard to predict because it can happen to any stock, there are some that are much more prone to doing it, as are many of the futures markets.

I used to trade currencies a lot, but I had to stop because I couldn't sleep. I'd stay awake till 3 or 4 in the morning to see how they were doing in London and Europe and then I'd sleep with one eye open, constantly waking up to check how they were doing on a computer screen next to my bed. It began taking a toll on me and affected my regular trading so I stopped doing it. If I do it now, it's a long-term trade with a small position I can handle not watching all the time.

Are There Any Recognizable Patterns that Repeat?

Because markets are driven by people who are creatures of habit you will begin to see patterns repeated over and over in different markets. For example, after a nice run-up on a five-minute chart in the S&Ps, you are very likely to see an orderly pullback before the next run-up. Some markets tend to always close in the opposite direction that they opened. Some will tend to reverse between 10:30 and 11ish. Some will close near their high or low and others tend to always close in the middle. Some react perfectly to certain technical indicators while others look like they move randomly. Keep looking for patterns and you'll find that a market tends to do things in a somewhat predictable way.

How Does It React to News?

The word news is generic and can mean many things including all the reports I've mentioned before. It also means every little thing that comes off the news wire, like a strike by coffee workers in Venezuela, the death of a CEO, an airplane crashing, or a popular toy getting recalled. If you are going to trade you should learn how what you trade reacts to certain news. Some markets will rally on the same news that will make another fall. Interest rates affect markets in different ways. Higher oil prices are good for some stocks but not for others.

As for reports, not only do you need to know that the crop report is coming out, but you should know how it will likely affect the price of soybeans and even hogs, which eat those grains. By knowing how it should react you can then be in a position to capitalize on the news. By the way, included in the hogs' diet of corn, soymeal, oats, barley, and wheat are some delicacies (according to the *Dallas News* 5/1/07), like blood and ground-up bone and meat byproducts from a variety of animals for the protein and calcium content. Feed can include the carcasses of unborn cattle, which are taken from slaughtered cows. The product is produced by grinding whole carcasses, exclusive of calf hides. Misshapen and leftover pet food is frequently added. Animal manure and leftover food and grease from restaurants are also sometimes included. Anyway some of the best trades are made when a market fails to react the way you'd expect it to and you go with what the market is telling you instead of what the news tells you. Like when you'd expect an interest rate cut to really make the market rally, but in reality it drops. Shorting at this time is a great trade because it means that the market has shaken off or taken into consideration the news and is heading where it belongs regardless of outside noise. Learning how to read markets after a news release is one thing that will definitely make you a superior trader, but I don't believe that it is something you can pick up in a book.

How Does It React to Sentiment?

Some traders like to look at sentiment indicators to help make their trading decisions. Such indicators could be the put/call ratio and the commitment of traders' reports that come out every Friday for various commodities. The theory being that when everyone is bullish the market has no one left to buy and it should turn. Some markets respond better than others to these indicators and a good trader will know how his market reacts to sentiment indicators if he chooses to use them.

How Does It React in Different Market Environments?

Different markets will react differently under the same conditions. For example in a range bound market one stock may constantly hit the support and resistance areas, while another may just float around aimlessly. Some markets are textbook examples of trend following, with regular size retracements and can be traded with much clearer signals and safer stop areas. I remember years ago that crude oil was stuck in a 2-dollar range from $18 to $20 for a long time, and it moved much differently when it was in that range than when it broke out and started trending. In an uptrending market it tended to rally regardless of whether it opened weak or not.

While it was range bound though, it tended to close the morning gap almost all the time and then trade aimlessly the rest of the day.

GETTING THE BIG PICTURE

Let's forget about the peculiarities of individual stocks, but let's look at the big picture of where a stock is. When you trade, you need to know where in time you are. Some traders have blinders on when trading and forget to see where a market is in its long-term picture. Before you make a trade you need to know what type of market it is because markets will react differently in different conditions. You should be looking at charts in multiple time frames to get both a short- and long-term picture of what the market is doing to help determine if the market is trending, choppy, range bound, and so on. You also need to know what the general direction of the market is. You may also want to be using indicators to help you determine where the current market is in relationship to the big picture. Once you know all these things you can make smarter trading decisions.

For example, is the market in a long-term rally but has currently surged and moved too far off its trend line and therefore due for a retracement before going back up? Is it near the support of a range bound, choppy market with clear support and resistance levels? Has it recently broken out of a choppy market? Is it in a position where a possible reversal is looming?

Once you can pinpoint where a market is and know all of its levels you can start planning trades with much less of a gambling factor than if you were just looking at a small amount of data. Good traders will use different technical indicators and systems depending on the market conditions. Their game plan will vary according to where the market is versus its long-term history. They will be able to make smarter decisions as to where to get in and out as the picture gets clearer. All this in turn will make them better traders.

CLOSING THOUGHTS

The better you know your stuff the better your chances of surviving are. It does require extra work learning everything you can about the markets you trade, but you will only be a better trader by doing so. Some of the things I mentioned you will only gain knowledge of through time by watching markets day in and day out. If you are lucky and have experienced traders who you work with, you may be able to learn faster. Just don't rush things and expect to know how the markets will react to every piece of news disseminated out there. And don't get stubborn about what you think should happen. Remember the markets are always right, and they will tell you where they should be—not the other way around.

When I was studying for my SATs I learned the word "parsimonious." Twenty-five years later, I don't think I had ever used it, until this sentence. Yes, it has nothing to do with trading but it was a thought I had while I was rereading these closing thoughts so I figure I'd share it with you.

CHAPTER 7

After the Close

A man rushes into his house and yells to his wife, "Martha, pack up your things! I just made a fortune in the stock market!" Martha replies, "Wow, should I pack for warm weather or cold?" The man responds, "I don't care. Just get out!"

So, it's 4:15 P.M. and the S&P futures just closed and you had a bad day trading, so what do you do? Go down to your local bar and get soused? No, you start preparing for the next day. Actually, first you should run to the bathroom as you probably have been sitting for four hours straight glued to your monitor. Then go take a quick walk to stretch out and clear your mind. If you work on a trading desk at a day trading firm most likely everyone will be gone when you come back. But the next hour or so could be the most valuable one of your trading day. You're thinking the markets are closed, I can't trade anymore, the day is over, why should I still be here? But it's only the end of the day for John and his loser friends. Great traders use this time to review their day and start planning for the next one. As soon as the market closes is when your trades are freshest in your mind, so why not spend some time after the close going over them? You can gain a lot of insight into your trading by reviewing what you have done and what's more, you can start getting ready for tomorrow by doing so. After you've gone over all your trades, you should take some time preparing tomorrow's game plan. This is a two-part process, which should be done both the night before and the morning of, but by spending time on it the night before you will get an incredible jump on it the following morning and will be able to see things much clearer during the trading day.

Some things you will be concentrating on are what's happening tomorrow, what will you do if such and such happens, which of your trades just aren't working, and what are you doing wrong. You can also spend time looking for places to adjust your stops to and review your money management and risk levels. It doesn't take a long time to do all this, and its worth is invaluable.

LET'S REVIEW

This chapter may seem out of order at times because it assumes you are doing things that I'll discuss throughout the book some of which will come later. However, I put it here because the best way to start your trading day is to get ready for it the night before. But before you start getting ready for the next trading day, the first thing you should do is go over all the trades you made or have on. You can do this in any order you like, but I prefer to start by looking at any trades I have that are still open. These are the ones I need to be the most focused on going into the next day, and I like to confirm that they are still good trades.

By "good" I mean that the reasons I put the trade on are still valid. I've been known to not get out of bad trades in hopes of them opening up the next day in my favor. This is always a bad decision as bad trades should always be gotten out of as soon as possible. Now this is different from a trade that is not making money but is still in the parameters of your strategy. I'm referring to trades that blow through your levels but that you have decided not to get out of.

If I still have a bad trade on after the day, I make a big note to GET OUT if it does not start reacting correctly as soon as the market opens. It's oh-so-common to look at a bad position and rationalize why it could work. For example, if it gaps down against you the next day, you may say, okay this is the worst it can get and it will close the gap. And you sit there and hope all day it does. Doing this could easily throw off your whole game plan for the next day as you will spend too much time babying a bad position and ignoring the good ones you have, which may end up turning bad.

GOOD KID, BAD KID

A great example of this is parents with two kids, one who is near perfect, a straight-A student, captain of the tennis team, doing community service, and the other is cutting class, failing some classes, getting into fights, smoking cigarettes, shaving half his head, and so on. The parents can spend so much time talking about and dealing with the bad seed that the good kid starts to feel abandoned. He starts getting depressed thinking that they don't love him as much as his brother and soon begins drinking heavily. Then he finds some of his brother's pot and because no one pays attention he quickly develops a $5 a day pot habit. So the moral here is to cut your losses, send the troubled kid to military school, and praise the good kid; odds are he'll make more money in the future than the troublemaker allowing you to retire earlier, as he supports you. The bad kid on the other hand is going to cost you money for years, military school, bail, lawyers, counseling, hair dye, and so on. So cut your losses and concentrate on your winners.

Now back from my tangent, as you are reviewing don't get complacent with good trades. Analyze them in depth and always think about how you will get out. As you review your trades there are several things you can look at as I'll describe in the rest of this chapter. I'll start with the open trades.

THE OPEN TRADES

Many of the situations below can apply to winning and losing trades, so I'm not going to separate them into two sections. Just figure out which applies to your situations as you read them. A winning and losing trade can be looked at the same way depending on how long you have held a position. A winning trade that gives back too much profit is no worse than a losing trade. You don't want to give back too much on a winning position by overstaying your welcome. Even if you close it out as a winner, if you gave back too much, in my eyes it's a bad trade at least for the last part of the trade. Though I prefer to review my winners first, it doesn't matter if you do them or your losers first or if you just go down your list of trades in the order that you put them on. Whatever way you do it, just be sure to give them all their fair due. If you are a day trader who closes everything out at the end of the day then the next few pages may not be necessary, but you paid for the book, so the read them anyway. If you trade one market or stock, the reviewing part will go faster and then you could meet John at Moran's quicker. As you do go over every trade keep in mind that the main purpose for doing so is to prepare for the next day's game plan.

Why Did I Make the Trade?

The first thing I do when I look at my open trades is to start with ones I put on most recently. I ask myself, "Why did I make this trade?" Throughout a trade's history you need to keep making sure that it is within your plan's scope. I want to make sure that the trade is part of my trading strategy and not some randomly put on trade. I want validation that I made the trade for a proper reason. If I did, great, I can move on; if not, I want to make sure it fits into one of my strategies. If it doesn't, I'll look to get out as soon as possible, as I do not want to hold a trade that contradicts my basic principles. Sometimes during the heat of battle of the trading day, you may make some random trade and then not get out of it because you had no plan for it. Hopefully this doesn't happen often to you, but when it does, be aware you are doing something wrong and remedy it as soon as you can.

Do the Reasons You Got in Still Hold?

If you shorted the Dow Jones because the 3-period moving average crossed below the 10-period one as in point A in Figure 7.1, make sure it's still the case. If it's not, it's time to reevaluate the trade. Don't wait until you are stopped out to get out of a trade that isn't working, if things have changed, it's okay to get out. In Figure 7.1 if you got out after the 3-period moving average crossed back over the 10-period one, instead of waiting for the stop to be elected you would have saved yourself about 200 points.

If it's still within the parameters that got you in, look to see if they may be changing, so you can anticipate an exit. Maybe the trade is still good but

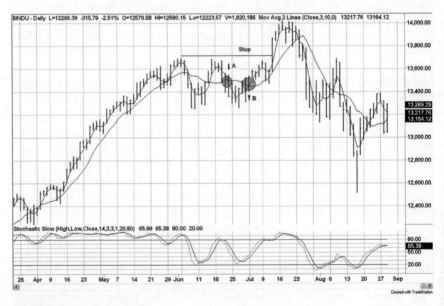

FIGURE 7.1 Daily Dow
Source: © TradeStation Technologies 1999. All rights reserved.

it's getting close to not being so, so you may have to watch it more carefully tomorrow. Make a note of this and keep it on your radar screen (I'm not referring to TradeStation's radar screen but to your personal one). Make sure if a trade is getting close to being one you have to exit that you are on top of it. In the example in Figure 7.1 you can see the 3-period moving average turning up and the highs of each bar getting higher prior to the crossover at point B. This could be a sign your trade may not be within the reasons you sold it for much longer, so you can start getting ready for action.

Is It Simply Not Working as Planned?

Another thing you should monitor is whether the trade is working like you planned. Yes, it could still be within your parameters, but maybe you were looking to get a quick move on the trade and after three days it's been stagnant, not doing a thing. You need to consider whether you still want to hold and monitor this dud? Your time and money could maybe be better spent elsewhere. So why not get out? The trade is not doing what you wanted it to, so you can consider moving on, though before you do make sure you gave it an opportunity to work. If you look at Figure 7.1 again you'll see this as well. Assuming you got filled on the short at the first circle, the market did nothing for the next few days. You expected it to go down right away and it hasn't. Even though the moving averages are still confirming a short, you may consider getting out as it's simply not performing as you'd like it to, especially on the fourth day. At this point, you gave it time to work and it didn't and now it looks like it may pop back up.

Is It Close to the Target Area?

Once your trade starts getting close to the target area that you should have established when you put the trade on, you should begin to monitor it more closely. The target area can be a number, like when the market hits 13,541 or it can be a technical target as in when the market reaches the top of a channel. It can be a time target as in exit after seven periods. Whichever the case, you want to be aware that it's getting close so that you can get ready to act on it the next day if the target is reached. You may, after reevaluating, consider moving the target, which is always an option, but make sure you have a reason for it if you do. In Figure 7.2 I used Fibonacci projections based on the up trend that started in July, to pick a target for a long using a breakout of a previous high. As soon as the market gets within about two normal days range from this target area (13,531), I would monitor it much more closely to determine when I need to get out. One thing you need to be on the lookout for is that it may fail to reach the target, in which case

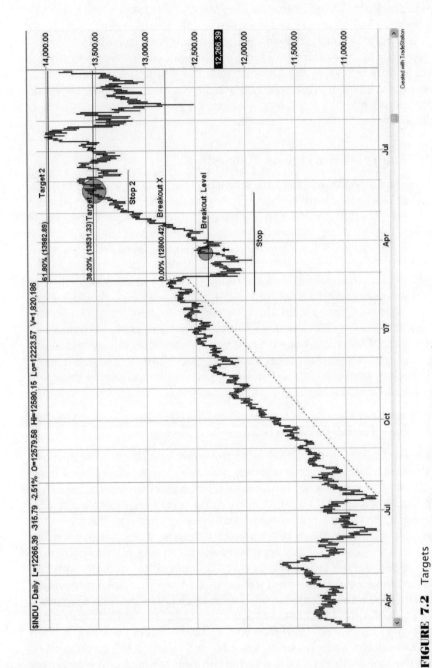

FIGURE 7.2 Targets

you need a backup plan as to what to do. I do this by constantly moving my stop up in a big move like this.

Has It Reached the Target Area?

Not only do you have to look to see if a trade is near its target area, you should also keep an eye out for trades that have already hit your target area. Let's say the market traded through a channel you had set as a target. You didn't exit because maybe the move was strong and you wanted to let your profits ride, which is a valid excuse. You now need to reevaluate the exit points. Should you come up with a new target and stop areas or should you get out, because your original level was hit? You could maybe keep the trade and use your old target as your new stop. You really want to be on top of a trade like this because there is no worse feeling then having a trade reach its target and then some, then getting a little greedy and before you know it goes against you and it turns into a loser. These losers are hard to exit because you keep thinking it will come back to the best levels of the trade and you end up just watching it fade away. Let's say in Figure 7.2 you did not exit at the target level and now the market is trading in the second circle. You need to now reevaluate the trade as a new trade and determine if you'd like to keep it as well as make a new target (target 2) and create a new stop level (stop 2). You may introduce new technical indicators to help you decide. I personally would have gotten out the second time it dipped below the 13,531 level. I would have given it one time to test the level and if it dipped below a second time I would exit. The reason being that I gave it a shot to work and it didn't right away, and it has already reached the target so why not get out?

Is It Approaching a Stop Level?

Just as when the trade is getting close to its target level, you also should be aware of any trades getting close to their stop levels. The closer it is to the stop point, the more you should pay attention, or maybe paying less attention is the better way to say it. Thinking too much about stops is a great way to cancel or move them, as the market gets closer to them. Sometimes your stops are mental and now is the time to either place them in or really watch the market so you can exit it if it does hit the level. If you are near a stop level, I recommend putting the stop in and forgetting about it. Do not try to second-guess it. If your original stop was well thought out, there is little reason to move it as the market gets closer. Most of the time you will end up losing more money by moving or ignoring a stop. You do, however, need to go over, review, and adjust stop levels on a regular basis. But I would not be moving them further away as they get closer for fear of getting stopped out. Look at Figure 7.3 and you'll see two different scenarios, the first is the long from the first shaded circle, which is the same from the previous example. As the market started getting better I would move the stops S2, S3, S4, and so forth, up along the with moving average until eventually the market catches up to it at S7 and you get stopped out; this is the proper way to move a stop. The wrong way is the other example. Say you shorted at the arrow marked Short and you placed a stop (Stop1) above previous highs. But a couple of days later the market rallies strong (oops). Now instead of leaving your stop in and taking it like a man, you move it up to Stop 2 to give the market room to breathe. All you are doing here is costing yourself 200 more points for no reason. As the market reaches the stop level you have reasoned to be good, leave it alone. I'll get into this in more detail later in the book.

Did You Ignore Stop Levels?

This section assumes you are a moron and let the market go through the level where you should have placed your stop. I'll discuss it later in the book, but you should not make a trade unless you know where you are getting out on both the winning and losing side. Maybe you had a mental stop, but froze and never put it on, or worse, you never even thought about

FIGURE 7.3 Stops
Source: © TradeStation Technologies 1999. All rights reserved.

one and just hoped for the best. Maybe you've been in the trade for a while and are making money and got a little lackadaisical moving a stop along to lock in a profit. Regardless of the reason, if you ignored a stop you need to put this trade on your "I must get the hell out of it soon" list and make sure you are on top of it first thing in the morning. If you go back to Figure 7.3 and for some reason you let the short keep going and did not enter the stop at Stop 2 and now it's trading above that, you really need to force yourself out of the trade the next day. Cutting your losses is something you need to learn and emphasize as you are making your game plan every day. Ignoring stops will definitely lead you down the wrong path, so should you find yourself in a position where you did ignore one and are now in danger, do not sit there and hope for the best; instead, get out and take the loss.

Should You Add to It or Cut Back?

Position size is another decision you should be thinking about as you go over every trade. If, as in the example in Figure 7.2, the market reached your target area and the trade is still working, why not take off some of the trade and lock in a little profit, but keep a little if you think it still has room. Maybe, on the other hand, it's earlier in the trade and the market just broke above the Break Out X line. Here you can have another strategy that kicks in when you break out of this resistance level. You are already in the trade with a nice profit and now you get confirmation of a strong trade with a new signal. In this situation you may want to consider adding to the position as the trade just got better in your eyes.

What, however, if the trade isn't really working as well as you had intended it to, but you don't want to get out in case it does take off? A good strategy here is to reduce the size of the position while still holding onto some of it, just in case it does end up working. Cutting back and scaling is one of the hardest things to do in trading, as you can probably make a case for both sides in every instance. No matter what you do never ever forget the cardinal rule of never adding to a loser.

Is Your Money Better Spent Elsewhere?

A part of the thinking process in the above scenarios when deciding on adjusting position size is that if you take off a portion of your trade, it will free up money to be used elsewhere. As you go over every trade keep that in mind and ask yourself, "Is my money better spent elsewhere?" If the answer is yes you may be better off getting out and putting on a different trade. Or at least keeping money on the sidelines for when a better setup does come along. You should not be in the habit of being maxed out, but many new traders have limited funds and can quickly reach their margin levels. Freeing up some money then becomes part of their everyday game plan.

Should a Trade Be Closed Now or Held Longer?

Which leads to the question, "Should I hold or get out?" If you have a purely mechanical system then you shouldn't override it and as such you should only get out when a signal is given. However, this book deals mostly with discretionary systems, which leaves a trader to make a lot of decisions. Althoughmost everything mentioned above comes down to this basic question. Ask it out loud. "Should I get out or stay in?" Keep singing the Clash's song "Should I stay or should I go?" until it becomes second nature. Ask yourself, "If I didn't have this position on would I get in now?" If the answer is no, you should get out and move on. Don't waste your time, money, and energy on positions you do not feel like you would have on if you had a fresh start. There have been many times where I've been married to a position I knew was wrong, but I couldn't make myself get out of it. I'd be long losing money and I knew that if I had no trade on I'd want to be getting short, because the market looked so bearish. Yet I couldn't bring myself to take a loss. Eventually I found that taking a loss is okay, and doing it will save you lots of money over time. So learn to do it. Now this doesn't just apply to losing trades, you could have trades that are winners but are no longer doing anything. You may want to reevaluate those as well every night, and if you believe or your strategies tell you it's done, get out and move on.

Has Volatility Changed?

As I write this, the volatility in the stock market has recently exploded. As you can see by looking at the Average True Range (ATR) in Figure 7.4, the S&Ps range has more than doubled in the last couple of weeks of trading. The average trading range went from under 12 points a day to well over 20 for the month of August. You must be aware of this as you trade because the dynamics of any trade made before this just got different. Targets and stops may need to be moved further away to make them realistic. The market may now be too dangerous for you to trade and you may have to reconsider your strategy. If you had a stop that was to get out after two consecutive days of negative closes and before you thought you were risking $2,000 dollars, well that risk may now be $5,000 and you may not be able to afford it. Likewise, you may have a fixed stop that is about $2,000 away, but now that can easily be hit by a modest intraday swing, so you'll get stopped out when technically you shouldn't have been. When the volatility changes dramatically you must reconsider your positions. Even if the

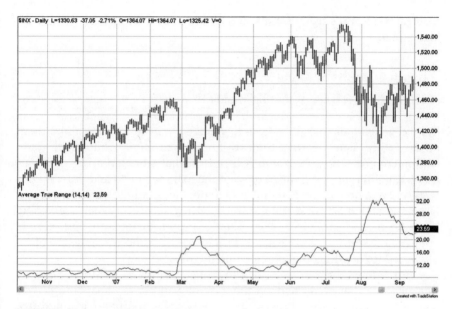

FIGURE 7.4 Doubling Volatility
Source: © TradeStation Technologies 1999. All rights reserved.

volatility changes to be smaller, you should still reconsider your positions. You may now want to add to your position or move your targets in to be more reasonable. Volatility may not have drastic changes often but when it does, be prepared to alter your strategy and game plan accordingly.

What Was in the News?

Another thing I think traders should look at is why the markets moved like they did. If you were in a trade that acted out of the ordinary, find out why it did so. It may not help you much on closed trades, but it's good to know if you still have a trade open. Though I don't like trading off of the news, it can sometimes change the nature of a trade, and you should be aware of it. Many news events are blips that will give a market a nice swing, but in the long run don't make a difference. But there are some that can be the cause of a market reversal, like when the Fed cuts rates more than expected, or a central bank tightens its monetary policy, or a company reports really bad financial news, or a CEO gets arrested out of the blue for accounting fraud. If news made something move, even just for the day, it's good to be aware of it so you can make a more educated game plan the next day. I always find trading how a market reacts to news to be a powerful tool, and you can take advantage of it if you incorporate that information into your game plan.

THINKING ABOUT TOMORROW

As you go over all your open trades, you need to keep thinking about them in the future. You will want to draw up different scenarios for each trade and make notes as to how you will react if that situation arises. I like to think up different possibilities of what the market can do and draw up targets and exit points for them. I'll anticipate if I will add to or subtract from a position. Doing this keeps me from getting surprised when something does happen. Maybe there is an earnings report coming out, and there is a chance it can cause your stock to move. As a good trader you will be prepared for anything that stock could do the next day.

For example, if you were long in Figure 7.5 you could start preparing for anything that could happen the next day and in the near future. You may say, "If the market breaks above the double top line I will add five contracts to my position, with a target of 14,300, and I'll raise my stop to under yesterday's low to the Stop 2 level. However, if it drops below the

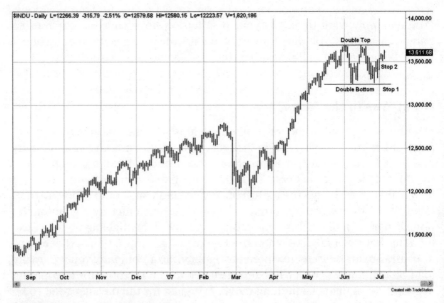

FIGURE 7.5 Drawing Scenarios
Source: © TradeStation Technologies 1999. All rights reserved.

double bottom, I'll exit all my longs and reverse and use the double top area as a stop. If the market stays within the range it is in now, I'll keep my current stop (Stop 1) and do nothing."

Planning out current trades will start to take the gamble out of your trading as it's much better to have all your scenarios planned out before they happen and surprise you. You can get more elaborate and consider what you will do if the market opens up 50 points and rallies or reverses after the up open or what you'll do if it opens below the support line. The possibilities are endless and the better you have them considered in your game plan the better you will do.

This isn't an end-all list of things to look for when going over your open trades. You may have special criteria you want to keep track of on your own, or you may have things that are specific to the way you trade or the markets you trade. I can't come up with every little thing, but part of trading is that you should always be learning and finding ways to improve, so work a little on figuring out other things to look for when going over your trades.

THE CLOSED TRADES

Did You Follow Your Plan?

After you finish reviewing the open trades, you then should go over the trades you closed out during the day. This is where the real learning begins. Again, you can do this in any order you like, but I like to go over all my losers first. I want to learn what I did wrong or right and reviewing is the best way to do this. The first thing you want to do is to make sure you had and stuck to a plan for the trades you made.

As you go over every trade ask yourself:

- Why did I make this trade?
- Did I have an entry plan when I got in?
- Did I have an exit plan for the trade?
- Did I follow my plan?
- What did I do differently and why didn't I follow that plan?

Having and following a plan is so important in being a winning trader. It is one thing you really need to keep on top of all the time. If you have a plan and have exit strategies in that plan and you consistently ignored them, then it's useless having a plan. You may need someone slapping you in the back of the head every now and then saying, "Hey stupid, what are you doing? Follow your plan." If you've ever watched the old *Pink Panther* movies, you'll remember Cato, Inspector Clouseau's martial arts expert manservant. Cato would constantly jump out of closets and sneak-attack Clouseau to keep his defensive skills and awareness sharp. Well, maybe we all need to hire a Cato to keep us on our toes and in line every time we deviate from our plan. It may hurt a little at first, but soon you'll be able to stick to your plan much better.

If you didn't follow your plan, ask yourself why not and what you should do differently next time to help you follow it. Find out why you put on every trade, and why you got out of them. If you are diligent about sticking to a plan, then you don't have much work to do here, but always review to make sure you stick to your guns.

The Good Losers

Some losing trades are good trading decisions that didn't work out and if you got out with a small loss when you were supposed to, I don't consider it a bad trade. A bad trade is when you let it get away or make a stupid, unplanned trade. Being able to take a good losing trade is the most important trade of all and this is a behavior I want to reinforce. The reason I think they are the most important trades of all is that your money is made as a total of all your trades—winners and losers. You will have losing trades, and you cannot get around that no matter how good you think you are. But if you are able to limit losses to a manageable amount and avoid the huge losses, your net profits will soar and you will be a better trader. I am more proud of getting out of something with a small loss that would have turned out to be worse, than I am about having a winning trade. Everyone can get lucky and make a great winning trade here and there, but only good traders know how to get out at the right time on the losing side. Even though I may have lost money on a trade it is a good trade if I did the right thing. When I review these trades I look to remember what I did to make me get out quickly so that if I see that situation again I hope to act correctly the next time as well.

Ones That Got Away

Next you can go over the ones that you just let go. These trades usually fall into two categories, either you overstayed your welcome and gave back too much on a winner, or you let a loser go and froze up as you watched it disintegrate. Either way they are going to really affect your P&L statement. It only takes one bad trade to wipe you out, even after 10 winners in a row, so try as hard as possible to not let it happen. You have got to learn to stick to your exit plans and constantly reviewing this will definitely help.

Don't be satisfied that you made money on a trade. If you had a 50-point winner that you turned into a 3-point winner, you screwed up that trade and gave back your money. At the end of the day, week, month, or year it's a total of all your trades that determines how you did, so don't take it too lightly if you take a small winner that was once a big one. You lost that 47 points, that was your money to be had. Find out why.

If I let a trade get really bad, I try to see why I did so, so I don't do it again in the future. As you look over the trade, look for the spot you should have gotten out and try to figure out why you didn't. It could be because you had no exit strategy or because you failed to follow one if you did, or because you got greedy and tried to get more than you could out of a trade. Or did you freeze up and hope a loser would come back? There are many reasons you could let a trade get beyond the point where you were suppose to get out. Figure out why you did so and work on not doing it again. These are the trades you need to work on the most on because they will draw down your account faster than the good trades will add to it.

The Good Winners

The last thing I review is my good winning trades and again I'll try to learn from them. Good winners are the trades you did everything right on and made some decent money with. Don't just look at it and say "good trade" and move on. Really delve into it. Ask yourself, "Why was it a good trade and what did I do right?" Did you just get lucky or did you really do something right. If you did something right, then make sure you keep doing it. By studying trades you may find that every time you make a trade with a certain setup it works great, but if a certain variable was changed a little it doesn't work as well. Only thorough reviewing will tell you things like this.

If you are a person who has trouble following a game plan, and odds are you are or you wouldn't have bought this book, keep track of how you did on trades where you followed a plan, had an entry point, and came up with a predetermined exit level. And then keep track of those trades you put on with little preparation. Next, compare them to see how they do. Hopefully you will see a big discrepancy and realize that you need to have and follow a strategy/plan when you trade if you really want to succeed.

GETTING READY FOR TOMORROW

Now that you have gone over all your previous trades, it's time to start focusing on the next day. As you reviewed your open trades you should have been adjusting your plan for them as you went along. But what about new trades you may want to put on? You can start looking at charts to see if there are any good setups you may want to trade. You can start creating entry and exit points for these trades. You can look to see if there are any schedule reports due. If so, figure out how you will react depending on what the market does. Say you are trading oil and the American Petroleum Institute (API) numbers are due tomorrow. If they are indicating a bigger buildup in reserves than expected, you would expect the market to drop. But after 20 minutes if it hasn't dropped then you will go long, otherwise you will short. If the numbers are weak, you will buy right away and give it a two-point stop.

Look at your charts and know where all the indicators, trend lines, and average true ranges are. See how the market closed today and figure out what you want to do the next day based on different openings. In the morning, you will follow up on this once you know where the opening is going to be, but it is better to get a head start the night before.

As you scan charts, have a note of what you are looking for. Are you looking for a breakout, a reversal, a bounce off of a channel? If you do find something you like, then be prepared by knowing where you will be exiting so you can estimate a risk and reward. Do your homework, look at different time frames, be realistic about what you can expect and what you can lose. Try to figure out how many contracts you will be trading based on the risk of the trade. This doesn't mean you will enter the trade in the morning, but you are giving yourself a potential trading opportunity that you have preestablished.

All this is a lot easier if you only trade one market; however, if you are one of those day traders who has 120 stocks on his screen and trades almost anything, this reviewing process is a little tougher. What I used to do when I traded equities was I had a scenario I liked to trade (I looked for trending stocks that have had a little pullback to a trend line) and I had my favorite stocks to trade. I would quickly go through them all and see which fit my setup. I made a list of the stocks that did and these are the ones I would look to trade the next day if they met further requirements.

By doing the things outlined in this chapter you will be well on the way to starting the trading day with a solid game plan. You will still have to make some adjustments to it in the morning, but you should now know how you will react to different situations in the market. You will have your stops and exit levels for existing trades. You'll have entry levels for new trades. And you'll even have targets and stops as well as risk and reward ratios.

REVIEW YOUR PLANS AND STRATEGY

Don't just review the trades but constantly check the plan itself for validity. You may be losing money and the reason may be that your plan is faulty so keep checking to make sure that it is sound. This is something you will definitely do during off market hours. It is not something you will do every night, but every now and then go over all your strategies and make sure they are doing what you thought they should. If they are, are you following them? Or maybe you just have strategies that were no good to start with. Doing this will help keep you on top of your game and ensure you are trading with a solid strategy.

CLOSING THOUGHTS

It doesn't take that long to do all these things; you can knock it out in 30 minutes to 2 hours depending on how much you trade. But regardless of how long it takes, it's worth much more than the effort you'll put into it. By going over all your trades, you will gain insight into your trading and you'll learn what's working and what isn't. Those who never review their trades will never learn what they do right and wrong. Instead, they will keep making the same mistakes over and over again. By preparing for the next day, you will get a tremendous head start on the day. Think how much better you'll trade if you come in with a game plan and scenarios for all your trades. No matter what curveball the market throws at you, you'll be ready. Hell, they will all look like hanging curves if you are prepared.

Now go and have that beer with John.

CHAPTER 8

Before the Market Opens

A man visiting New York City decided to take a tour. At one point in the tour, they went to the World Financial Center (which is on the Hudson River). The tour guide showed them some of the giant yachts docked at the pier, and said, "Here are the yachts of Wall Street's biggest stockbrokers." "But," asked the naive visitor, "where are the yachts of the investors?"

You did all your homework the night before and you think you are ready for the markets to open so you can start trading. Well, you still have some work to do, plus you should review what you reviewed the night before so you are on top of your game. Just like a football team looking at game films to get ready for a game, traders need to prepare for their trading day as well. Yes, you did a lot of prep work the night before, but the markets are dynamic and a lot can happen between then and the morning. Plus you want everything as fresh as possible in your head, so you should review your work form the night before with the added information of knowing where the market is likely to open.

TO EACH HIS OWN

What makes writing parts of this book a little tough is that I don't know how you trade, so I can't customize a plan for you explaining how you can review and get ready for the trading day. Every trader will have a different pattern that will benefit him the most and you need to figure it out on your own. If you are just a sugar trader, your process will be much different—and faster—than that of a person who trades 264 stocks throughout the day. The same holds true for your holding time frames. And whether you are a purely technical or fundamental trader will also affect these things. I have seen all types of traders over the years. I've also changed my style many times, from just trading one market like the S&Ps to trading every commodity there is to day trading 200 stocks a day, back to trading just one market again and holding for days and weeks. Game plans and preparation will differ dramatically from one trader to another, so not everything in here may be for you, just take out what you can.

GETTING THE NEWS

Though I don't put much faith in reading the news, I do like to keep abreast of what's going on in the world and in particular anything that may affect me. There definitely are events that can change how your positions will do. For example, the Fed cut the discount rate unexpectedly on the morning of Aug. 17, 2007, (the up arrow in Figure 8.1). The market had had a miserable month before that and there had been growing concerns about problems with credit companies like Countrywide so the Fed stepped in to give the market a boost. If you had been short going into this, you needed to reevaluate your thinking fast. Although if you were short you should have started reevaluating the day before when the market rallied back from a 300-point drop. One piece of news was all it took to make the market about-face and eventually reach new highs. If you had tuned it out you might have given back or lost a lot of money.

Not everything will cause such drastic moves, but you should be aware of what is going on. You should stay informed on how things like oil, interest rates, inflation, and unemployment are affecting the market. Part of your routine either in the morning or the night before should be to make a list of what reports are due and when. Some reports have a tendency to move the market so you may want to sit on the sidelines for those, while for others that don't really mean much, you may decide to keep a position on. Just be prepared for any fundamentals that may move a market. An important reason to do this is that if a report comes out that may cause a larger than normal volatility swing, you may want to be prepared to widen your stops or exit points—unless of course you want to be filled prematurely. You may also deem the market too risky and decide to watch it from the sidelines before getting back in.

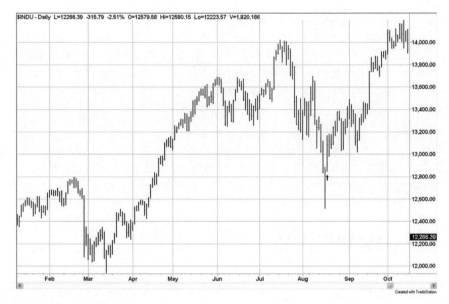

SINDU - Daily L=12266.39 -315.79 -2.51% O=12579.58 Hi=12580.15 Lo=12223.57 V=1,820,186

FIGURE 8.1 Unexpected Rate Cut
Source: © TradeStation Technologies 1999. All rights reserved.

KNOW YOUR MARKETS

You should know the markets you are trading. I can't tell you every report that can affect what you are trading, so make sure you know your stuff. Each commodity market and stock group moves on unique reports and news. Some major events can affect all markets but each one in a different way. It's your duty to know this. If you trade crude oil, or oil driller stocks, learn what drives them and know when any reports that affect them will come out. Have a list and be ready to react to anything that may occur when they come out. As you gain trading experience and through back testing you should come to know how markets will likely react to different reports. Once you learn how the markets should react to different events you will do better—especially when they fail to react to news as you would have expected them to, as this is always a great trading opportunity. It takes time and experience to gain this knowledge, but trading is not an overnight thing, so don't worry if you do not have it yet. If you are going to trade off of news-related events you will, however, need to acquire this knowledge.

LOOK AT OVERSEAS MARKETS

If your markets are affected by events that happen in Europe or Asia, then you should review to see what they did. Sounds simple right? Well it is. A lot can happen overnight, so spend the few minutes it takes to see what the world markets did. You can take the easy way out and just get the macro picture by watching CNBC, but spend a little more time and read through headlines. It is so easy to get news at your fingertips these days that there should be no excuse for people who don't do it. Even if you do not trade off of news, I find it helps to know why things did what they did. The days of trading the markets during regular daytime hours are long gone. Now you have to be ready for moves 24 hours a day. This can lead to both trading opportunities and dangers as well. The trading opportunities will be self apparent; the dangers come when the market blows through your stops during the night or opens much differently than it closed the night before.

HOW ARE THE MARKETS OPENING?

After looking to see what the markets did overnight, your next and more important duty is to see how they will open in the morning. Look at your positions in the morning and reevaluate them once you have a good idea of how they will open. Walk through all your open positions and justify why you have them and adjust any levels you may have to. Look to see if the market is opening near or through a stop or exit level. I wouldn't advise you to keep a trade that made you feel uncomfortable if it no longer fit in your game plan or exceeded it. If the market is close to an exit level, you will have to fine-tune your game plan for what to do and be prepared for action. Don't just stop with the ones you no longer feel comfortable with. You want to look over all your current positions for an opportunity. Sometimes, if a market opens up strongly in your favor it could be the kiss of death, as it can reverse for the rest of the day or more. Look at the shaded circle marked X in Figure 8.2 and you'll see where the S&Ps open up about eight points, leaving a gap from the day before. This was also an all-time high in the market. John, who is long, is dancing in streets and ecstatic. He starts making plans to buy a yacht and a house in the Hamptons. But the market has different thoughts and after a brief attempt at a rally, it closes the gap and keeps going down for the next 2 months dropping 170 points. John now has to put his plans aside and sell his car to meet a margin call on his trade.

FIGURE 8.2 Opening Gaps
Source: © TradeStation Technologies 1999. All rights reserved.

There are many opportunities in the market after the opening and you could use the opening call to find them. One example is that there are people who love to look for gaps in the morning and then trade in the opposite direction looking for them to get filled. I showed a bunch of examples of gaps that closed in Figure 8.2. They do not always work, but if you combine a gap with a couple of other variables including timing an entry and a stop, you can make money by trading gaps. Once you know where the market is going to open you can start making a game plan for these types of trades. I'll discuss how I do this in Chapter 11.

MAKING ADJUSTMENTS

As you are evaluating your positions, now is the time to think about making any necessary adjustments to them. Because the markets changed overnight your game plan for these positions could be totally different in the morning. You may now need to decide whether to exit a position or maybe move stops and targets. You may have to recalculate risk on a position and possibly lighten up or add to a position. If you are trading on tight margin you may have to look at your positions and decide to get rid of a few of them so that you can trade something else that has better potential. Maybe after sleeping on it you've decided you no longer like something; now would be the time to adjust your game plan so that you can exit the trade. As a trader you need to be flexible in your decision making so that you can adjust your game plan to suit the market. If you are a stubborn person who can't change, you will have trouble succeeding.

WERE THERE ANY BIG MOVES OVERNIGHT?

One of the things you need to look for is to see if there were any big moves in the position you have. If the move was against you, there is a chance it may have blown through your stop levels. In that case, you will need to decide if you will let yourself get stopped out on the open or do you take your chances and try to get out at a better price? Normally the best answer is to get out, especially if it blew through your well-thought-out stop. When you get these big overnight moves it can really screw up your plans. If you were long Yahoo!? in Figure 8.3 and were prepared to lose $2 dollars a share on 5,000 shares for a total of $10,000 on a trade but there was a tremendous move before the market opened, then you may be out $30,000 when it opens. The drop came after reporting lackluster earnings the night before. It's hard to take this kind of loss so some people will tend to ignore their original stop level and hope for the best. This can be a very painful process and you could end up holding a bad position on what was supposed to be a two-week trade for two years until it comes back.

The other situation that arises with the big moves is that a position you were in makes a nice move in your favor, either blowing through your target or getting close to your target much faster than you anticipated. Then you have to decide: Do I want to hold and get greedy trying to get more out of it, or take the money off the table? This one is even harder to figure out because it really could go either way. It could be the beginning of a big move, or it could do what I've seen time and time again, which is it has a great opening and then just goes the other way the whole day or even starts a major reversal like in Figure 8.2. When you get to these decisions you have to step aside and ask, "What would I do if I had no position?" It's too easy to think blindly with your position. It's kind of like being in a bar at 3:00 A.M. drunk and thinking the person you're talking to is someone that you would like to... well, you know that I mean. Taking a second to think with a clear head and looking at your trades with

FIGURE 8.3 Blowing through a Stop
Source: © TradeStation Technologies 1999. All rights reserved.

an unbiased opinion can make you quickly reevaluate your prospectives on things.

LOOK FOR POSSIBLE TRADING SITUATIONS

The morning is the best time to look for new trading opportunities. I like to sit down and pour through charts in different time frames and look for potential entry levels. I look for trend and channel lines, Fibonacci retracement levels, and potential breakouts. I do this for the 5-minute, 60-minute, daily charts, and weekly charts. I look for support and resistance levels, I look for previous peaks and bottoms and any patterns I can find. I also like to analyze the indictors I use, which are moving averages, Relative Strength Index (RSI), Moving Average Convergence/Divergenc (MACD), and stochastic and average true range.

Though I did this the night before briefly, I do it in more detail in the morning because it will be fresher in my head and of course things do change overnight. Plus, you have the advantage of knowing roughly where the market will open, which is something you cannot know the night before. As you are doing this, look for patterns that can help you. You may see a possible breakout area, or a spot where you can possibly get a reversal. The market may not give you what you are looking for, but at least you know what the possibilities are and will be prepared to act if it does what you think it may or fails to do what you expected. Remember, markets that fail to do as they are supposed to become great trading opportunities for traders.

I've shown a few examples in Figure 8.4, which is a 60-minute chart of the S&Ps with a MACD indicator. Assume you came into this period short. On the morning of Nov.13 you can make a case for exiting the short at circle A. Here, I notice divergence between the market and the indicator, suggesting it may be time to exit the trade. Besides, the market closed very weak the night before and now is called to open 20 points higher. I'd give it a half hour and if it didn't head lower I'd exit the trade. A couple of days later on the 15th, I found another opportunity to short as the market was not able to break higher on the 14th and formed the beginning of a trend line and sold off at the end of the day. With the market having a lower open on the 15th and then the histogram of the MACD going back to the zero line and a place to have a tight stop, I'd be willing to take a chance on shorting this at point B.

FIGURE 8.4 Looking for Trading Situations
Source: © TradeStation Technologies 1999. All rights reserved.

Similar to point A, at point C on Nov. 27 you also see divergence between the indicator and the market, so you can take this as an opportunity to plan an exit that morning on the lower open should the market go positive on the day. Finally, on the morning of the 28th you look to see that the market will open above the trend line and that the MACD lines have crossed over to the upside, which gives you a situation to trade if you trade breakouts. Here you can place a stop below the trend line that got broken and sit back and relax. If you like to trade gaps you could have shorted this open, but this one wouldn't have worked out, which is why you need to know in advance where you will get out if you're wrong.

DRAW UP SCENARIOS

One thing I like to do in preparing for the trading day is to draw up scenarios of what could happen. As I look at my stuff in different time frames, I make what-if plans for the market. For example, if the market is supposed to gap lower, I'll have a game plan for what will happen if it continues to go lower. I'll also have a plan if it gaps lower and immediately starts to rally. Then I'll have plans for what to do if the market fills the gap and fails, or if it continues to rally strongly after closing the gap. I'll go through this all in detail in the next chapter, so I'm not going to show an example here.

Look at charts and the news (if you rely on fundamentals) for all your positions and possible trades and draw up scenarios and have a plan for what you will do if the market breaks a level, or bounces off a level, or if it fails to react to something,and so on. The market is very unpredictable but if you are prepared for those unpredictables and have different strategies for them, you will be ahead of the game. If you know in advance what you will do if so and so happens you will be trading with a much clearer head and have the basis of a solid game plan, which will give you a tremendous advantage when something does happen.

ADJUSTING SIZE

As you are drawing up different scenarios for what can happen make sure to include how it will affect your position size.

There are four basic choices you can make with your position size:

1. Do nothing.
2. Exit the entire position.

3. Add to your position.

4. Reduce your position.

Your position size can be affected by changes in volatility in the market, by changes in total other positions that can affect how much you can risk on other trades, changes in your account size, changes in how the market looks, or the risks involved. It can also be affected by whether you have multiple systems that can give you signals to add or subtract from your position size.

One example of how your size will be affected is if you are tightly margined and have a position in crude oil that you like, but you see something you really like in soybeans.

Now you have a choice and need to ask yourself: Do I exit the crude and get into the beans, or do I forget the beans, or do I get out of half my crude and buy some beans? This is one of many scenarios you should have thought out before the market opens so you are prepared to execute trades when it does open without having to do much thinking.

MAKE YOUR DAILY GAME PLAN

During the last part of the morning, before maybe going to the bathroom, you should complete a game plan for the day. You have gathered a lot of information since the close yesterday, now take it and do something constructive with it. You should have started laying out the basis of your game plan the night before but now take the extra 15 minutes to assemble all your information into a proper plan for the day. Don't just have a mental plan, but write it out. You are more apt to follow something if you have it on paper in front of you. If you trade 10 stocks make a list of them and include entry requirements, how many shares you will trade, what your targets are, and where you will exit if you are losing. Have all your what-ifs clearly written out. I like to print out charts and draw arrows and circles on them to make it clear where I am getting in and out.

You can be a guy who trades one market and has trades that last two weeks. However, you should still update your game plan every day, as you need to make adjustments because you never know which is the day you will be getting in or out of your position.

If you are a purely systematic trader you won't be doing as much work. You should simply rely on your systems to give you all your signals. It's your job to follow them and adjust the number of shares/contracts you trade. The other type of trader is the day trader who makes hundreds of trades a day. Actually there are two types of day traders.

One is the day trader who is a pure scalper trying to get the bids and offers and make a tick here and there. His game plan relies on his discipline; he doesn't need to spend too much time studying the market and make a plan every day. Basically he may just want to know the direction of the market and then scalp in that direction. His trades can be random, but he has the discipline to get out right away when he is wrong.

The other type of day trader is the active guy who trades looking for dips to buy or rallies to sell or whatever it is he looks for during the day. Maybe it is shorting when the tick reaches a certain level or buying when the two moving averages cross. His morning preparation won't help him much in picking out trades. He has the markets he like to trade and is just waiting for opportunities during the day. His strategy is the same day in day out, so his game plan won't change much from day to day. Even though it seems like these traders may not need to spend time studying the market and making a game plan, they should. They still need to do things like look for general market direction, support and resistance for individual stocks, changes in volatility, and check to see how much they should be risking.

CLOSING THOUGHTS

This is pretty simple: The better prepared you are for the trading day, the better you will do. Take the time each morning to go over anything that may help your trading. Reevaluate your positions, see how the markets will open, draw up scenarios, and make a game plan for the day. That's it. Now it's your choice to do the work and eliminate some of the gamble from your trading and become a better trader or not do it and rely more on luck than skill.

CHAPTER 9

Drawing Up Scenarios

A long-term investment is a short-term investment that failed.

A s part of your prep for the trading day, you should have started the night before to draw up scenarios for what could have happened and then fine-tuned it in the morning. One important thing a well-prepared trader will have done is gone over the market and tried to out-guess it by imaging everything it could possibly do. You need to know what you will do if it keeps going in your favor—will you add to it or start lightening your positions? What will you do if a trend line gets broken? What if it reverses midday? What is the worst-case scenario? Not only must you do this before the market opens but you need to do it throughout the day as well, as the market can be a lot different at 2 P.M. than it was before the open or at 10 A.M.

As I continue, I'll show you how I would do it for the Dow Jones Mini futures contract that I like to trade. You, however, should apply it to what-ever you trade.

KNOW YOUR MARKETS—REVISITED

This is where the chapter on knowing your markets comes in helpful. If you are going to trade something, you should know what makes it move, what its typical trading range is, whether it has patterns it follows, and so on. It takes time to get really acquainted with a market, but it's time you should put into a market if you are going to trade it. For those who trade a couple of hundred different stocks, you will never do as well as a guy who specializes in just one or a handful of stocks; those guys know their stuff inside and out. They know pretty much everything they need to know that will help them be prepared to better trade and monitor their position. This puts them in a much better position to make money than a guy who is all over the place.

As you are making the morning game plan, make a list of variables that can affect your positions (if you have any on) or the market you are about to trade. For me, it could be that there is a Federal Reserve interest rate announcement today at 2:15, or the market is approaching its 50-day moving average, or the stochastics are at an overbought level and starting to turn down. This list will change every day as market conditions are always changing. It's part of your homework to be prepared to know what can happen. You should know which reports affect your markets and by how much, and you should know when they are coming out. There is nothing worse than being surprised by a report that moves a market in a big way. For example, if you trade crude oil you should be aware that every Wednesday there will be a report released by the American Petroleum Institute regarding inventories. This report moves the market and usually violently. You do not want to be caught unexpectedly on the wrong side of this move. You probably wouldn't want to get caught on the wrong side even if you were expecting the report, but at least then you would have made your own bed.

GETTING THE BIG PICTURE

If you have open positions, start with them. Let's say I'm long the Dow Jones, the first thing I want to know is why I got into the position. This shouldn't be hard to do if you have kept your game plan from prior days. But before I continue, I need to backtrack and go through the thinking process that got me into the position. I'll show you how I'd go about drawing up scenarios that led to getting into this position first.

First, I know I want to take primarily long trades. You can see in the weekly chart of the Dow Jones Industrial Average, Figure 9.1, that the market has been in a nice bull market for close to five years now, and the rallies are much more powerful than the pullbacks. This is typical of a bull market. Though there are several places where one would get hurt going long, for the most part the market is a strong one and should be bought. The one thing I'd prefer to see if I'm looking to get long is that the market was closer to the trend line as there is room for a 1,000-point drop while still remaining in a strong uptrend. The fact that it could drop so much and still

FIGURE 9.1 The Big Picture—Weekly Dow Jones
Source: © TradeStation Technologies 1999. All rights reserved.

be in an uptrend is one of the scenarios I'd have if I were to make a trade. As I look at this chart I see two scenarios: one is this possible drop, but the other is that it is in a strong uptrend and it looks like it may take off and make new highs.

I'm looking at the actual index here and not the futures. As I mentioned in Chapter 6, I make my decisions using the actual indices and then trade the futures, as I believe it's a truer indicator of the market's big picture.

GETTING A BETTER PICTURE

Next I'll look at a daily chart to get a better picture of what's going on. The market has been in a downtrend the last two months, but finally it may have had a move that could break that trend and begin sending it back up again. The Dow had a pretty huge day, jumping about 350 points, which followed a day where it jumped about 200 points after closing on its low the day before (see Figure 9.2). During this day, the market crossed the downward trend line of the past two months, the stochastics turned positive and started crossing over the oversold area, and the market rose above my two moving averages. With all these things looking good, I would

FIGURE 9.2 Getting a Closer Look—Daily Dow Jones
Source: © TradeStation Technologies 1999. All rights reserved.

consider this could be a sign of reversal toward the upside. But this is just one step in my confirmation of going long. I need to look at other time frames to confirm that I should be going long. The daily chart alone would give you a signal deep into the move, so I also look at other time frames to get a better picture, anticipate a trade, and time an entrance point. By taking it down a time frame and looking at the 60-minute futures chart, Figure 9.3, I was able to get a jump on the trade, but you can also use it to both confirm a trade and to start planning an entry.

When I look at the 60-minute chart, the first thing I notice is that the market has made two successful lows on Nov. 21 and then again on Nov. 26, while the stochastics indicator has not. This divergence is one of my favorite reversal signals. I'm looking for a pattern to get me long, and this is a great one; however, I don't want to jump the gun so I will wait for it to break the downward trend line. On Nov. 27, it closes just above it but not significantly enough to give me a signal. I know I'm on to something though, so I'll plan to possibly make a trade on the next day if it breaks this line on the open. If I did want to get in early the close above the trend line would have been a place I could have chosen to do so.

Come the next day as I'm doing my pre-market homework, I see the futures are called to open somewhat higher. The open would cause my moving averages to cross to the upside, which is a buy signal for me. Now

I need to start to draw up some scenarios. There are a few things that can happen. First is that the market opens higher and then closes the gap, going negative and back below the trend line of the 60-minute chart. Or it closes the gap but then rallies. It could also open higher and take off with the momentum of both the breaking of the down trend line, and the daily stochastics (Figure 9.3) showing it is coming out of oversold territory. The market has plenty of room to take off and this may be the push it needs to do so. The last scenario I would consider is that it opens higher, tries to go higher, and then fails. My plan for the morning is that I'll look at the 5-minute chart (Figure 9.4) and see what it does for the first 30 minutes. If the market is higher than where it opened at that point I will get in and for now my stop area will be at the low of the move from two days prior, but I could fine-tune this later. By the way, for the purpose of the rest of the book if I say put a stop at the low of, or something similar, it means at a comfortable level below that spot so that I don't get filled by the market should it retreat to near that technical spot, I want a little cushion to be safe. On the upside, if I hold this trade long enough I think it could go above 14,000. The reward-to-risk ratio is a little more than 2:1, which is good but not great, but I know I can raise my stop once the trade is established, putting the ratio much more in my favor.

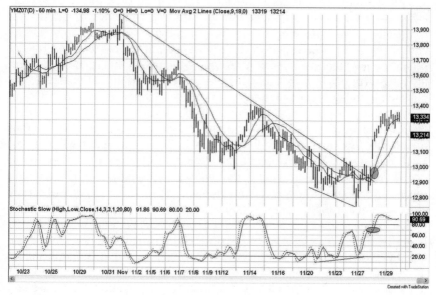

FIGURE 9.3 Finding the Trade—60-Minute Dow Futures
Source: © TradeStation Technologies 1999. All rights reserved.

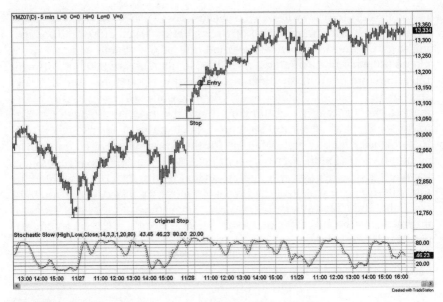

FIGURE 9.4 Entering the Trade, 5-Minute Dow Futures
Source: © TradeStation Technologies 1999. All rights reserved.

As you look at Figure 9.4, the 5-minute chart of Dow futures, the market does open higher and goes straight up, never backing off at all in a very bullish day. I place my order to buy at 30 minutes after the bell rings and get filled at 13,165. So now the trade is on and I have to start drawing scenarios for what to do with it. For now, I have an emergency stop and my long-term target is at least a new market high, which I believe is very possible in the next couple of weeks. However, I want to move my stop up for this trade as the original stop is just too far away. For a tighter stop I want to move up to just below the low of the day, because if the market breaks the low of the day, I believe it will fill in the gap, at which point I will reevaluate. Though I know my stop and my target I have one other criteria for this trade and that is that it closes in the top half of its trading range for the day. Otherwise, in my opinion, it is a failed attempt at a rally and break of a trend line, and I don't want to be in. If at 4 P.M. it's below the middle of the trading range I will get out, otherwise I'll hold on. As I plan to hold this trade for at least a few days, I'll end up spending more time looking at it every night and morning to see if things have changed, rather than during the day. I do, however, go over all my trades and potential trades at lunchtime and before the close to make sure they are still valid trades and that I want to hold them. This is a typical thinking process of how I'd enter a trade. Before I do, I'll have all the angles covered so nothing will surprise me. I'll do this every day looking at the markets I like to trade, looking for some opportunities. Maybe I can't always find a great setup like this, but there are always trades to be made, even if some of them are only for a couple of hours. It's tempting not to want to short a market that has been down trending for the last two months, but I always have to think longer term and try and find places to buy. I will, however, short on occasion if I see a fantastic short-term shorting scenario with a tight stop.

This whole scenario-making process can be done by the active day trader as well, but using a slightly different approach. Like I did before for this scenario, a day trader should analyze his markets and determine from which side of the market he will be trading. Yes, you can trade from both the long and short side throughout the day if that is your style, but I prefer to have one side and concentrate on that. If I'm trading from the long side, instead of reversing when the trade is done, I'll sit out till the next opportunity.

Once you have determined a side, you have to keep in mind that markets do have major turnarounds at times or can be trading choppy, which means you'll be better off buying and selling. As part of your scenarios, you have to be aware that these things can happen. And constantly throughout the day update your scenarios depending on what the market is doing. I'd say you should do it an hour after the market opens, at midday, halfway between that and the close, then about 45 minutes to an hour before the close, and if you plan on taking anything overnight once more in the last 10 minutes.

Getting into a trade is the easiest part of trading. Next come the harder parts: monitoring and knowing when to exit. This is where money is made or lost, so don't let down your guard after you are in.

END OF THE DAY

If I'm considering holding trades overnight, the last hour of trading is critical to me. This is when I have to decide for sure if I'm going to keep the trade overnight or not. It's not until the last 15 minutes of trading that I make that final decision. Most of the time it coincides with the evaluation I did in the last hour, but I have changed my mind a few times in the last few minutes. During this hour, I want to make sure I know what lies ahead for me. I'll make sure to know if there are any reports that could affect the position. If so, I want to make sure that doesn't change the risk involved. I'll go over my indicators and see if anything has changed to the point where it changes my outlook. I'll confirm that the trade is acting the way I had intended it to when I put it on. If I bought into the Dow and I was expecting a strong move that day and didn't get it, I would consider getting out even though it may be within my target and stop levels and I could be making some money on it. It didn't act the way I had expected it to, so why stay in? During this end of day evaluation I could say something like, "It's acting great. If it stays above 13,250 I'll keep the trade, if not I'll get out." Or I might say, "Everything is still as planned, even though I'm down a little on it, I wasn't expecting it to shoot out the gate, and I still believe the trade will do what I expected it to so I'll hold it overnight."

I don't reevaluate long-term targets and stops at this point. That will be done later. This time is just spent deciding If I want to keep the trade based on its performance, how things may have changed, and whether there may be something coming up the next day I may have missed earlier. I usually know if my intentions are to get in and out of a trade in the same day or hold it overnight before I put on the trade, but things change throughout the day and it's important to change with them. This doesn't mean you should make a long-term trade out of a short-term trade that failed.

BACK TO MONITORING OPEN POSITIONS

Okay, I have spent about six pages, more or less depending on how it comes out in print, explaining how I got into a position, which probably should have gone in Chapter 11 on entering trades. Anyway, now that I have a position, I need to start monitoring it. And I have to do it I every evening and morning. You saw before how important it was for my entry to know that the market was expected to open higher when making my scenarios. This is why the morning period is critical to planning out your day, as you simply cannot know the opening call at night. The best way for me to monitor my positions is to start making up scenarios of what can happen every day. You shouldn't just forget a trade once it's on and expect to either get stopped out or filled at your target. You have to actively monitor it.

If something is working for me, I'll tend to hold it for as long as it works. This could be a few days or two months. I let the trade decide how long that is, regardless, I take it one day at a time. When I made this trade my intended target was for the market to make new highs. This doesn't mean I will not exit it sooner if it is not working. After putting on the trade it looked like I was going to be right, but it ended up not working out that way. As you can see in Figure 9.5 the rally ended up failing and we never did make those new highs. But that's okay, not every trade will work out as planned, but I stuck to my plan, which is important. The trade took off like a bandit the day I made it (the shaded circle), the market was up over

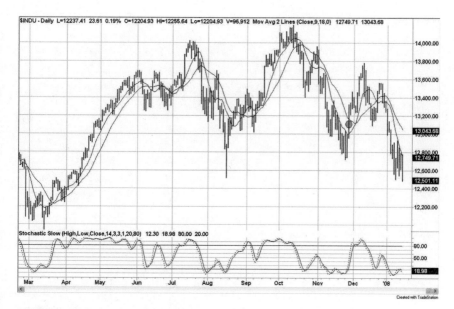

FIGURE 9.5 A Look Ahead
Source: © TradeStation Technologies 1999. All rights reserved.

350 points for the day and I had 170 points in it, which is a nice cushion. But you never want to let how much money you've made affect your trading decisions as you make up scenarios.

So that first night I have to start looking at the market and think, "What do I want to do now?" My first concern is not to turn it into a big loser, because one scenario is that it could completely turn around and give back the 350 points plus some the next day. The market had been pretty wild the last half year so anything is possible. First thing I want to do is make sure my stop is a good one, which will give the trade room to work. For now, I'm content with my stop below the gap, but I will want to start raising it soon.

That's pretty much it. I'm still looking at a nice move in this market, and until I see something that may change that opinion, I'll stay long. It's too soon in the trade to add to the position or take some of the profit. My main concern is that it is working and that I'm protected.

ONCE THE TRADE IS ON

December 5, 2007

Let's move forward to later in the trade (Figure 9.6) where I do have choices to make. It's a week after putting on the trade and it is doing okay,

FIGURE 9.6 Drawing Scenarios: 1
Source: © TradeStation Technologies 1999. All rights reserved.

nothing stellar, but I'm happy with it. After a quick initial jump up, it has consolidated in a sideways pattern, but the lows have been getting slightly higher and it just closed near the high of the area. I like the congestion area because this could mean the market is poised to explode upward. The stochastics at overbought levels are actually a bullish sign, as long as they stay up there. As far as my scenario goes at this point, the market can take off to the upside, consolidate more, or break downward. If it breaks to the upside I want to move my stop up to just under the congestion area (A) made by the recent low of the days. This, unless something unforeseen happens, locks in a profit for me. If the market consolidates more or it drops, I would use the lower moving average as my stop level (B).

December 10, 2007

Next we move three days further (Figure 9.7). If you are counting along and are thinking December 10th is five days later, don't forget the weekend. The market has finally taken off and looks like it may head up toward the new highs I had aimed for. As I make a new scenario at this point I want to move my stop and not risk 500 points per contract, but there really is no place to put one that would be a proper stop. Given the recent big moves in the market, anywhere between where it is and the lows of December 5th is fair

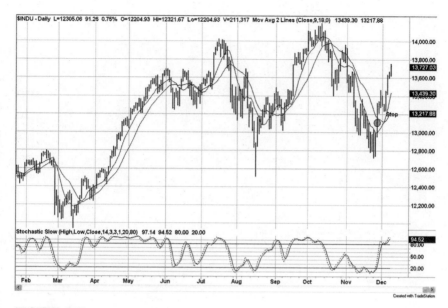

FIGURE 9.7 Drawing Scenarios: 2
Source: © TradeStation Technologies 1999. All rights reserved.

game for the market to hit while still being in its up phase. I'm concerned that it is moving too far off its moving average and is due for a correction of a few hundred points. Tomorrow at 2:15 the Federal Reserve Open Market Committee will make an interest rate announcement, which could move the market, substantially, either way. I am leaning toward taking 50 percent of my trade off before this announcement and locking in a profit looking to get back in should it retrace afterward. Though my initial target was much higher and it's doing what I had intended it to do, I will take some of the gamble out of this position by exiting half tomorrow. With the other half I will stick to my previous stops, regardless. My rationalization for this is that I still believe it will go up, but I want to reduce my risk. I will go back to 60- and 5-minute charts to exit this portion of the trade. If the market does rally after the Fed announcement, I will look to get back in so that I'm at my full position size. I'm not concerned about missing out on some profits, the balance of not taking a beating if I'm wrong makes it a zero gamble proposition for me.

December 11, 2007

Yikes! The market crapped out, dropping 350 points for the day (Figures 9.8 and 9.9). I ended up taking half of my position off near the high of the

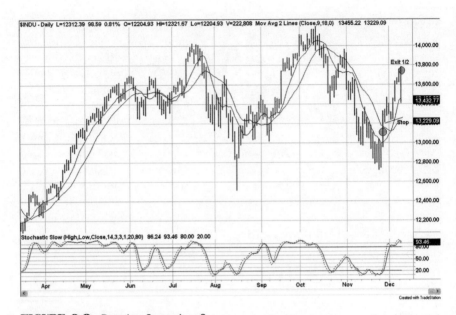

FIGURE 9.8   Drawing Scenarios: 3
Source: © TradeStation Technologies 1999. All rights reserved.

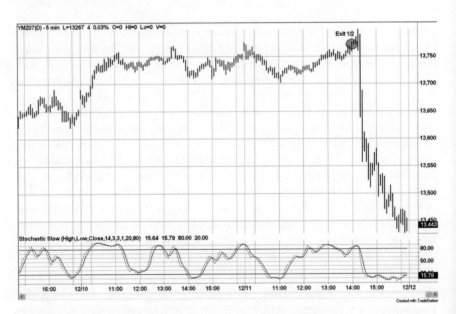

FIGURE 9.9   Exiting Half the Trade, 5-Minute Futures Chart
Source: © TradeStation Technologies 1999. All rights reserved.

day, just before the Fed announcement came out. My rationalization and scenarios of what I was looking for will come in a few pages. I held until 2 P.M. because the market gave me no indication I should get out beforehand. (I sold it at 13,761 for close to 600 points on this part of the trade.) My main reason for taking this portion off was that the market had just had a great run up recently and that could have been in anticipation of a rate cut. If so, once the cut hits the market it may sell off in the old "buy the rumor, sell the news" manner. The market was sitting at the top of its range just before the Fed announced a cut of the fed funds interest rate by one-quarter of a percent. But the Fed gave no indication that further interest rate cuts are likely, just a wait-and-see attitude. Traders were a little greedy and were hoping for either a half-point cut or further indications of rate cuts. Not getting exactly what they wanted, traders threw a tantrum and the market plummeted. Though it had a huge move down, it's not an extra out of the ordinary move given the recent volatility of the market and the fact that it is still in its recent uptrend. I also believe this is an overreaction to news and that the market will shake it off to continue this leg of the up rally. It's also the end of the year and portfolio managers want to look good and will try to rally the market in the next two weeks. However, now I need to be really attentive as a 350-point drop could mean the move is ending. If it goes below the congestion area of a few days prior, I have to exit the rest of my position. My best-case scenario is that this was just a little blip on the charts and that it continues up, in which case I want to re-add the contracts I exited. Many traders would have exited the whole position before the Fed announcement, but I try not to trade around news items if I'm looking to hold long term. I can't decide if I should be happier for grabbing close to the highs on half and looking like a guru, or kicking myself for being a schmuck and not exiting the whole thing before a risky announcement. If I had been day trading I would definitely not have had a position on during the announcement. I would have looked to enter the market afterward without a long-term bias and just looked to capture the day's move. A little later in the chapter, I'll look at this as a day trader would have and you can see my analysis there.

After the market closed, I looked at all the scenarios the market could muster up and decided as long as the market was higher 30 minutes after the open, the next morning I'd re-buy the contracts I had exited, using my initial stop area. This is a great opportunity to get back into the trade, while having taken a few bucks off the table.

December 12, 2007

The market is expected to open much higher, about 250 points higher (Figure 9.10). There were a few scenarios I now considered. The ones that

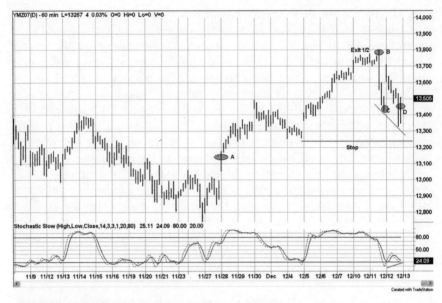

FIGURE 9.10   Getting Back In: 60-Minute Futures
Source: © TradeStation Technologies 1999. All rights reserved.

stick out to me the most are one, the market could sell straight off, in which case I would hold my position until I got stopped out. Two, it could rally and shake off the drop from yesterday, in which case I'd like to get back in. And three, it could just float around doing nothing, in which case I need to reevaluate later in the day and look to re-buy if it closes positive for the day. After the strong open, it ended up selling off most of the day, dropping some 370 points from the high to low and going negative for the day. However, in the last hour of trading it had a sharp turnaround, rallying 170 points off of the low. When it crossed back above yesterday's close point C, I reentered the position I had exited the day before at point D (13,452). One reason I felt comfortable doing this was the divergence between the market and the stochastics, indicating the down move may be ending.

December 14, 2007

The market has been consolidating the last two days (Figure 9.11), and it is holding its lows of the days in a steady area. Today it closed near the low of that range, and it's getting closer to both the stop area and the longer of my moving averages. It already broke into the moving average band, and is only 40 points from the lower average, and the stochastics have turned

FIGURE 9.11 Drawing Scenarios: 4
Source: © TradeStation Technologies 1999. All rights reserved.

lower. There is a good chance I will get stopped out of this trade tomorrow or in the near future. Regardless of what happens though, I will not lower my stop because I think it is a properly placed one. The one scenario I'd love to see is for the market to open lower, test the moving average while staying above those lows from the week before and then have an upward reversal day. (This means it makes a lower low than the day before and then goes positive on the day.) If this is the case I will add 50 percent of my position size to my trade. I'll do this because the risk if I'm wrong is quite low at this level and the potential on the upside is quite high.

December 17, 2007

Monday morning, the market is called to open about 70 points lower (Figure 9.12), which would be below my stop area. I reevaluate the market and my positions, but nothing has changed I will give it a half hour after the open to see if it can rebound first, if not and it is below the stop area at that point, I'll exit the trade regardless.

The market opens lowers and though it doesn't sell off right away, it cannot rally, so I stop myself out at 13,252 (point X) with a profit of 87 points on the remaining portion of the initial trade and a loss of 200 on the second long I made. Plus, I had already locked in a 596-point profit on the

FIGURE 9.12 Stopped Out, 30-Minute Futures Chart
Source: © TradeStation Technologies 1999. All rights reserved.

first half that I had exited earlier, for a total of 483. Though my initial trade wasn't stellar and didn't do as expected, overall it turned out okay. It was a well-thought-out trade all along the way, and I don't regret giving back 600 points. First, I could never have known when the high was going to be and second, I stuck to my game plan on the trade and if it had worked I would have done quite nicely on it. I will now sit on the sidelines looking for another opportunity to go long.

THE DAY TRADER

It's a lot easier for an overnighter to make up scenarios than it is for the more active day trader who gets in and out in every 10 minutes. But the day trader has to do this as well. He still needs to draw up his scenarios every day for what his markets can do to give himself an edge and an idea about what he wants to do. He may realize he is in a choppy market for a while and constantly has to figure out when that choppiness is over so that he can change trading strategies, because what works in a choppy market will not work in a trending market. The morning scenario is important as there are many trades a day trader can make based on how the market will open. It doesn't matter if the market opens higher, lower, or flat, once you know how the market will open you can start making up plans for what you will do in the morning. You should have a plan for getting into and out of the market without hesitation based on your scenarios.

As the day progresses you should be updating your scenarios as you get into new positions. The day trader has to think fast, but he can take advantage of the market by being prepared for it.

MAKING SCENARIOS FOR THE NEWS

Let's go back to the situation where you know that a major report or news event will move the market. In my trade above, I made the choice to exit a portion of my trade and keep the remaining portion, ignoring the news to come. Some may call this gambling, but I considered my trade as a longer term one and took into account the news that may affect the market; besides, I was going to lock in some profit on the trade by getting out of some. Though it was a gamble going into a report, it was a calculated gamble. But if you were a shorter term trader or a day trader, then you would have to trade around this kind of news. I'd say about 95 percent of all good day traders are on the sidelines just before a Federal Open Market Committee (FOMC) interest rate announcement, as it is such a gamble.

So what's the best way to trade this? Why, make scenarios of course. First figure out what the Fed can do. They can leave rates alone, raise them, or cut them (and if they cut them they can do so by one quarter or one half a percent). Then comes the Fed's statement, which can hint at further increases, or cuts, or their intent to do nothing. The market consensus was for a 25- to 50-basis point cut in rates (with 25 being more likely) with hope for further easings. That's a lot of scenarios and combinations to be prepared for, plus you need to double this as you actually should wait to see how the market reacts to this news to really make the best decision.

Given the recent economic slowdown and lending problems, it is highly unlikely that rates would rise or stay the same, but if they do, I'd expect the market to really plummet and I'd want to get short as soon as possible. If the market gets a 50-basis point cut and expectations of further cuts, you could expect the market to explode. Everything in between is where it's hard to figure out. A 25-basis point cut with expectations of further cuts would be quite bullish, while a 25-basis point cut with expectations of no further cuts could be anywhere from slightly bullish to bearish but most likely bearish—though I wouldn't have thought it would be as bad as it turned out. I had thought the market would maybe sell off about 100 points or so and then rebound in the next day or two, which is the main reason I did not get out of the whole trade. One other point to remember is that the market had just had a nice run up the last two weeks, and any good news may have been discounted in the price already, so there may be no place to go but down.

These are all preannouncement scenarios; now we have to see what the market can do. I'm aware that the market is near the high of the day as well as its high for the last month and a half. At this level there is probably going to be some action when the news comes out. Either it will skyrocket toward maybe new highs and then perhaps do an about-face, or it could just sell off if the market doesn't get what it wants. The way I trade these announcements is to sit back and do nothing for the first 10 minutes and then look to see a direction confirming or disconfirming the news. Many times you will get whipsaw moves, which tell you nothing, before the big move comes. Also, I'm not against trading against the trend on big news days as I see them as a one-day news-related move that can be taken advantage of and not as a change in direction.

As you can see in the two-minute chart of the day (Figure 9.13), the initial reaction (shaded circle) was to go up but that failed in a couple of minutes and sold off with no looking back as soon as it was announced that

FIGURE 9.13 FOMC Result, 2-Minute Futures Chart
Source: © TradeStation Technologies 1999. All rights reserved.

there were no future expectations of rate cuts. If I had been day-trading, I would have gone in with an open mind. If the market broke new highs I would get in on the long side with my stop below the low of the day. If it failed to rally while getting the 25-point basis cut, then the proper decision would be to go short. This, with the disappointment of no future expectations of rate cuts, could make for a great short. Because I wasn't day-trading and had a long bias, I chose to ride it out and look for a buying opportunity to reenter the portion of trade I had exited.

GENERIC STUFF TO LOOK AT WITH OPEN POSITIONS

How you look at the market during off-market hours will depend on your open positions. A person who is long and one who is short could both have positive outlooks on their position and may have different criteria and expectations they look for. People with different indicators or strategies will look at different things to help them decide what they want to do. The best I can do is give you some basic questions you should answer to guide you with drawing up scenarios.

Are the Conditions You Entered the Trade for Gone?

One of my main criteria for getting out of a trade is that the reason I got in no longer is in play. Say you were playing poker (Texas Hold 'em) and stayed in to see a flop because you had two clubs. You were looking for a flush, but then if no other clubs came out you should fold, assuming you didn't improve your hand with a good pair or three of a kind, or something like that. The reason you folded is because you didn't get what you were looking for. Beyond that, you are just hoping you get the cards you need to win and hope is never a good strategy. The same holds for trading. If I'm long because of a breakout of a trend line and then that breakout fails, it's time to get out. As you read this you may be wondering what this has to do with drawing up scenarios. When you are making your game plan and scenarios, you need to note at what point the conditions you entered for would no longer be there and what market scenario would get you to that point.

What's the Worst-Case Scenario?

Though one can never really predict the worst-case scenario, you should be prepared in case it does happen. If the market has been ranging an average of 100 points a day for quite a while, you wouldn't expect that one day it will drop 400 or 500 points. But it does happen every now and then. It happened to me in late February of 2007 (Figure 9.14), when I put on an options position that got decimated in two days. You also occasionally get a day when the market is down 200-plus points at 2:30 P.M. only to close positive by 150 points. Though we can't plan for these events, you should have worst-case protective stops in the market just in case. And every day that the market is down or up big, you should keep in mind that there is a small chance it could reverse big and have a backup plan in case it does. It's kind of like living every day like it's your last; one day you will be right.

Now, let's forget about the extreme moves because they don't happen that often. But even thinking about normal moves, you should get yourself prepared for being dead wrong or the market turning on you. If you are long and making money, you should have a scenario for what you will do if the market decides to prove you wrong. For example, in the trade I showed earlier in this chapter my worst-case scenario is that I am wrong and the market drops, continuing its downtrend. I was willing to risk to the low of two days before I got in (this is where I had planned to put my initial stop), which, with slippage and all, would have been close to 400 points. When I raised my stop to the low of the day, my worst-case scenario

FIGURE 9.14 Out of the Ordinary Move
Source: © TradeStation Technologies 1999. All rights reserved.

hadn't changed, but my new stop would get me out beforehand. In either case, I'm prepared for the worst, so it won't come as a shock should it happen.

MY $8,000 NOONER

I remember one day when I was day-trading stocks and I had just started dating a girl who lived two blocks from my office. She called me up and said she was home from work that afternoon and asked me if I wanted to come over. I think I was out the door before I hung up the phone. I had maybe 10 long positions on at the time, which were all doing okay in a boring, sideways market. So I didn't think much about leaving them alone, besides, I had stops in them (though not tight stops). I put on CNBC when I got to her place just to keep track of the market, which didn't go over all that well. After about an hour or so, a report comes out about an anthrax scare. My first reaction was, "Ah crap, I'm gonna get killed." My second reaction was, "Ah crap, how am I going to leave. She's gonna kill me." I had my stops in, so I decided to stay. I later rushed back to the office where I had been stopped out of everything with an $8,000 loss (which was a big loss for me).

Though this is a scenario you can never really plan for, you always need to have the unexpected in mind and be protected should it happen. The worst of it was that it was a false scare and the market came roaring back up later. That feeling was even worse than her e-mailing me and saying I was a jerk and she didn't want to see me again. Anyway, the moral of the story is that if you are going to have a nooner, make sure you're protected.

Where Should My Stops Be?

As part of the scenario process, you need to constantly reevaluate where your stops should be. You need to ask yourself, "Do I need to readjust my stops?" This could be done to make them tighter so that you lock in a profit or take less of a loss. Or it can be done to move them away if the market calls for it, although it's not a good idea to move stops farther away simply because you are close to getting stopped out. There are some situations where, after a day or two, you are very likely to get stopped out, even though you are still correct in your trading decision. Maybe it's because volatility changed and your old stop became too tight. If this were the case, I would do one of two things. Either get out because conditions have changed, or change the stop to a proper level given the new volatility.

Most times though, you should look to move your stops closer. As you go through your different market scenarios, concentrate on where you will get out if the market doesn't go your way. One thing I want to note is that depending on the trade, I can have different stops based on the scenario. Let's say I'm long the market and have a protective stop in. I also may have a system that gets out of a long trade if the market gaps open higher and then goes five ticks below unchanged for the day. In this case, I have my original stop, which is based on the reason I got in, but if the market does open higher then I'll have a new stop at five ticks below unchanged. If the market does not gap higher then this stop is not even put into play. If the market does gap higher but doesn't go negative afterward, then I revert back to my regular stop for the next day unless I move it for some other reason.

Is the Market Near a Stop or Exit Point?

The closer you get to your stop or exit point, the closer you get to action time. This is the time you have to really draw up the tightest scenarios to confirm what you want. Avoid the temptation to move your stop or target simply because you are close to it. But the markets are dynamic and change with the wind, so the target you had in mind two days ago, may be totally irrelevant today, and you need to make sure you have the proper scenarios of what it can do now. You need to be totally alert as you get closer to a stop area. In my example above, I knew the market was going to stop me out on the open. But I had a scenario that called for me to remove the stop for a half hour to see if I could get a turnaround. As long as you are disciplined to get out when that 30 minutes is up, I think it's acceptable to do this. The problem comes when you do not actually get out when you say you are going to.

Should You Add to or Lighten Your Position?

This is one of the main reasons you want to draw up scenarios. Every day and every hour things change. The initial position you may have had may no longer be as strong or it may be stronger. By keeping abreast of the market changes you can be in a better position to lock in a profit, limit a loss, or see a new place to add to your position. The person who puts on a trade and then ignores it, is really only trading half-ass and putting on an unfinished trade. Nurture the trade and you will get a lot more out of it.

What Is This Indicator Trying to Tell Me?

Indicators not being a set-in-stone science, leave a lot to the what-ifers' imagination. You can ask yourself, "What will I do if the trend line gets broken? What if it holds? What if the five-period moving average crosses the 20-period one, while the RSI is rising? What if the stochastics indicators are oversold but stuck in oversold territory? What if they are rising and all of a sudden turn? What if the market breaks a 10-period congestion area? What if it breaks then fails?" I can go on and on with this for the next 12 pages, but you get point. Make scenarios of whatever can happen and you will be so much more ready to trade them when they happen than if you came in blind.

Traders all have their things they look at when evaluating positions and there are many ways to come up with scenarios. I like to know the average true range (ATR) of the markets I trades. I'll know that if it stays within its average range I will think one way, but if it breaks it, the market is presenting a different scenario from how it normally acts, so I start looking at it from a different point of view. Some people like to know where the pivot point (the average of the previous day's high, low, and close) is. They trade one way if it's above the pivot point and another if it's below, and yet another if it dances around the pivot point area. Whatever indicators you like to use, draw up scenarios as to how you would react depending on what they say.

What If It Reverses Midday?

Are you prepared for a huge reversal during trading hours? Though not an everyday occurrence, it does happen, and it can be violent. I've seen several times where commodity markets go limit down and then reverse later in the day to go limit up. I've seen the Dow be down 150 points at 2:30 P.M. and then rally 300 points. I've been on both sides of these days, where one minute I'm down $12,000 and then end the day up $10,000 and vice versa, I've also had a couple times where I played it perfectly and caught both moves. One that sticks out was simply using my multiple time frames and seeing a support line in the 60-minute chart that wasn't clear in the daily or five-minute chart and combining it with a stochastic indicator that just crossed over from oversold. The things I did best here was not get married to my position and included it as one of my market scenarios as the day unfolded. It's hard to predict these moves until after they are well on their way, as they start out looking like a normal dip or bounce in the giant move of the day. You could have a great short trade on and be down 150 points in the Dow, and before you know it, it's only down 100 points and you are tempted to short more as you believe it is just a bounce and a new shorting opportunity. Then all of a sudden the market is down 50, then down 10 and then up 40, and so on until it closes up 150. These moves happen so fast you have no idea what hit you. Just know it can happen and have stops to help you avoid a disaster. You need to be able to think fast and reevaluate at the drop of a hat without being stubborn if it does.

CLOSING THOUGHTS

This chapter ended up being longer than I had planned, okay a lot longer, so I guess it turned out to be more important than I had thought. There's a lot to recap in it, but I don't want to make it much longer. So I'll just say, it's really, really important to draw up scenarios of everything that could happen, before and after the market hours and then a few times during the day as well. Keep an open mind and try to be able to look at the markets from all sides. Yours is not the only opinion out there. Even if you trade the wrong opinion, you should know what the market can do and be prepared for it. The more you can imagine what it will do, the more likely you are to reduce your risk and capitalize on your trades.

CHAPTER 10

Taking the Gamble Out of Trading

One day, at a restaurant, a man suddenly called out, "My son's choking! He swallowed a quarter! Help! Please, anyone! Help!" A man at a nearby table comes over and says he was quite expert at this sort of thing. He walked over, wrapped his hands tightly around the boy's testicles, and squeezed. Out popped the quarter. The man then went back to his table as though nothing had happened. "Thank you! Thank you!" the father cried. "Are you a paramedic?" "No," replied the man. "I work for the IRS."

O riginally this chapter was called "Making the High Probability Trades," a title that I may have lifted from that other book I wrote. They are both basically the same concepts, but now that I have finally chosen a title for this book, I'll go with this new chapter title, even though trading without gambling is only achieved by making the high probability trades.

ALTERNATE TITLES FOR THIS BOOK

I've written this book out of sequence and I'm down to my last four or five chapters now. With so many other things on my plate I've been at this on and off for a year and a half, mostly off. But now I'm concentrating on finishing and glad to finally see the end zone, and then I can go back to having some free time. Though we are about at the halfway point of the book, I'm more than three-quarters of the way done. If you're wondering why, it's because I wrote most of the chapters that did not have charts first. I've also been writing two chapters at a time, one at home where I have my charting software and one on my laptop wherever I happen to be. For example, I'm working on this chapter and Chapter 17 (which may become Chapter 16) at the same time. Hopefully when I go back to review everything, it will make sense and flow.

Well anyway, it took me a while to come up with a title for this book, about two years more or less, mostly because I didn't give it much thought. The working title was *Trading with a Plan*, but I never liked that much as it was too generic. The other working title amongst my friends and family was, "This $&%*@#^ Book I Don't Think I'll Ever Finish."

Here's a list of other titles for this book I though would do well:

Harry Potter, Market Wizard and His Trading Secrets

The World's Greatest Trading Book Ever

Trade Your Way to Riches, Yachts, and Bikini-Clad Girls with Implants

Higher Probability Trading II

Trading For Really, Incredibly Stupid Dummies

Trading for an Even Better Living

The whole goal of the previous chapter was to get you to make the best thought out trades you possibly could by taking some of the surprise out of the market by being prepared for any scenario. If you want to take the gamble out of trading, then you really need to plan out every trade and only take the ones that in the past have had a high degree of success and/or have a reward to risk level that makes them worth it. I'm still debating whether to have the following chapter be titled "Have a Reason for Every Trade" or to combine it with this one. The reason I'm debating it is because you cannot make a high probability trade unless you have a good reason to make the trade. Because I will rely on that concept in this chapter I may not have enough to write a full chapter on it later. I also may have stolen a little for this chapter from the previous chapter and from another one later on reviewing and managing trades. We'll see what happens as the chapters unfold. Sorry, if anything gets repeated, but it is probably important.

GOOD TRADES CAN BE LOSERS

Though the trade I made in the last chapter didn't work out as well as I had hoped, it was still a high probability trade in my opinion. It had all the ingredients of a good trade and as perfect a setup as I could want. Though

I made money on the trade, it fell short of my expectations but I thought I acted correctly on it the whole way. Not all good trades will make you money. Sometimes you'll put on what looks like a great trade that ends up going against you, but so what. You did your best and you stuck to your plan. Not all trades are going to be winners, so don't sweat it if it you don't make money on every well thought out trade, it's part of the game. This was a good trade despite not being a blockbuster one. I couldn't control the market environment. It's two weeks later now as I write this and the market has gotten worse (Figure 10.1, shaded area is area from last chapter). I lost a little on a second attempt to get into the market with basically the same thinking process as my previous trade. There have been accelerated fears of a recession, problems in the financial sector due in big part to bad credit problems, and concern about upcoming earnings, plus crude is at $100 a barrel. These things have taken their toll on the market this week. But I'm not going to worry about it and I'll look for another place to go long, with the knowledge that if we do get more recessionary news we can go into a major downtrend. But I'll look to get long in places where the setup is right and the risk is low as long as the long-term picture is up.

One headline today from the Associated Press showing how weak things are is "Stocks Fall Sharply Amid Worries over Investment Bank

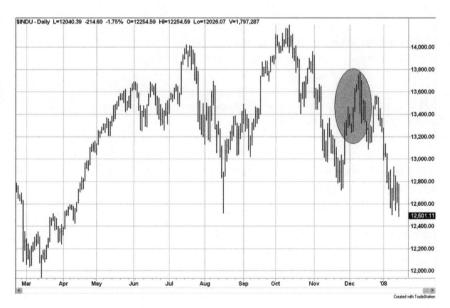

FIGURE 10.1 Daily Dow, Still Going Down
Source: © TradeStation Technologies 1999. All rights reserved.

Writedowns, Anxiety About Earnings." Here are the first few paragraphs of the story:

> *Wall Street plunged again Friday amid renewed fears that the financial sector's troubles with bad credit won't soon end and that some consumers are buckling under the weight of a slowing economy. The major indexes each lost more than 1 percent, including the Dow Jones industrials, which finished down nearly 250 points.*
>
> *The arrival of quarterly earnings reports has investors worried about how banks and brokerages have fared after suffering losses in the collapse of the subprime mortgage market. Traders appeared to grow more pessimistic ahead of reports due next week from the nation's biggest financial institutions. Merrill Lynch & Co., Citigroup Inc. and JPMorgan Chase & Co. are slated to weigh in next week.*
>
> *Adding to investors' unease, Merrill Lynch might take a $15 billion hit from its exposure to soured subprime mortgage investments, according to The New York Times. The nation's largest brokerage is also said to be seeking another capital infusion to help shore up its balance sheet.*
>
> *Investors also grew nervous after American Express Corp. warned that slower spending and more delinquencies on credit card payments will hamper profit throughout 2008.*

Closer to home, my girlfriend works for three more days at ACA Capitol holdings. They are an asset management and credit protection company. Standard & Poor's downgraded them to CCC status, which I think stands for Crappy Credit Company. The whole company is getting taken over by the regulators, and they are letting everyone go next Wednesday. Plus, no one got a big fat juicy Wall Street bonus this year, so, yes, I know there are problems out there.

I don't normally trade on news, but I am smart enough to know when it can have an affect on the market. However, I'm still looking at charts to make my long-term decisions until they tell me otherwise. I still believe the market is heading higher so I don't want to short yet, but I'm scared to go long as the down days could be brutal. So my best bet is to sit on the sidelines until something tells me to buy. Chapter 16, which I wrote a month ago, is on trading rules. One rule that didn't make it in there, but was a close runner–up, was that no position is a position. Don't be afraid to do nothing. Since half your trades are probably going to be losers anyway, if you were good enough to sit those trades out, you'd be the best trader ever.

The reason I believe I should still be buying can be seen on the weekly chart of the Dow in Figure 10.2. We are still above a five-year major trend line and until we clearly break it, I'm going to be thinking bullish and looking at down moves simply as waves and buying opportunities. If we do break I will definitely become a bear, as I love shorting.

I think I'm done with my three-page tangent. You can never make a completely gamble-less trade, because there will always be outside factors (like news events or a giant player liquidating a huge position) that you can't control. What you can do though is take as much into consideration as possible, and plan a proper trade, and then stick to that plan. Trading is not about how you do on one trade, it's about how you do at the end of a lot of trades. And if you can constantly do the right thing, you should make out all right in the long run. That should be your goal: to consistently make the highest probability trades you can in order to take of the gamble out of trading.

TWO PARTS TO A TRADE

Before I continue, I want to make sure everyone knows that a proper trade is actually composed of two trades: the entry and the exit. The exit is

FIGURE 10.2 Weekly Dow Getting the Big Picture
Source: © TradeStation Technologies 1999. All rights reserved.

further broken down into two parts: the risk and the reward. Getting into a trade in a superb manner means absolutely nothing if the exit is done in a half-assed way. When planning out a trade, your plan is not complete unless you have the exit in mind as well. I'm going to short because there is fear of recession and my girlfriend is out of a job is not a well thought out trade. It's the start of the thinking process, and it may be a good argument that you should follow up with more details. Ask yourself, for instance, "If I do short, where exactly will I get in? Just at the open tomorrow, or do I want to time a trade based on so and so an indicator?" Next you need to know how much you will risk. This is without a doubt the most important part of the trade. Without knowing where you will stop your losses and how much is at risk, you should not trade. Repeat that sentence over and over again. It is the key to successful trading. Once you have a stop area in mind, you can't just say, "I'm going to short and risk 200 points." You need to have some idea of when you are getting out with a profit or what you are looking for in order to get out. It is possible you don't have a target and you can simply ride your winner saying, "I'll get out when it stops going down," but at least you should have some strategy for knowing when that is. Maybe it's if it bounces back 20 or 35 percent, or when the 50-day moving average is crossed. I'll go through this in more detail later in the book; for now, just know you are gambling if you put on a trade without accounting for all those factors.

SAME MARKET, TWO VIEWS

By my definition, a good trade is one that is well thought out win, lose, or even not taken. I'm going to give an example of how two people looking at the same market at the same time can have two different opinions for a trade that can both be considered good trades with little gamble in them. I'm going to stick to the Dow and a little bit further out from the trade in the previous chapter.

GOING LONG

Jan. 7, 2008

We are at close to a crossroad in the market where the long-term uptrend may be ending and the short-term downtrend may be taking over. I know a lot of the news is bearish, which can weigh the market down, but I tend to discount the news and trade technicals over the news when they give me different opinions. I start by looking at Figure 10.2 again. On this weekly chart of the Dow Jones you can clearly see an uptrend going back five years. That alone should make you want to think long. If you look at the stochastics in that chart you will see it is getting close to bottoming out and is at the same level it's been for the last three bottoms. So the down move may be ending very soon, presenting a great place to go long. The horizontal line, which represents the previous low, seems to have held with the latest drop, another indication the market may be done going down.

Now look at the daily chart (Figure 10.3). There seems to be an area of support and resistance between 12,500 and 14,000. We are at the bottom of the range, with prior congestion in the same area as at the bottom of this last down wave. These are two good signs of a possible return to the upside. When you add the possible turnaround in the stochastics, you have another indication. However, it's still too early to jump in. For starters, before making a trade you need to measure the risks and rewards of it.

As far as potential profits, there are a few targets you can look at. The first would be above point A, with the second being above point B; however, the ultimate target would be much higher and I would use Fibonacci projections to get it. Due to space limitations I can't show it on the chart, but the low to high of this five-year move is about 6,800 points. I would then multiply 6,800 points by .38, giving me about 2,500 points, and I would add

FIGURE 10.3 Jan. 7 Daily Dow
Source: © TradeStation Technologies 1999. All rights reserved.

that to the previous high of 14,200, so that my first super long-term target would be 16,700. This is a long-term expectation and may take two years to achieve, but it's a possible target that I would consider staying with a long bias until it's reached. All of these targets are not "get out when reached" targets, but are target areas where I would reevaluate. If a target gets hit and it still looks bullish, I obviously will stay in and come up with a new target level.

Next comes the risk. I see a few areas of support that I could use for stops. The first is pretty close and it's under the low represented by point D. This is now a double bottom that the market has recently created, but the stop is so close that I'm very likely to get stopped out if I use it. Next is the low represented by point E. I like this one better as the market has traded above it for about 10 months and a break below it could mean we are headed lower. I'd place a stop 50 points below this to be safe at just under 12,450. If it breaks this level I think it will test the five-year trend line (X), so my next stop would be just below that trend line. This will be a trailing stop; currently it is a safe stop at 12,050. The low at point F is another place to have a stop but because this is below trend line X, I'll ignore it. My intentions would be to get out if line D gets broken and look to get back in as it nears the trend line.

Before I make the trade, I want to confirm with the S&P weekly chart (Figure 10.4) to make sure everything matches up. In the S&P chart the

FIGURE 10.4 Confirming with the Weekly S&P
Source: © TradeStation Technologies 1999. All rights reserved.

market had reached its five-year trend line on Friday (1/4) and now on Monday morning it dipped below, but didn't follow through and bounced back over it. I like this. It's a sign of a false break out and that the down move may be over. The market is also above the previous low point A, however, the stochastics have some downside room left and this may be enough to drag the market below the trend line. It will become important to watch the S&Ps as the trade progresses, as they are closer to a turning point in the overall market direction than the Dow Jones is. If they break the trend line then the Dow may follow.

My initial trade would be to go long three units, which I could scale out of at the different target levels. I like to trade in units of three. This could mean 15 contracts (3 units of 5) or 21 contracts (3 units of 7). Now all I need to do is to time the trade to get the best entry possible. I will risk to point E (Figure 10.3) and my target is still above point B. At the current levels I'm risking 300 points to make 1,300 points. Looking at the smaller time frame charts I will look for a safe signal to enter on. This to me is a low gamble–high probability trade. I have a setup I like that has a good chance of working and a 4.5 to 1 payout ratio if I'm right. When you have a trade as well planned out as this with a great reward to risk ratio, you are trading without gambling. A little bit of luck will always help, but you are no longer shooting for the moon with a long shot or a stupid trade.

I planned this trade out in detail and then waited for a place to enter. I had a few scenarios that I was looking for to get in and I never got them. The market just kept going down for the next couple of days as you can see in the 60-minute Dow Futures chart (Figure 10.5). One of the scenarios I had made for myself in order to get in was to wait for the market to cross above the downward trend line you see in the chart. This did not happen in the next couple of days. In that time the S&P broke below its five-year trend line (Figure 10.6) which was a scenario I had for not getting in, as it may lead the Dow to break its line as well. Not taking this trade turned out to be a great decision. Had I not been so thorough in my planning, I might have decided otherwise. Even had I just taken the trade I would have been stopped out a week later with roughly a 300-point move against me, which I was prepared to lose.

GOING SHORT

Now let's look at it from someone else's eyes. My friend Bruce is as bearish as can be. By the way, I mention Bruce several times throughout this book, His name is Bruce Tandy, and he has been day-trading stocks for

FIGURE 10.5 Jan. 9 60-Minute Dow Futures
Source: © TradeStation Technologies 1999. All rights reserved.

FIGURE 10.6 Jan. 9 Daily S&P Breaking of Trend Line
Source: © TradeStation Technologies 1999. All rights reserved.

over a decade now and is one of the few people I know who makes money doing so. Though he is a day-trader he does take longer term positions at times as well, though he is very fidgety when he does. When he doesn't trade long-term he does trade with a bias based on his market opinion.

He cites many of the bearish news factors I mentioned above for his thinking from the short side. This has put him in a bearish state of mind, and though his views are different from mine, they are valid as well. He's looking to short and thinks the market may drop 2,000 points. He tells me there is a head-and-shoulders pattern seen in Figure 10.7 at Points A, B and C, and expects this wave will be the one that breaks the market down. And not just a little but to below 10,000, and then there is nothing holding it back for another 1,000 points or so after that. He sees that the 50-day moving average has crossed below the 200-day moving average and that the market is below both of these averages for the past week. This coincided with the break of the triangle at point Y. His stop is above the downward trend line (line Z) formed by the triangle. This will be a trailing stop for him, which he will keep moving down as the market drops. He is also using the 50- and 200-day moving averages as an indicator to stop himself out, should they cross or if the market is above both of them. He also is risking about 300 points with the goal of possibly making 2,000, though he needs

FIGURE 10.7   Daily Dow from the Short Side
Source: © TradeStation Technologies 1999. All rights reserved.

to see how it reacts at both lines E and X to make a proper assessment. He likes his trade more now that the S&P has broken its five-year trend line.

These are two different approaches to trading and both were good ideas. Of course, only one person can be right, assuming he doesn't screw up the trade by not getting out. It's 10 days later and the market has dropped considerably as I write this (Figure 10.8). The market has mostly been weighed down by more bad news. He is still short and I'm waiting for a sign to get in. The Dow is on the five-year trend line, but the S&P has broken its trend line and both markets are below their 50- and 200-day moving average. So I'm no longer as bullish as I was; now I'm considering shorting but I'm waiting for an opportunity to do so as the risk/reward is too large now. I'd also consider going long if I see a bottoming pattern or a break of a high, or something else I like. The only thing making me think a lot is that the Dow has not broken its five-year trend line, though I think we are heading lower as every other major support I had got broken. Until then I'll sit at my computer looking at charts and making believe I'm busy so my cranky, newly unemployed girlfriend doesn't ask me to do anything around the house. I tend to write the book at night so I can't use that as an excuse.

By the way, I ended up going short two days after writing this; I'll show why in the next chapter.

FIGURE 10.8   Daily Dow 10 Days Later
Source: © TradeStation Technologies 1999. All rights reserved.

WAITING FOR THE RIGHT OPPORTUNITIES

I mentioned above how no position is a position. You will be much better off by sitting out of the market while waiting for the perfect setup than by trading nonstop. Even day traders can benefit from this. Why make 100 trades a day, when if you learn patience and better timing you can make 25 to 40 trades that have a higher probability of working? This is a lesson I wish I had learned when I started trading because I was so impatient it was pathetic. I needed to trade, regardless of the situation. If I wasn't long, I needed to be short. There was no lunch break and I traded until the bell rang. For me, action was more important than timing. Luckily I outgrew that. Now I've leaned the importance of waiting for the right market opportunities before jumping into a trade. Things like looking for trends, timing, waiting for pullbacks, not being impetuous or making rash decisions have helped me. I'm a natural born gambler and it was fun always being in the market—the same as it was being in every hand when playing cards or betting on which elevator would come first. But only when I learned to sit some out did I stop being a gambler. Professional gamblers are not really gamblers; they have taken as much of the gambling out of their play as possible and have learned to play the odds and wait for the right odds. As a trader you need to do so as well. When you can stick to a game plan and have to account for every trade, you will automatically cut back on your trades. The trades that remain should be the best of the crop. You won't be right on all them, don't worry about that, just wait for the best ones and you will be right more often than before.

MEASURE THE RISK-TO-REWARD RATIO

So how do you actually take the gamble out of the trade? The answer is very simple: Only take trades where the odds are in your in favor. This means you need to know a combination of a few things first. These are the percent of winning to losing trades and the amount you can make versus the amount you would lose if you were wrong. The first part assumes you have a back tested strategy you are using. If you are trading a computerized system then that ratio is pretty simple to get, just back test your system and the software will tell you what it is. (This ratio could be misleading at times. It will be a measure over the life span of the data you tested; however, it could be quite different in sideways markets as opposed to in trending markets. You could think it was right 62 percent of the time, but in reality, it's only correct 40 percent of the time in trending markets and 77 percent in range bound, choppy markets).

If, on the other hand, you are trading a manual, somewhat discretionary system like I have been using, you still need to go back, look at charts and come up with a percent right to wrong ratio. An accurate ratio won't always be possible unless you can convert it to a computerized system to actually test it. My approach to these trades was more of a thought-out process with several indicators, parameters, and market patterns that I know do work well. I do not have an exact ratio of how many times this setup works versus how many times it doesn't, but I do know from experience, however, that it a profitable approach I take and that I'm right about 40 to 50 percent of the time.

Once you know your system's win/loss ratio then you need to compute your maximim loss to potential win ratio. This is more important than the win/loss ratio, as you can make money with a system that is only right 30 percent of the time, if your wins are large enough, compared to your losses. If you figure out your max loss to potential win ratio for every trade, it means you are planning out your trades properly and coming up with both stop and profit targets. It's very simple to do, and if you do this every time, you are way ahead of the pack. I always try to get a three to one risk ratio before I consider a trade, anything below that I find to be not worth the trade. But that's just me, your ratio could differ.

Now, many people who are going to be reading this will think that my risk of 300 points on the Dow is way too much. But, I'm willing to take a risk, it's the way I trade. Some people cannot trade this way as it's against their risk threshold, but because I do go for big winners, I can. That is my style of trading and may not be suitable for all people who can only stomach a 50-point loss. When day-trading, Bruce trades stocks like a fiend and panics if they go five ticks against him. Everyone has his own style so go with what works for you.

Don't make a trade just because the risk is low and the rewards could be great. If there is little chance of that trade working then it's probably not worth taking the long shot. You have to do some math, and it is not an exact science unless you have a back tested system with accurate win to loss ratios. Even then, make sure you account for the slippage in the trade as many people forget to do. I have been guilty of this—looking at the charts and getting my numbers and taking the slippage and commissions for granted. If you want to be exact don't do this.

There is no perfect ratio, just make sure that the profit/risk ratio times the win/loss ratio is greater then .50 before you even consider making a trade. If it's below that you're playing against the odds and it's like gambling in a casino where you have no edge; you are just hoping for luck. I like for this ratio to be at least 1.50.

Here is the formula you need:

$$W = \text{win percentage} = \text{\# of wins/number of trades}$$
$$R = \text{risk ratio} = \text{potential win/potential loss}$$
$$W \times R = \text{the "should I take the trade" ratio}$$

For example, if I know my system is right 50 percent of the time and my risk is 300, to make 900 then the formula would be

$$W = .50$$
$$R = 900 \div 300 = 3$$

Then

$$WR = .50 \times 3 = 1.50$$

GETTING THE EDGE

This is the formula you need to know in order to get the edge in trading. It's similar to counting cards in blackjack. Blackjack is one of the most popular games in a casino because when played properly it has the smallest house edge (advantage) for the casino of all the casino games. It has a house edge of less than 1 percent. The key phrase here is "when played properly." Many players give up a huge advantage to the house by playing hunches, not playing the game properly, or taking insurance. Once people start doing this, the house edge can go up to over 5 percent.

Someone who knows how to count cards can turn the edge around and put it in his favor by as much as 1.5 percent. This doesn't mean he will win every time, but over the course of time and many, many hands, a card counter will have an advantage over a casino. Counting cards is hard work and the casinos frown on it, so I think you are better off learning to trade while making sure all your trades have a proper "should I take the trade" ratio.

WAYS TO GET THE ODDS IN YOUR FAVOR

Getting the odds in your favor, taking away the gamble, or making the high probability trades is not about math, but it is about making the correct type of trades over and over again. There are a few simple things you can do to help get you there, and it really only takes a little time to do but a lot of discipline to keep to it. I mentioned all this before so I'll recap it quickly.

Use Proven Strategies

Sounds like a trivial common sense statement, but it's not always done. Before you use a strategy or indicator in a certain manner, make sure you know that it works. The best way, of course, is to back test your ideas. Don't use someone else's ideas without back testing them yourself first. You should also understand what you are doing. Just because somebody told you to short when a stock rises 33 percent over its average daily range, you shouldn't just trust them. Make sure you understand what that means, and then make sure that it actually works. Even if you read it in a book, it may work great in a book using two-year old charts, but it may not be worth anything in realtime trading. After you have established that you have a proven strategy, then trade and follow it. Hey, if the strategy works, don't tinker with it in midstream. When you start playing with it or changing parameters or ignoring signals, the strategy is no longer being followed and won't work like you thought it would.

Follow a Plan

Not a lot new to say here. If you plan every trade and stick to that plan, you should definitely put the odds in your favor. Your plan, however, has to be sound and should make sense for it to work. I'm sure there are people out there who make trading and game plans every day and can't make a cent. It's most likely their plan is not real-time trading worthy or they can't follow it.

Know Your Risk and Reward

Do not make any trade without knowing this. It is part of planning a trade and will determine if you should make the trade or not. I don't think there is much more I need to say regarding this as I just spent quite a bit of time talking about it above.

Know Your Exits

This is another no-brainer that I'll talk more about two chapters from now. You cannot get an accurate risk/reward ratio if you do not know how and when you are getting out. I believe planning the exit is more important then planning the entry. So don't trade without knowing where you will get out. Exits do not have to be set in stone but I use them as guidelines and targets to shoot for. I adjust my stops all the time and I will move my target depending on what the market does. I'll get out anywhere in between if it is not working.

Have a Reason for Every Trade

I decided not to devote a full chapter on having a reason for every trade, because by this point in the book, that horse is pretty much dead, and there is not much more I can add to it without mutilating and disemboweling that poor beast. I'll also slip it into the next couple of chapters as I discuss getting in and out of trades. It should be pretty obvious by now that you should not make a trade unless you have a legitimate thought-out reason for it. Don't trade out of boredom or to capture a quick move that came out of nowhere. Think about trading less and being more selective and you will do much better—even if you are day-trading. You may not have time to plan every trade when day-trading and your individual trades can be random, but they should all follow a thought-out process you use to make trades or from the homework you did earlier in the day or the night before or from a system you use.

I can remember quite a few times where I came in thinking I was going to be trading the market long that day and then for some reason or other, I decided to catch a few ticks on the downside while the market retraced for a few minutes. There was no reason for these trades except greed and boredom and they ended up costing me dearly, as I then would nurse a bad position all day. Ah, but those were my younger, stupider days.

Money Management

I didn't mention money management in this chapter, but I will later. Other then pure luck, having a solid money management plan is the only thing that will keep you afloat when trading. No matter how good your trades are, if you do not know how much to risk, you are gambling. No trade is a gimme. No matter how confident you think you are, there is a chance of losing on it. If you get too confident and trade over your head you are likely to get killed. That's the bottom line. I thought my trade in the previous chapter was a gimme, the setup was perfect and I made a few bucks on it, but I could have easily missed my chance to get out and if I had traded too much size I would have been hurting.

Discipline

I'll end the chapter mentioning discipline. None of the above can be accomplished if you do not have the discipline to work hard, make a game plan, stick to it, keep to money management, and so on. Trading and successful gambling are all about discipline. You need to have it if you want to make it as a trader.

CLOSING THOUGHTS

To be a great trader you need to learn to take as much of the gamble out of each trade as possible. By playing the percentages and having well-thought-out trades, with predetermined stops and exit targets, you can begin to accomplish this. I was able to show how people can have well-thought-out trades from both sides of the markets. And yes, one of them will be wrong, but that is not what is important, because it is impossible to be right all the time. Your goal is to consistently, right or wrong, make quality trades or to sit them out. This is where having and following a proper game plan helps invaluably. The problem people have is when they do not plan out a trade, as these trades really are no more than a gamble.

CHAPTER 11

Getting In

A stockbroker was filling out a job application when he came to the question: "Have you ever been arrested?" He answered no to the question. The next question, intended for those who answered the preceding question with a yes, was, "Why?" Nevertheless, the stockbroker answered it: "Never got caught."

Though I decided to skip the chapter "Have a Reason for Every Trade," it doesn't mean that I won't talk about it in this chapter in the context of how to properly get into a trade. Actually, this chapter looks like it is going to be a bit of recap of the first half of the book. And this is not a bad thing as it will not hurt to drive some points home. Getting into a trade is composed of several factors, which I'll go into below. First, I want to stress one thing and you can probably guess it: *You should have a reason for every trade you make* and not just the entry but the exit as well. I have spent the last two chapters showing in detail my thinking process on how I would make a trade, so I will try not to be repetitive and not go into as much detail in some instances. However, the best way for me to get my idea across is with an example of a real trade, and what better way than to continue where I left off in the last chapter.

SPOTTING THE OPPORTUNITY

It didn't take long to find a reason to make a trade. I ended up abandoning my long bias and got short the Dow today (Jan. 11, 2008) and as of now

I'm pretty happy with the trade. But one good day is not what I'm in it for. The first step in making a trade is to spot something that you want to get involved with. This could be an individual stock, commodity, or market sector, or it could be a pattern you see, or a news event. For me, since I do not look at a lot of markets, I tend to look for patterns I want to trade. Now don't get me wrong and think I only trade the Dow. I do look at other markets on a regular basis. I look at crude oil, the Euro, the U.S. dollar and different interest rate financials every day, and I'll also occasionally look at the grains. I will put on trades in them every now and then in the order I listed them, if I see a pattern or am alerted to something I like. Nevertheless, about 80 percent of my trades are made in either the Dow or S&Ps. The other commodities are things I do on the side with less volume when something really strikes my eye. Some people trade only one item and they just look for something to trigger a trade. Others have a system or pattern they use and then scour the markets looking through 400 stocks to match that criteria. No matter what your style is, you cannot make a trade until you spot something that says, "Hey, buy me." In my case with the Dow, I had spotted that the market was probably going down and I've decided I wanted to now be short. A good trader knows when he is wrong and can change his mind. John, our bad trader, on the other hand, decided the market is going up and will stick to that belief until he proves the market right or runs out of cash.

Now back to my trade. The opportunity I saw, actually the latest opportunity as I missed the first one when the 50- and 200-day moving averages crossed and then a second opportunity when a few days ago the market broke below bottom A and trend line A for the first time. The market rallied about 300 points after that break and went back above those support levels, but now has retested and broke through again this second time around (Figure 11.1). By this time, the S&P had broken its five-year trend line. And I thought this to be a great opportunity to go short.

PLANNING THE TRADE

After you spot the trade you want to make, you next need to figure out your game plan for getting into it with the least exposure and best strategy you can come up with. After finding the opportunity for a good potential trade I had to sit down to plan it out. In the planning of the trade stage you will come up with a strategy for the trade. It is here where you will determine amongst other things how you will actually get into the trade. It's one thing to just see an opportunity and it's another to pull the trigger properly. Many

FIGURE 11.1 Spotting the Opportunity Daily Dow
Source: © TradeStation Technologies 1999. All rights reserved.

people freeze up when it comes time to get in, and others are too willy-nilly about it, just going on impulse as soon as that opportunity is spotted. They do nothing to help themselves get the best price they can. You need to plan your entrance into a trade trying to get the most out of it that you can. You don't have to get the best price of the move, just try not to get the worse price. If you miss an entrance then you have to make a new plan for getting in on the next opportunity.

This happened to me on this last trade. The market had dropped quite a lot over the last few weeks before I got short. I didn't recognize the original opportunity to get short and only did so after a big move. I had to then plan the best entrance I could, given where we were at the current time. Along with getting into the trade it's at this stage where you need to start thinking about the exits. But I'm going to give that its due in the next chapter—just assume that I have taken it into consideration at every step of the way in this chapter.

As I planned my trade I knew I wanted to wait for a good, safe opportunity to get in. I don't like to make a trade as soon as a level is broken; instead I wait for some sort of retesting of it. I'll go through all the planning stages of the entry in the next few sections.

DRAWING SCENARIOS FOR GETTING INTO THE TRADE

With planning the trade comes drawing up scenarios that should be included in your prep work for getting into the trade. If you have a proper game plan with different scenarios for the entry of a trade, it can definitely save you money. It first of all can help you find an actual entry level. With proper role playing you can come up with different target areas as to where you will enter the trade depending on what it does. It can secondly make you realize, "Hey, maybe this trade is not such a great idea." What can look good at first glance can seem like a risky trade when scrutinized more carefully. Maybe you can see there are too many things that could go wrong and decide the trade shouldn't be taken.

In my trade, I had made a few entry scenarios. You have to look at the 60-minute chart, Figure 11.2, to see my thinking process for entering the trade. I'm going to use the futures chart for this and the trend line drawn is derived from the trend line made using the actual index. Once the market broke Trend Line A and Bottom A (shaded area A) on January 8, one of my scenarios was that it would drop like all hell until it tested Trend Line B, again derived from the Figure 11.1. At which point there were several

FIGURE 11.2 Making Scenarios 60-Minute Dow Futures
Source: © TradeStation Technologies 1999. All rights reserved.

other scenarios, but I'll worry about them later. Another possibility was that it would dillydally around the current level until it figured out where it was going. The other main scenario I had was that it was a fake breakout and would soon rally.

My decision to wait to get short was made from the 60-minute chart. I noticed that there was a divergence between the down Trend Line D and the upward slope of the bottoms of the stochastics. I also paid attention to the fact that the market had gotten too far below its moving average and I expected it to bounce back closer to it. Both of these are usually signs that the most recent wave is ending. This potential bounce provided an opportunity to get short at a better price if I waited. I wasn't scared about missing the move if I was wrong. These were my original scenarios and then it took two days to get a scenario where I wanted to get in. That came on the morning of the 11th after a decent two-day rally starting the latter part of two days before. During this rally the market did retrace to a place I found acceptable. If you go back to Figure 11.1, you'll see how on the 10th it went back above Trend Line A. And despite breaking above it, the market did retrace toward the end of the day. The market ended being up 120 for the day, but it didn't close near its high, selling off more than 100 points at the end of the day. You can see it clearer in Figure 11.2 Point B and in Figure 11.3 (a five-minute chart) right before the gap. This, to me, was a bearish sign, and gave me the go-ahead to get ready to possibly enter the next day.

FIGURE 11.3 Timing the Trade, 5-Minute Dow Futures
Source: © TradeStation Technologies 1999. All rights reserved.

On the 11th, knowing that the market was expected to open lower by 50 points or so, I had two main possibilities. I'm now looking at a five-minute Dow futures chart (Figure 11.3) to further make my scenarios. One was for the market to rally after the open, closing the gap, and giving me two new scenarios: either it continues its upswing or it backs off. If the market did break up and go above Trend Line A, I would back off and wait. If it closed the gap and stalled I would reevaluate.

The other initial possibility was that it just went straight down. In which case, I would use a 30-minute breakout trade (shaded area A) to get in. As you can see in Figure 11.3 the market went pretty much straight down the whole day. There are many more scenarios that could have happened, and I don't want to spend the next 10 pages going through them, but these were 2 main ones with some subscenarios, I was looking at. Soon, I'll go into how I actually timed the trade.

DON'T CHASE THE MARKET

Before I get into timing a trade, I think it's important to learn not to chase a market. If you miss a trade's signal or first opportunity, you will put yourself at excessive risk and be subject to excessive slippage as well if you just jump in. Sure, you may miss a trade completely if you wait or never be able to get as good a price as you could have. But when the risk becomes too large, the fundamentals of a trade change. I've seen too many times when someone rushes into a trade, especially after an announcement of some sort comes out, only to then watch the market come flying back in his face. Look again at Figure 11.3, and you'll see that the market broke up above the line called Breakout A and took off. It rallied 100 points in about 8 minutes. If you rushed to get long you could very likely have gotten filled near the high of the move, only to watch it drop 150 points in your face immediately. You are much better off waiting for the market to consolidate or to retrace back to the congestion area from before the breakout. By doing this, your risk is clearer and smaller and your slippage becomes not much of a factor. If you rushed in, your slippage could be 30 to 50 points, which comes out to a nice chunk of change.

TIMING THE TRADE

Timing a trade is a crucial factor in making money that many people do not take as seriously as they should. I have found that when I take the time to time my trades, I can turn many trades that would have been losers into winners, small winners into large winners, and not make a few trades that would have ended up as big losers. Yes, I have missed moves, but I've learn to say, "So what?" and move on, as I believe that I have made or saved much more money in the long run with the ones that I got a better price on or ignored. The reason for my love of using multiple times frames to get into and out of trades is that they not only help me to get the big picture but more importantly they help me time my trades.

In my trade, though I knew I wanted to go short, it took three days after getting my initial alert that I went short at 12,712. That's a long wait for many people, but it paid off. Even if I lose money on the trade, I at least got it at a better price, at least 100 points better. I didn't have to endure a 300-point move against me and a safe stop was closer.

Being that I was 1,500 points late getting into the down move, I had to find a safe way to get in. I did so by thinking of my entry as a day-trade. I choose to use my ever popular 30-minute-after-the-open breakout system. I'll go more into that in a short while. By doing so, I got short when the market broke below the range it established in the first 30 minutes of trading. If I was wrong, I'd get out at the top of that range. Risking about 100 points, however, I actually gave it a bit more room in case it decided to close the gap (see Figure 11.3). I ended up timing this trade as I would a day-trade, and I would get out as a day trade if I was wrong. However, if I was correct, I was in for the long haul. Because I was able to time the trade as I did, I was able make a low-risk high-potential trade.

LOOK FOR PATTERNS WITHIN THE LONG-TERM TRADE

When looking to establish an entry, I like to first look for the long-term direction of the market and then I try to find a shorter term tradable pattern within that longer time frame. This could be in either the same time frame you are looking at or a shorter time frame. The reason for doing this is as I mentioned above to time a trade and reduce risk. I just showed how I used a 30-minute breakout system on a 5-minute chart to time an entry into a longer term trade. I needed to get into the market and I need a way to do so with as little risk as possible. This was just a pattern I was looking at in order to time my trade better. I could have chosen another pattern as well. I could maybe have gotten in after the break of Trend Line A on the open, with a stop at the high of the move the day before. But there was more risk involved if I did that as the stop would have been about 200 points away.

Here are a couple more examples of finding patterns within patterns.

The grains have been on a tear the last year and a half. They have reached all-time highs, due in part to strong demand from China, alternate use of them in making ethanol gas, and a very weak dollar. Look at the weekly soybeans chart, Figure 11.4, and you can see the steep upward move. If you had missed the move and wanted to get in much later what can you do? The only way to trade this, assuming you are going to go with the trend, is to wait for a pullback and then find a smaller pattern within that big uptrend to get in with. You may think it's too late to get into the trade, but the thing keeps going higher and higher as people are still driving it up. One thing I took away from reading *Reminiscences of a Stock Operator* by Edwin Lefèvre is just because a market is too high doesn't mean it cannot go higher.

In Figure 11.5 at the first set of ovals there is a pattern I like to trade. It's very simple. I look for a retracement in the uptrend and then wait for the stochastics indicator to cross over the oversold line. I know I'm wrong if either the stochastics goes back into the oversold area or the market takes out the lows it made when the stochastics bottomed out. I can also look at the pattern in the second set of ovals. Where the market tried to go lower and couldn't, as soon as the stochastics cross back up, I would go long. Now the trade I'm looking at has not happened yet. I'm waiting for it and what I'm waiting for is for this current dip to repeat one of these two

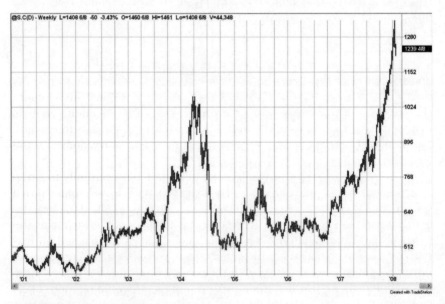

FIGURE 11.4 Weekly Soybeans
Source: © TradeStation Technologies 1999. All rights reserved.

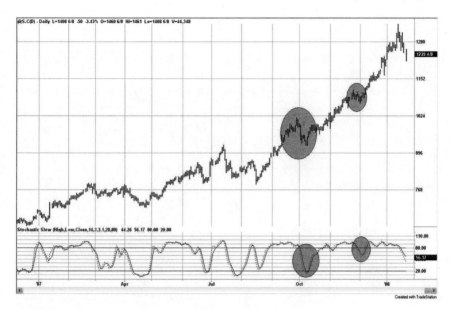

FIGURE 11.5 Continuous Daily Soybean Jan. 21, 2008
Source: © TradeStation Technologies 1999. All rights reserved.

patterns; when it does I will get in. It takes me all of one minute a day to see if the market is close to fulfilling one of these scenarios. I had been looking at a continuous chart of soybeans for the big picture, but I would use the current most active month to actually time and make a trade.

The next step is to take it down to a smaller level, to either time a better entry or to day-trade. I'm going to use the active front month for this part of my analysis. I'll use the 60-minute (Figure 11.6) and the 5-minute (Figure 11.7) charts to see these patterns clearly. The 60-minute chart is just to show the strength of the uptrend and to spot areas of retracement. The points A and B correspond to the patterns and entry points in the 5-minute chart.

For the first pattern you would need to be watching carefully to get in as it happened at the end of the day. The market gapped lower, traded down toward the moving average on the 60-minute chart, then rallied to close the gap and tried to sell off again. The second sell-off wasn't as strong as the first and had formed and broken Trend Line A, indicating the sell-off had failed. As soon as that trend line gets broken, you have a buying opportunity. You can also confirm this with the crossover of the stochastics. Now this happens in the last five minutes of trading so it would be more of an overnight trade than a day-trade. As you can see, the next day the market exploded. This is a great example of how using two different time frames

FIGURE 11.6   60-Minute Soy Futures
Source: © TradeStation Technologies 1999. All rights reserved.

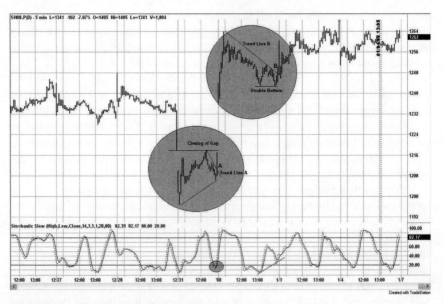

FIGURE 11.7   5-Minute Soy Futures
Source: © TradeStation Technologies 1999. All rights reserved.

you can see different patterns that will signal a terrific trading opportunity. Your stop could be the day's low and your target would depend on your holding time. But using the longer time frames you can easily find good targets to shoot for.

In the second example, the bull market is still the same, but the pattern I see is a little different. We still have the market selling off and forming Trend Line B, but this time I see a double bottom and a divergence between the lows of that double bottom and that of the stochastics, indicating the last move down was not as strong as it looked. As soon as that trend line gets broken, you have another entry level with a small stop loss just under the double bottom.

These types of trades are the best you can make in a strongly trending market. Just look for any sell-off and then find a pattern that you can use to get into the market that has a low risk area. By finding these low risk entries in the direction of the major trend, you are giving yourself a better chance of making money.

KNOWING THE RISK

This leads me to the point that the entry is only as good as the risk. Entering into a trade and leaving yourself at risk for too much is not a good trading decision. Win or lose, if you are exposing yourself for more than you can handle you will probably end up getting hurt in long run. You must know the risk you are going to take before you get in. As you are thinking through a trade, think risk first and then profit, and only then should you concentrate on getting in if the risk/reward ratio is worth it. All your planning and making of scenarios is what will help you establish the risk. Money management is what all good traders have in common and money management cannot occur if you are unaware of the risks. This may sound obvious to you but in my days as a broker I noticed many an amateur trader not give risk its due consideration. The bottom line is that knowing your risk will help in evaluating a trade more than anything else I can think of.

DECIDING HOW MUCH TO TRADE

Not only do you have to know your risk and where you are getting in but you have to know how many contracts you will be trading. Not every trade and not every market is the same. There are times when you can be more aggressive and other times when you may want to trade lighter than normal. I'll go over this more in the money management chapter later in the book. For now, I'll say that position size cannot be done properly if you do not know the risk and the potential of the trade working. If a trade has a great setup and a small risk I may consider putting on more than my typical size trade. The key is getting out if I'm wrong. It's also at this stage where you need to decide if you will be adding to the trade and by how much at any set levels or patterns. Don't just add to a trade because you are making money. If you are going to add to a trade it should be as well thought-out as your initial trade was, as in reality it's a whole new trade.

CLOSING THOUGHTS

The last thing I can think of is that the entry of the trade is like giving birth. The planning of the baby came way before he entered the world. Okay, not every baby is planned and some are the result of a lot of alcohol, but let's ignore those. Pregnancy is a nightmare or at least living with a pregnant woman can be. And labor is no joy, especially if your wife is doing it naturally and squeezing your hand till your fingers turn blue. Before the baby is born you're thinking, "Oh my, $140,000 for college," but on the other hand you say, "At least now there is someone to take care of me when I'm old and pooping my own pants; it's a good risk/reward ratio." But after the baby is born, now that is when the hard work actually begins. All the monitoring and worrying whether he'll get into the right preschool and having to come up with scenarios if he doesn't. Well that's just like putting on a trade. Just because the trade is on, doesn't mean you can relax. You need to monitor that trade just like you would your firstborn, constantly checking it and asking, "What will I do if his fever gets to be 104?," or "We are going out for 4 hours, is 25 diapers enough?," or "is 2 gallons of sun block enough for his face?" and so on. It's not till the baby goes off to college when you can relax, just like the only time you should relax when you have a trade on is when you exit it.

CHAPTER 12

Getting Out

Fred made lots of money shorting the market recently, and he decided to buy an extravagant sports car. Out of curiosity the dealer inquired how he made his money and Fred told him from trading. The dealer was surprised and said, "In this bad economy? And Fred said, "Yes, I was shorting as companies were going out of business and made a killing." The dealer asked, "Since you made your money at the expense of others, have you thought about giving it to charity?" Fred thought for a moment and said, "No, but I'll tell you what, I'll buy the car. You can give the money to charity afterwards."

L ike the previous chapter, this one will also recap and expand on topics from earlier chapters. This book is not about exit strategies themselves, but more on how to implement them. I spent a lot of time in *High Probability Trading*, discussing different ways of establishing stops and profit targets, so I won't reiterate them here. This chapter, however, will help you become a better trader by stressing the importance of pre-planning the exit and keeping on top of it as the trade progresses.

PREESTABLISH YOUR EXIT STRATEGIES

I've mentioned this several times thoughout the book, and I cannot stress enough how important it is: You must know your exits before getting into a trade. Having an exit strategy planned out while you are planning the trade will lead you toward the path of success. You need to know what you will

do on both the winning and losing side. Don't let the exit surprise you. Plan
it out in advance. These exits do not have to be chiseled in stone. They act
as guidelines to help you evaluate whether a trade should be taken or not
and as an initial target. Once the trade is on, you should readjust them if
need be to better mirror ever-changing market conditions.

Getting out of a trade is more important than getting into a trade, because that is where you will make or lose money. Keep in mind you will
never make money by getting into a trade. You only do so when you get out
of it. It's the same with losing. You only really lose money when you exit a
trade. Though paper losses are real and should not be ignored, it's the exit
that determines the actual loss. In the long run a proper exit strategy can
make the difference between making or losing money.

Your job as a trader is to lose as little as possible when wrong and
make as much as you can when right. If you spend the time determining which trades have the greatest potential with the smallest possibility to hurt you, you will start achieving that goal. Unfortunately many
traders put on a trade first, and only then start to weigh out everything that
could go wrong with the trade or make a true estimate of how much they
could make.

Think of it like you wanted to cheat on your spouse. If you are going
to do it, make sure you plan your actions and your alibi before you do it.
If you have to come up with a lie as you are being confronted for coming
home at 5 A.M. smelling of cheap perfume, you may not think great under
pressure, and you'll crack. However, if you've established a fictional weekly
poker game at Frank's house every Thursday night, and his wife happens
to sell cheap perfume and you carry a sample with you just in case, then
you have a preestablished alibi and your chances of succeeding will be
much better.

CUTTING LOSSES AND LETTING PROFITS RIDE

This is one of the best known of all the trading expressions. And it's said
for a reason: It will make you money. As you go through the stages of a
putting on a trade and preestablishing the exits, keep the phrase in mind,
and only put on trades that can give you this setup (big profits, little losses).
Don't trade anything where the stop has to be too far away and you are
only looking to get a few ticks out of the trade. You will not succeed this
way. You need to be able to let your winners take off. If you know you get
antsy and cannot hold something for 10 points don't make trades where

the proper stops are 8 to 12 points away. That's just too much to give away if you are wrong. You'll never know until you get out of a trade what your profits are really going to be, but you need to have an estimate of what they could be. And you need to be able to let it do it. Getting out too soon is a another deadly sin that you'll need to overcome to be a great trader. By having those preestablished targets you can learn to let a trade do its thing. There will be times when a trade stalls in a gray area between your target and your stop. Then you need to decide if you should let it develop or if the trade is dead and you'd be better off getting out instead of waiting for the stop. That's the tricky part of trading, and you can end up kicking yourself when you decide the wrong way, but I'm a believer that if it is not working as planned and you gave it enough time and evaluation, you get out and look for another opportunity.

USING STOPS IN YOUR GAME PLAN

Having exit strategies will help you avoid the big losses, which is a key to trading. It's okay to lose on a trade, it's losing too much that's the problem. But you can solve that problem with good exit strategies. By having thought out a stop before getting into the trade, you can eliminate the problem of losing too much. You, of course, need to know how to properly place a stop and how to stick to it. Too close is no good, because you will get stopped out repeatedly when in reality you shouldn't have been. Too far on the other hand means you will suffer large losses you should have been able to reduce. You also need to know how to move a stop, both as the market volatility changes and as the trade progresses. As the market moves, it will show you new levels to place your stop. This is especially true in a trending market where you can keep sliding your stop with the trend line. As you make new scenarios once your trade is on, keep thinking about where the new stop should be.

In your pretrade planning process you need to consider what can go wrong and make sure you are protected. Stops are made to help traders know their loss limits and to stick to those limits. One thing you need to do is not get lazy because you have a stop. Stops are not the end all to putting a trade on. You still have to constantly watch and baby the trade. When you get complacent because you have a stop in, you will miss opportunities and get stopped out and end up losing money instead of taking smaller losses or even winners beforehand.

This leads me to another point. Should you actually place the stop into the market or should you keep it mentally? Place it in the market. Most people are not disciplined enough to react to a mental stop the proper way when the market nears it. They start doing last-minute rationalizations as to why they should not get out. If you have any doubts you can keep to a stop, place it in the market. There will also be days that can surprise you and unless you have a stop in the market you will get a monkey wrench thrown into your plans. The only time I recommend possibly having a mental stop is in a thin market where the floor traders can shoot for your stops in quiet trading.

You are going to have times when you get stopped out and the market completely turns around and goes in what would have been your favor. The most likely reason for this is that your stop was too close. But if you had the right stop and it happens, don't bang your head against the wall or lose your composure and make stupid trades. The market is unpredictable and it will get you at times. You need to learn to take it in stride when it happens and prepare for the next trade with a clear head. When I used to play college tennis, one of the things my coach tried to drive into my head was to not let a bad shot get to me. It's common for players to get on edge after they just miss a shot and then start hitting harder in anger. His words of wisdom were that it was just one point and that I should not let it bother me or affect the way I play. And he was right; those players who get rattled after a miss hit tend to lose much easier than they normally would.

PLANNING YOUR RISK

As you make your risk part of a game plan for a trade, you will have to decide a few things including:

- How much are you willing to lose?
- Where is the proper place to have a stop?
- How and when will you adjust a stop?
- What kind of stop do you want to use?

As you look to put on a trade, you should first stop to consider how much you can lose. This is the number one priority when putting on a trade. I'll show this example from a day trader's point of view as well, as they have to think about risk also. I'll look at the Dow again a few days later from where we left off in the previous chapter. Though I like to look at both the Dow and the S&Ps, I'll simplify things here by mostly referring to just the Dow. The Dow and S&P charts look pretty much the same the last few weeks; they have done nothing but gone straight down. Look at Figure 12.1 and you can see the recent sharp decline.

FIGURE 12.1 The Decline, Daily Dow Jan 22
Source: © TradeStation Technologies 1999. All rights reserved.

THE SETUP

The market has been down for the past five days straight and today, January 23rd, it started the day no different, opening lower some 200 points. Looking at Figure 12.2, a five-minute chart of the Dow futures, and you'll see the trading scenarios I'm going to look at.

Yesterday morning the big news before the opening was that the Fed unexpectedly cut rates by 75 basis points a week before its scheduled Federal Open Market Committee (FOMC) meeting. This was the biggest cut in 23 years. You'd expect a euphoric explosion on this news, but instead it gapped lower close to 400 points, mostly on recession fears. It opened so much lower because traders got nervous that if the Fed was this scared that it had to cut rates by so much and unexpectedly and couldn't wait a week to do it, then we may be in some deep shit. Despite the initial pessimism, as soon as it opened it rallied to close the gap as the effect of the rate cut settled into people's minds. However, the market ended up being down about 125 points for the day after spending most of the afternoon trading sideways with a late day sell off as recessionary fears crept back in.

FIGURE 12.2 5-Minute Dow Futures Jan. 23
Source: © TradeStation Technologies 1999. All rights reserved.

A GRAIN OF SALT

I take all the news with a grain of salt. I'm also a person who likes to look everything up, so if you were wondering where the expression "a grain of salt" comes from, here is what I found. It's been used in the English language since 1647 and comes from the Latin "cum grano salis," which dates back to the year 77. It comes from a book called *Naturalis Historia*, by Pliny the Elder, who was a must-read back in the Roman days. Somewhere in his 37-volume book, he mentions the discovery of a recipe for an antidote to a poison. In the description of the antidote, he states it must be taken fasting plus a grain of salt. Threats involving the poison were thus to be taken "with a grain of salt" and therefore, less seriously.

Now back to my original tangent about the news. Traders are fickle. One month they get a rate cut, and the market plummets because the wording isn't as perfect as it should be. Today they get a huge bonus rate cut plus they expect another one next week and the market plummets, then rallies, then plummets again the next day only to rally once more. See why it's so freaking hard to trade the news?

TRADING THE GAP

I'll show a few examples of a trade one could make with the key being knowing your risk. For starters, and you could see the setup in both today's and yesterday's charts, a very common day-trade is to trade against the opening gap. You would exit when it closes the gap. Though it works better when it gaps against a major trend and you trade into the trend, the trade can be done against the trend as well. There are several ways to enter the trade: one is on the open, another is after 30 minutes. That doesn't matter here, what matters is you know where you will get out if you are wrong. There are several ways to set a stop loss on a trade like this; it depends on the trader as to which he'll use. Some will use an exact dollar amount and others may use a technical level, others may set a time limit for when they'll get out if it is not working.

No matter what method you use, you should be able to come up with a rough estimate of how much it will cost if you are wrong. Let's assume John was trading and he was impatient and put the trade on at the opening bell on the 22nd. Now here are a few methods you can use to place a stop and help him out, because John has no stop of his own.

Method 1: The Time Stop

One method is to let the market trade for 30 minutes and if it's lower at that point or anytime later on he exits. You can estimate how much this will cost by taking a 30-minute chart and getting the average trading range for 30-minute periods. Looking at Figure 12.3, you can see that this has been about 40 to 90 points recently, with the range getting larger every day, and it has spiked up at the open to 120 points and later in the day reached 135 points. Knowing this, you can estimate that at worst it may cost 150 points if you held for 30 minutes. And most likely it will be 70 to 100 points. It's not exact but nothing in trading is, and it's a pretty good way to get an estimate on average over time. Yes, there will be times when it goes haywire and you'll take a beating, but you need to play the averages. You may want to add a worst-case scenario stop just in case something drastic happens.

Method 2: The Fixed-Dollar Stop

Another method is to have a fixed-point loss or monetary loss. You can either say, "I'm willing to lose 50 points and then I'll get out, or I'll risk $2,000." These are both the same because the latter assumes you are smart enough to trade the right number of contracts to make it a rational gamble. If you trade ten contracts on average and you are willing to risk 50 points

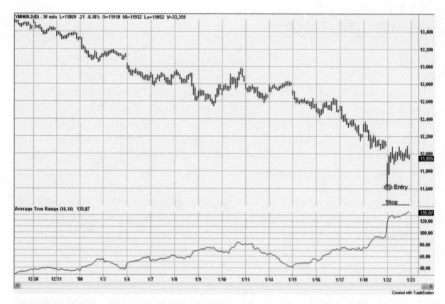

FIGURE 12.3 30-Minute Dow Futures Jan 22
Source: © TradeStation Technologies 1999. All rights reserved.

($250 per contract), your risk is $2,500, so if you want to keep it under $2,000 you need to only trade 8 contracts. The point value you choose to risk can be determined by using average true range or a standard deviation move from the normal, or just something you feel safe with. An example would be that if you know that a typical move in a day is 150 points then you can use that 150, plus a cushion, to determine where the stop should go.

Method 3: The Technical Stop

You can pick a stop by using a technical level in the market. This is usually a support, resistance, or congestion level or a recent high or low. For example, today I can use the low from yesterday's move as an indicator that I'm wrong, see Figure 12.4. In a straight down market you may not find much to look at on the charts to give yourself a safe level to place a stop, but if you have one use it.

Method 4: The Technical Indicator Stop

Another way to place a stop would be to use a technical indicator to help you establish it. Going back to the first gap day you can say that if the stochastic dips below the recent low in the stochastics (horizontal line in Figure 12.5), you will get out. This type of stop makes it the hardest to mea-

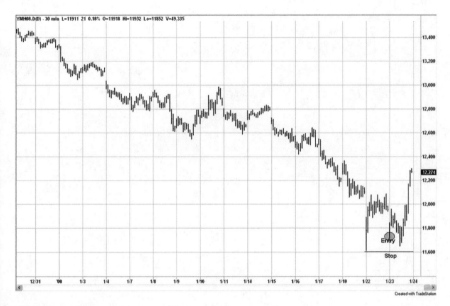

FIGURE 12.4 30-Minute Dow Futures Jan 23
Source: © TradeStation Technologies 1999. All rights reserved.

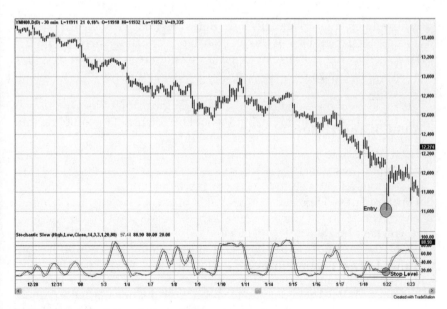

FIGURE 12.5 30-Minute Dow Futures Jan 22
Source: © TradeStation Technologies 1999. All rights reserved.

FIGURE 12.6   Another Trade, 5-Minute Dow Futures
Source: © TradeStation Technologies 1999. All rights reserved.

sure how much you will actually lose. But with enough trading experience you can get a decent idea of the relationship between the market and the indicator and what it will take to get it down there. I think about 3 or 4 more 30-minute down bars and it will reach that point, possibly costing up to 200 points.

If I had to choose one of these methods for exiting this type of gap trade, I would use the first one, but I would be abreast of the other factors and exit if the trade did not seem to be working.

ANOTHER TRADE

This isn't the only day-trade you can find in the last two days. Let's assume you took the gap trades and exited when the gaps were closed in both situations. My first reaction would be to go short because we are in a downtrend and just closed the gap. The news of the rate cut wasn't a major factor to me because the market completely shook it off by opening lower, and I believe the subsequent rally was a normal technical reaction to a gap open.

Let's say I shorted (Figure 12.6) at point S1 as soon as the gap was closed and the stochastics crossed out of the overbought area. This would be at about 12,050, with the target being the lows 400 points away. As a day trader I would place my stop above the congestion of the end of previous day shown in the gray box, or use the stochastics to tell me I was wrong or I could place a stop above the trend line of the last two days.

I could also use a 30-minute chart or a 60-minute chart to come up with a stop. For this trade I'm going to start my stop above the congestion area at 12,220 (Stop 1) and plan to move it down as the market goes down. I'm currently risking 200 to make 400 and I'm going with the major trend so I like this trade. The market went sideways to down the rest of the day testing the high two other times. It was a good day for traders who like looking at oscillators but I'm sure many people bought the peaks and sold the bottoms at each move. As I look through the day's action it is most likely I would have stayed short until the end of day, as I would not have been stopped out.

A CRAZY DAY

When I started writing this today the market was where Figure 12.6 leaves off. Luckily I don't have time to day-trade much until I finish the book, and I'm happy with my short position. But today is the kind of day people can get their heads handed to them.

I'll use the high of yesterday as my initial stop (Stop 2) for any shorting situation. I could adjust it when I get in again or as the market moves, but my worst-case scenario would be that. Let's say you wanted to short at point S2, when the market broke below the day's trend line. Depending on your style you could have placed a stop at Stop 3 or Stop 4. The more of a winner you are going for the more room you can give yourself. What you cannot do is give yourself 200 points if you're looking for a 50-point winner. I personally would have set my sights first for the low of the day and then yesterday's low.

As the short started working I would consider adding to it as it broke the lows of the day and moving my stop down with the recent trend line it was making. Yes, the Dow was already down 300 points but it's been in such a bad tailspin lately and it couldn't hold the rally yesterday and volatility was blowing up, so I believe it could still go lower. But as a day trader you need to be careful about just how much lower you think it can go. This is all about drawing up scenarios and the closer you get to the target the better those scenarios should become. Yes, there are some days when the market will drop 500 points or so, but that's happened what? A handful of times in history. Odds are not likely you will get that kind of a huge move, but on the other hand the market had all the ingredients for it to do it now. It's a tough call to add to the position when the market is down 300 points, so I would have chosen against it. But if I had added to it, I'd be diligent about a tight stop in case I was wrong.

Anyway, where Figure 12.6 leaves off I sat down to watch TV with my almost two-year-old daughter and though it was a riveting episode of "SpongeBob" we were watching, I fell asleep on the sofa. When I woke at about 3:30 I was shocked to see what the market had done during my nap. From being down 300 it was approaching being up 300 points. Look at Figure 12.4 or Figure 12.7 and you'll see this incredible late-day rally. I was also shocked to see how much damage one unsupervised toddler with one yellow crayon can do before she eats half of it trying to destroy the evidence.

This is one of those days where if you do not have a stop, you can get destroyed in the market by not paying attention. You can also get hurt by repeatedly shorting throughout the rally thinking that the up wave was ending any minute now. If I had been out of the market, I know I would have looked to get short at points A and B (Figure 12.7), thinking it was the greatest setup for a trade, using the stops from earlier in the chart and boy would I have been wrong.

FIGURE 12.7 The Turnaround, 5-Minute Dow Futures

Forget about the market, the one thing I really did need to do was come up with a good excuse to give my now even more extremely cranky unemployed girlfriend whose stocks haven't been doing so hot lately and who was just coming back from yoga, as to why the walls and Siena's tongue were yellow. Luckily, Crayola makes nontoxic crayons that come off the walls with a little WD-40. Not having a good excuse, I then needed to go over my real position of being short for the last two weeks. I had just given back almost 600 points from the peak value of the day, and that is a lot of "paper" money to give back. I would never enter a trade with a 600-point stop, so I don't like giving that much back, but I do have to consider the volatility of late. The market was still below my stop level but that kind of bounce needed to be reevaluated. This is the kind of day that can end up being the turning point in a market's major direction. I wanted to make sure I didn't miss anything, and so I needed to review the trade in all the time frames. I'll go through this in the next chapter. By the way, the stops in Figure 12.7 are for day-trading purposes, not for my longer term trade.

I'm sure if someone else was writing this book he would use this chart to show you the perfect market setup in hindsight and how he captured the whole move from point A or even better, and what you could have done to do so as well. That's why I think a lot of books are a bunch of crap. Yes, if you look at enough indicators with optimized parameters you can show how to catch this move from the bottom, but I think I'm one of the few authors you'll find to admit that he was wrong. I was napping so I don't know what I would have done at the bottom. I can see the crossover in the moving averages and stochastics indicating a buy, but I know for sure I would have been shorting aggressively when the market reached the trend line and had its little dip. And I would have been stopped out above that trend line and most likely not have gone long because I'm thinking bearish, and I'd think the up move was probably out of steam and I'd probably short again.

One last thing I need to stress, if you are actively day–trading, wait for the market to close to take a nap or you may just miss something.

PLANNING YOUR TARGET

Knowing where to put a stop is only a piece of preplanning an exit. It's the defensive part of trading and it saves your butt. But if you are going to make money you need to know how to get out with a winning trade. Again, you start thinking about this before the trade is even made. As you are contemplating a trade and you have figured out how much is at risk, then look to see how much you can make. This is much harder to do then picking a stop. A stop is a worst-case scenario that you can see by looking at a chart, it is a fixed amount you are willing to lose. But a target is a guess that you hope the market can achieve. For example, I showed how grains were at all-time highs. There is nothing to tell you just how much higher they may go. You can maybe measure waves and have an estimate as to where the next wave is going to be, but this is a pure guess. You can have a back tested strategy for the Dow and know on average the winners are 800 points. But this is an average of 50-point winners and 2,000-point winners. And again, it's just a guess. You may be long crude because of a certain thing like an increase in demand from China. You don't know when that demand will die down or if there will be enough supply to meet it. So how do you get an estimate? You look for technical support and resistance areas, you use trend lines, Fibonacci numbers, Elliot wave theory; you can use a variety of technical indicators and most of all you guess. Even if you are wrong, at least you have something to work with. Me thinking the market may drop 2,000 points is just a guess based on a support level and measurement of a wave. I have no idea if it will get there, but at least I have something to base my trade around.

HOW WILL YOU EXIT?

When you plan your exit you also need to plan *how* you will exit. If you are working with a purely mechanical system, you really don't need to think much, just enter the orders and let the trade do its thing. It will get you out when it's ready. But when you think your trades through, like I have, you need to know what it is you are looking for to get you out of the trade. Is it the end of a drought? Is it when the market goes down for three days in a row? Is it when you get an outside reversal day? Is it when the market goes below its 50-day moving average? Whatever it is, you need to know this in advance. Yes, you can and should change your opinion once a trade is on and the market gives you more information to work with, but at the beginning you need something to go with. You need to know if the trade has room to work and is worth the risk you are about to take by putting it on. Consider the long trade I made a few chapters back. I really thought the market had room to go to new highs and this justified the risk I was taking. I was wrong, but so what? I still managed to make some money. I realized the market wasn't going to get there so I had to rethink. But if I was just long because I thought the market was going up with no thought as to where, then I don't know if I would have been able to tell I was wrong.

THE IN-BETWEEN AREA

Next comes what is the most likely scenario and that is the gray area between your stop and your target. The stop should be a last resort method of getting out, but if the trade is not working you should be out before it gets there. You also need to consider what will be your exit if your target is not reached. Here is where money is made and lost most often. You made what was a well thought-out trade, but now it's not working entirely as you planned. You need to realize it and get out. It doesn't matter if your stop or target hasn't been reached. I have stated several times that you should get out when the reason you got in is no longer there. You need to exit when the trade tells you to. Getting out of a small loser is one of the hardest things for a bad trader to do. He rationalizes that it's not a lot of money, it's better than it was an hour ago, he wants to at least cover his commissions, and he has a stop in place. Once you can learn to let go of a nonworking trade, you can move on. Bad traders are scared to take a little loss, and I've found it's one of the hardest things to get people to overcome. But learning to lose is crucial. I read somewhere once that losses are to trading like exhaling is to breathing; it's just part of the game and it needs to become second nature to you as you can't do one without the other. Trading is not about how much money you made or lost on one trade. It's about how you did over the course of a time period. If you can get $1,000 more by taking a winner before it retraces or a loser before it gets stopped out, and you do this repeatedly, you will increase your odds of making money.

Another scenario is that the market is getting close to the target and looks like it will go right through that target. I consider this as a new trade that you have to rethink everything for. You don't need to get out and get back in, but you need to think about it from scratch. You had a goal and it was reached, now what? Am I overstaying my welcome? Is the market still looking good? Was my target too close? Do I want to let it retrace a bit? Do I need to move my stop? How will I make sure I do not blow this and give back my profit? It's a lot to think about, but if you are going to stay past your target you need to reevaluate the trade.

CLOSING THOUGHTS

Just as I spend quite a bit of time planning and looking at different time frames and scenarios to get into a trade, I do the same when I exit it. I don't just get out on a whim. I need a reason to do so and then I evaluate and draw up scenarios the same way I would as if it were the start of a new trade. Don't take the exit with any less seriousness that you would the entry. I know I wasn't very specific in how to actually pick stops and profit targets—I did that all in my first book—this chapter was more about why you need to do it and how you should plan getting out of trade. If all you get out of it is that you need to spend more time planning your exits than your entry, then I've done my job. Oh, and don't fall asleep when your toddler has a crayon handy.

CHAPTER 13

Reviewing and Managing

A market analyst is an expert who will know tomorrow why the market reacted as it did today and why the things he predicted yesterday didn't happen today. Apparently put on this earth to make weather forecasters look good.

So far I've showed you how to plan for getting into and out of a trade. But what about the time while you are in the trade or trades? This is the time you cannot let your guard down and you must constantly review and manage your positions. It doesn't matter if you are day-trading or keeping stuff for weeks. You need to constantly evaluate your positions, the market, your money management, your exits, and ultimately your plans. I've already touched upon this in Chapter 9 on scenarios.

AFTER THE TRADE IS ON

If you want to be a great trader you need to be on top of your trades all the time. It's not just putting on a trade, picking a stop, and placing an order for an exit. There is a lot of work to be done before you get out. Yes it's important to have a predetermined exit before getting in. But the markets are so dynamic that you need to constantly update your plans. Every night as you are going over the day and preparing the next day's strategies, take the time to go over and review your trades in detail. Look at the charts and check the news if you like. And then start drawing up those scenarios, moving stops and targets and making any adjustments necessary.

I got out of my short trade yesterday with an okay profit. I had gotten in at 12,712 and made over 400 points on the trade—nowhere near the thousands of points I was hoping for. But things had changed and I was getting concerned the market might bounce back and I didn't want to wait to be stopped out. I'm currently looking for a new shorting opportunity, but I believe I will wait until the Federal Open Market Committee (FOMC) meeting and its interest rate announcement later in the week to do so.

I bring this up because I exited the trade only because of constant reviewing and managing my position.

Where last I left off, the market had had that huge intraday reversal move and that was my first concern. As I was going over my position that night, the short was still within my original stop level, but I was concerned because many times this type of move is indicative of a market reversal. Another indication of the end of the move can be seen in Figure 13.1. It's the weekly chart showing that five-year trend that just got broken. But what I'm looking at here is how wonderfully the market bounced at the 38-percent Fibonacci retracement level. For you skeptics out there, these levels do really hold a large percentage of the time. There were a few other factors that got me to get out. I was concerned that the stochastics in Figure 13.2 might be breaking above the oversold level and that the trend lines I had were telling me maybe it's time to get out. As you can see in Figure 13.2

FIGURE 13.1 Fibonacci Retracements, Weekly Dow
Source: © TradeStation Technologies 1999. All rights reserved.

FIGURE 13.2 Reasons to Get Out, Daily Dow
Source: © TradeStation Technologies 1999. All rights reserved.

Trend Line 1 is too far away and a snap back could be possible and Trend Line 2 is too steep to be good for a trailing stop and could easily be broken. The same held true for the moving averages, because of the previous big drop the market was too far away from them and very likely to snap back to them.

My real stop had been placed above a congestion area (the oval marked Stop in Figure 13.2), which is the only legitimate place to have a stop on a long-term trade. But with the huge drop in the market recently, it is a little on the far side now. Even though it is pretty much where I entered the trade, I didn't want to give back too much profit.

Though we were below every place I would put a stop, my concern now was to play it safe and not turn a winner into a loser. This didn't mean necessarily getting out, it just meant being very sensitive to the trade and getting out if I didn't believe in it any more (and I was starting to have some second thoughts about it). There was one more thing looming in my mind and that was that Fed was expected to announce a rate cut in two days at its FOMC meeting. The consensus was another 50 basis points and if that happened there was potential for the market to really go up, but in the interim I believed the market might go up on the rumor and then we could sell the fact once it happened if it failed to follow through. There are other scenarios involved which I'll get to soon.

I also decided to look at Fibonacci retracements from the high in October to the low just made (Figure 13.2). I figured the market had a good chance to go up and test the 38 percent level, which was about 340 points away. I didn't feel like giving that up if I didn't have to.

The night of the big intraday move as I was analyzing my position, I reverted to the 60-minute chart (Figure 13.3) to start fine-tuning my potential exit. It was here that I drew the downward trend line and decided that if the market broke this level I'd be getting out before my major stop level was hit. Though this trend line may look like an obvious place to have a stop, do not forget it's a 60-minute chart and a trend line here is not as strong as in a daily chart. This same trend line in the daily chart was much too steep to use and can be easily broken, but because I'm having doubts, I need a tighter place to get out.

Though the market rallied the next day (1/24), it was a congested rally (see the shaded area in Figure 13.4), and barely closed above the trend line. It reached close to, but below, my stop, which is always cushioned from the actual indicator.

The following day was the crucial one. That morning I knew the market was called to gap higher by about 100 points (level A in Figure 13.4), which would put it above my stop (Stop 1). As I made my game plan I decided I was going to cancel the stop and use my 30-minute gap trade to get out.

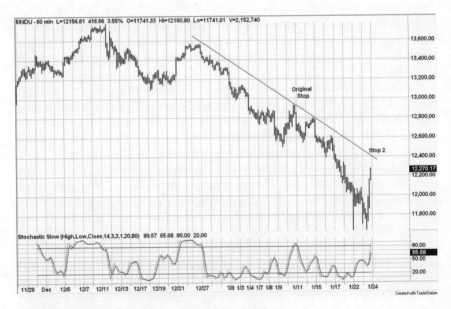

FIGURE 13.3 Going Over Stops 60-Minute Dow
Source: © TradeStation Technologies 1999. All rights reserved.

FIGURE 13.4 Fine-Tuning the Exit 60-minute Dow Futures
Source: © TradeStation Technologies 1999. All rights reserved.

If the market was higher than the open after 30 minutes I would get out regardless, hopefully though it would close the gap and go lower—which it did in a strong way. In my reviewing that night I decided my stop should now be slightly higher than it had been and used the high of the day, which was slightly higher then the previous day's high. This is one of the few times I would raise a stop, and I did so because it was technically correct to do so.

Actually at this point, I started liking my chances of the trade working out well again. The next morning (B), though, the market was due to open only slightly lower. With that information I made a scenario where, if the market took out the lows of the previous day, I would add to my trade by one-third the amount of my original trade, with a stop if the market went positive. With this trade my stop was so close that it was well worth the chance. I liked that the stochastics on the 60-minute chart were heading lower with room to spare and maybe that the recent rally may have just been noise. I also liked that yesterday was a downward reversal. I wasn't taking chances though, I had my stop in for my current short, and if the market did go up after the open I would not add to my short. If the market rallied a bit and fell I was prepared to add to the short as well when it took out the low of the day.

So what ended up happening was that the market went lower at the open but turned around soon after and rallied the rest of the day. I added to the short as it broke yesterday's lows, but then quickly got stopped out with a 55-point loss as it went positive. And a little later I exited the rest of my position when the stochastic turned back up. The trade ended up having a 435-point profit on it. Not what I was hoping for but still it was a nice trade. I got out at a decent level as the market had a strong rally that day and the next (C).

LOOKING AHEAD

This all leads me to tonight. I know that tomorrow the Fed is expected to announce a rate cut. I still want to short but it's a crucial point and I have quite a bit of planning to do before I can do so comfortably. I have to draw up all the scenarios of what could happen and how to react if the market does one thing or another. I've done this already once in this book so I won't spend five pages doing it again. But the main possibilities were:

- That they cut 50 basis points and the market rallies or it fails to rally.
- If they cut 25 basis points, the market should plummet.
- If they cut 75 basis points, I believe you'll see a quick, huge jump up and then a sell-off is possible as people realize it was done because the Fed is really nervous about the economy and a recession is a coming.

The only tricky scenario is if they cut 50 basis points as expected. My reaction will be to look for a place to short if we sell off or if we rally I'll look for a stall in the rally to short. If we just go straight up, I'll sit out. I'll use the Fibonacci retracements as my initial stop areas. It's late and I'm off to bed now. I'll let you know tomorrow what does happen.

It's actually two days later now, I didn't have time to write yesterday, but the news was as expected with a 50-basis point cut and the market rallied about 230 points off that initial news. However, it failed to hold the rally and closed down 35 points, selling off a couple of hundred points in the last hour of trading, as people feared the economy was in danger. See Figure 13.5 of a five-minute Dow futures chart. I ended up getting short at 12,592 because of the break in trend line X, and the trade was looking good going into the close so I held overnight.

I did my usual reviewing the night before, and I'll spare you those details except to say that I placed my new stop above the high of the session. This morning, however, I had stuff to think about as the market was going to open down 150 points or so (see Figure 13.6).

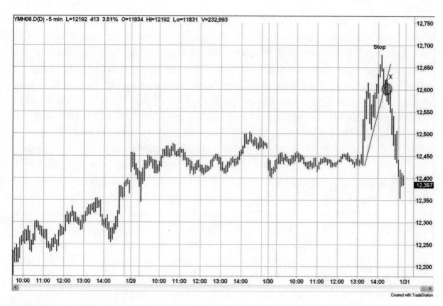

FIGURE 13.5 5-Minute Dow Futures Jan. 30
Source: © TradeStation Technologies 1999. All rights reserved.

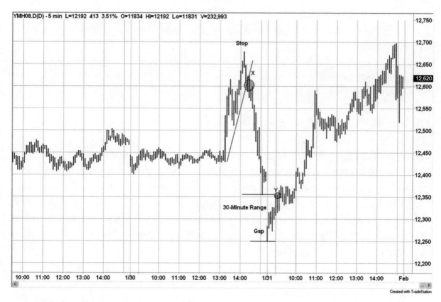

FIGURE 13.6 5-Minute Dow Futures Jan. 31
Source: © TradeStation Technologies 1999. All rights reserved.

My first reaction was to do a little "I'm in the money" dance with my daughter, but then I realized that the market would most likely close the gap and rally. So I decided to use a 30-minute breakout trade for a stop, which should give me a profit but nowhere near what I was looking for. If I got stopped out, I'd reevaluate and look to short again. I ended getting out at point Y, which I was happy with and then, sure enough, the market rallied and closed the gap and then rallied another 200 points closing really strong as investors now thought the interest rates cuts would make a difference. These fickle traders are making this one tough market to trade long term. The intraday moves have been pretty damn big every day and the news has become really wishy-washy. I really believe that analysts just make up the reason the market has moved after they see what the market has done. I have noticed, however, that the opening gap trade has been working like a charm. I'm going to start trading this set up more aggressively until it stops. Now most of what I just wrote may seem to you like it belongs in other chapters like drawing scenarios, getting in, or getting out. But what you can get out of it here is that by constantly reviewing the market and your trades, you can start to see things more clearly. I have just noticed that those gap trades in the morning are working like they were textbook examples. When you can find patterns that are working, trade then and don't be scared to be aggressive. The stops in these trades are not that large and they have been paying off. So keep reviewing and when you pick up gems like this take advantage. Although you can probably bank on the fact that now that I've decided to trade these more aggressively, they'll stop working.

As for my long-term opinion, it is still short, but I need to wait out this recent up move.

REVIEWING YOUR TRADING

There is more to just doing a simply review of your positions every night. You should be reviewing all aspects of your trading—from your entries and exits to the game, trading, and money management plans themselves. You won't become a better trader just by trading, you need to be proactive and question everything. You can learn to be a better trader just by taking a little time every day to review. There is a lot to review, but it will not take long and it's worth the effort.

Review throughout the Day

Reviewing is not just something you do when the market is closed, it should be done during trading hours as well. The markets change and what can start out as a down day can easily turn around at any point. You should take time out several times a day to do an analysis of your positions and the market. If you do not keep up with the market you will increase your odds of failing.

Closed Trades

At the end of every day I go over every trade I made and try and learn something from it. I look to see why I got in and why I got out. I look to see that I adhered to my stops, targets, and plan for it. I look to see whether my money management plan for it was wise. I'm always trying to learn and one of the best ways to do so is to review my trades showing me my strengths and weaknesses. You will learn a lot more after hours than while the market is open and you will learn a lot more from closed positions than open ones. The reason for this is that when a position is still open, you think with that position and you can have skewed thoughts based on that position, but after you are out of it, you can more clearly see it and what you did right or wrong with it. Don't just file a trade away after you are out of it. Make sure you learn from it.

Managing Position Size

Forget about deciding if you should keep the position or move a stop and so on, one key area you should review is the position size itself. The trade is not over when you put it on, it needs fine-tuning along the away. Getting in and out of a trade is a simple way of trading, and as you become better, you may want to scale in and out of a trade. You may want to add to it when the odds are in your favor or take away from it when you reach levels where the odds of it working are getting worse.

Every night when I have something on, I look at it from that point of view. If I want to add to the trade I'll think of it as a new position or have a new reason to get in. I don't just add random amounts either. I will never add more than my initial position, and usually a third or half of it, unless it's preplanned. There are times when I'm looking for a certain level to get into a trade full blast, and I'll put on a small position until that scenario hits. I'll then put on my normal size trade. This is preplanned and not a random adding to a position; otherwise, when I pyramid I make sure to do it in smaller quantities.

Adding to trades is often done wrong, and people tend to get top-heavy on a trade as it goes in their favor, with the result being as soon as it turns around they have the most shares at the worst prices, which quickly go against them. They end up taking a nice trade and somehow wind up losing money on it. Even worse are the idiots who insist on adding to losers. A simple oft-repeated rule that will make you money in the long run as a trader is: DO NOT ADD TO LOSERS.

Cutting back on positions is much harder to do than getting in. If something is going your way, do you want to let it ride or lock in some profits? It's a hard choice to make and you can easily go back and forth and come up with reasons for both. I find getting out of a portion of my trade to be one the hardest things for me to do. I reason that if I'm still in the market that means I like it, so why get out of a little of it? Or if I'm going to exit a portion, why not do the whole thing? And if I'm losing on the trade my natural instinct is to think if I get out of a portion of it, it will take twice as much of a move to get my money back.

There are several reasons for exiting part of your trade. First, if the risk or volatility increases and you have to move your stop, you should cut back, because you are no longer risking the same amount. Another reason to scale out is if you've reached your target but the trade still has some umph in it, and you think you can make some more on it. Since you reached your target you can take some profits and use the rest as the casino's money to try and get a little extra out of it. If you are wrong you still walk away with a nice win. Another reason to sell a portion of your position is because you are overextended and may want to free up some money to put into another trade, but you still like this trade. And last is that you are losing on the trade or it isn't working as expected, but you still want to be in it just in case so you lower your exposure to be safe.

Multiple Positions

This brings us to what to do when you have on multiple positions. Taking care of one trade is hard enough. But for people who trade many things at once, you really need to look them over carefully every night. It's much harder to actively trade 10 positions than it is one, so your homework has to be better. You need to have a clear plan of what and how you are going to do. When you are trading multiple positions, having a game plan will make your trading so much easier. If you do not spend time reviewing your trades properly you will have a much harder time trading them.

One area that is key is knowing, when you have 10 positions on and are losing money, which you will exit first. John likes to get out of the ones he is making the most money on so he can lock in some profits and expects the others to turn around. This is just the opposite of what you should be doing. As you review your positions, you may want to rank them in order of best to worst and know the ones you will liquidate first.

The Markets You Trade

You also want to review and make notes of all the markets you trade, because you may find you do better in some than others. You may want to trade more aggressively in the ones you historically do better in. You may also want to consider not trading the ones you cannot make money in. This doesn't apply just to individual stocks and commodities but to market conditions as well. If you make notes and find that you are a much better trader in a trending market, then you should trade more aggressively in them. You can take a further step by analyzing how you do in an uptrend when you buy versus when you sell. You may also find that you trade some commodities better in a choppy market and others you trade better in a trending market. By reviewing what you trade and the market conditions, you can open your eyes to a lot of things that you would be unaware if you didn't do it.

Money Management

I have a chapter on money management coming up soon, so I'm getting a little ahead of myself here. But what you want to do as you are reviewing your trades is to make sure you are always sticking to your money management plan. It has happened several times to me where I started trading after a break from trading with say $10,000 in my account. I remember I did this after finishing graduate school. I laid out some great money management formulas and started trading. Next thing I know I'm making money and have doubled my account. But I kept adding to open positions and increasing my total number of contracts traded. Where I was risking up to two e-minis when I first started trading, I then pushed it up to five and six contracts and even had some trades with 10 contracts. I doubled my account but was taking on three to five times the risk. As soon I hit that inevitable cold streak, it didn't take long to bring my account down to $3,000. Then I began trading four contracts on a regular basis trying to get it back up to my initial $10,000. So then my account size was a third of what I started with and I was risking twice as much money. I completely changed my money management strategy, and I wondered why I always lost money in the long run. I've seen this happen to many people. It is a horrible trading situation that you need to avoid. If you take the time to review your money management rules and how you are responding to them and then have the balls to tell yourself you are breaking them and to stop doing so, you will have a better chance. The hard part though is to discipline yourself to stick to the plan—when winning or losing.

KEEPING A JOURNAL

It's highly recommended that you keep a written journal of everything you do while trading. For those who are lazy and don't want to do it you'll pay the price, by not being a better trader, quicker. You learn a lot if you write down everything you did and why. Even if you decide you do not want to jot everything down, you should at the least make mental notes of your trading. Some of the things you may want to know are:

- Why did I make the trade?
- Did I trade too aggressively?
- Did I overstay my welcome?
- Did I not follow my game plan?
- Did I follow my game plan?
- Did I trade the proper size?
- Did I risk too much?
- Did I have a good reason for the trade?
- Was I lucky or smart?
- Did I make money?
- Did I do something wrong?

You can add to this list but if you can come up with answers to all these questions you will start to see patterns in your trading that can make you a better trader. You should make any notes you can to help you. Something like, "I got out even though we didn't hit my stop because I panicked," or "I got stopped out because I put my stop too close." You then need to periodically review these notes so that you can start seeing patterns in your trading.

Why Did You Make the Trade?

As you are reviewing, if you have to ask yourself just one question, I think it should be this one. Why did you make that trade? You should be asking it before you actually make it. But it's as important to know why you made it after the fact. There will be many times when you are trading that you will act on impulse or emotions and it's only after the market is closed that you can actually give yourself a good answer for it. You may find that the answer is not worth the trade and then you'll realize that you ought to be getting out of it, instead of holding it in hopes you get vindicated. My main goal for this book is to get you to have a reason for every trade you make. If you start keeping tabs on yourself you'll be able to see if you are achieving that goal.

Is My Trading Plan Working?

The last part of reviewing that I like to concentrate on is the game plan and the trading plan. You will not make a dime trading if these two things are not working for you. You may think you have a great trading plan and that your game plan is perfect. But are they? If you keep making the trades as per your trading plan and they are not making you money, then maybe something is wrong with the plan itself. It may be time to reevaluate and see why it's not performing as you had intended it to. The same goes for your game plan. You may find some flaws in it if you review it on a regular basis. But another aspect you want to consider as you review your trades is are you disciplined in making and then following the game plan? You may actually have a great trading and game plan, but your discipline may suck and you cannot follow those plans. You may think you are following them, but as you review your trading you may find that you didn't do everything as planned and let a stop slide or took liberties putting on too many positions. You'll never know this stuff unless you review all the time.

CLOSING THOUGHTS

Being a successful trader is not just about putting on good trades, it's how you nurture those trades, and what you learn from them. Never ignore a trade once it's on. There is always something going on that may give you insight on getting out of a trade, or getting a better price, or even changing your outlook on the market. If you are adhering to this book, you will have begun to do homework every night, as you prepare for the next day. As you do this homework make sure you spend time reviewing all you can about your trades, yourself, the markets, and your plans. Take nothing for granted as you can learn from everything you do. And remember, the better educated you are about yourself and your trades the better you should do.

CHAPTER 14

How to Keep from Overtrading

You know you trade too often if your inbox has more e-mail trade confirmations than all the spam you received last year combined, if all the stocks on the CNBC ticker are in your portfolio, and if your broker sends you a picture of his kid in college as a thank you for being a customer.

Overtrading is one of the deadliest things a trader can do. I know it's always been one my biggest problems. Overtrading can come in several forms. One is simply to just trade nonstop, making trade after trade after trade, with no breather in between. For some scalpers this may be their strategy, but for most people, it reflects a lack of discipline and is a commission-generating evil monster. Overtrading can also be a result of having too many positions on at once. At a certain point, having too much on will distract you and be unmanageable. For some people this could be more than 4 positions, for others it could be after having 20 at once; either way, when you get above a level you can handle your trading will suffer. There is still another level of overtrading and that is having too large of a position size resulting in having more at risk than you can afford to lose. When you have on more than you can afford, you will tend to make irrational decisions. I've seen it happen over and over again. Once in a while you will catch something in your favor, but for the most part when you are wrong you will take a beating that will make you curl up into a little ball. I'm proud to say I've been guilty of and have gotten hurt by all of these scenarios.

WHY HAVE A PLAN

One of the most important reasons I can think of for having a plan is that it will keep you from overtrading. Actually I should say it *should* keep you from overtrading. Chronic overtraders will always find a way to revert back to their old ways as I'll soon explain. When you have your daily routine planned out ahead of you, it's a lot easier to keep from doing stupid things like overtrading. If you have to have a reason for getting in and out of every trade, you will begin trading less than if you just traded randomly as the mood suits you. Chronic overtraders, more than anyone else, need the discipline of a trading and game plan if they want to cut back on their trading and have a shot at becoming great traders. I can't stress enough how important this is. So I'll say it again: Chronic overtraders, more than anyone else, need the discipline of a trading and game plan if they want to cut back on their trading and have a shot at becoming great traders.

DON'T FOOL YOURSELF

Some bad traders are really clueless and may think that because they do have a trading plan and are keeping to it they are not overtrading. However, they are dead wrong if they mistakenly put rules and parameters in their plan that let them overtrade. This is more common than you'd think. If part of your trading plan is to have 5 positions and trade up to 20,000 shares of stock risking $2,000 on each, you could be putting yourself at danger if you can't afford to trade like this. When you make your daily game plan you may keep adding too many shares or positions or trading in a time frame that may generate too many trades, simply because you think it's okay because it falls within the parameters of the trading plan. Sure you may believe you are fine because it's in your plan, but don't fool yourself. Make sure your plan is solid before risking too much or else you may hurt yourself.

YOU DON'T ALWAYS NEED TO BE IN THE MARKET

I used to be a trading machine and was always looking to make a trade. If I wasn't long a market I had to be short because I if I didn't like it long, then it must be a good short. The notion of sitting on the sidelines waiting for a good trade to approach was foreign to me. My systems were always reversing my position and I always seemed to be in the market. Not just for one market but for as many markets as I had margin for, but more on that soon.

Some people can trade successfully with these types of systems, when of course they are back tested. The problem, though, lies with the traders who do not have a proper strategy for doing this and sometimes start chasing the market as they continue to be wrong and "need to be right." They do not know how to take a loss and make 12 bad trades in a row trying to finally get it right. This happens a lot in choppy markets or when a trader is facing losses and is pressing and doubling up trying to get his losses back.

An example of this could be shown in Figure 14.1, which is a somewhat choppy S&P market. Let's say John rushed in and shorted two contracts on the weak open in the morning (S1). He holds and holds hoping to be right and then finally 10 points out of the money, he gets long on that last gasp up (B1). He now believes the market will rally and he wants to make his cash back so he buys four contracts to do it quicker. At this point it finally starts to back off. Now he panics and decides he was right the first time so he shorts six contracts at S2. Once again he picks the worst level and the market rallies, so now he buys eight contracts (B2) and the process continues. By the end of the day he has traded about 4,393 contracts and committed two overtrading no-nos. The first is making too many trades

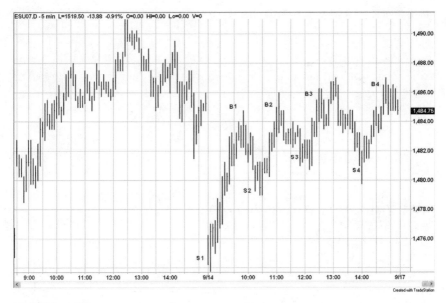

FIGURE 14.1   Choppy Market, 5-Minute S&P Futures
Source: © TradeStation Technologies 1999. All rights reserved.

and the second is trading too many contracts. Each can hurt on its own but combined, "ouch!"

The proper way to trade this kind of choppy market is just the opposite of John's method. You should be putting buy orders at the bottoms and sell orders at the tops. By having a game plan, you could stop yourself from doing it the wrong way. But you have to be disciplined to follow the plan, and most overtraders lack that discipline. A plan can simply tell you if you lose X amount in a day or have four consecutive losers to call it quits for the day. It can also say never trade more than five contracts at any time; these are straightforward ways it can help. But if you were well prepared coming into the day, there are other ways a game plan can help.

I'll show how Harry, if day-trading, could have cut the number of trades John made in half and walked away with a nice day. Harry takes times to look at the big picture of the market Figure 14.2 and makes a game plan recognizing that the long-term trend was up. The market recently had a decent down wave, but now looked like it might be starting to go back up. He also recognized that it was in a congestion period, so there was a chance of choppiness. His game plan then says he will buy the S&Ps on dips and it will not include shorting. Because he was only buying, he would be able to cut his trades in half, hopefully the worst half. Because he recognized that the market may be range bound, he called for using stochastics to identify

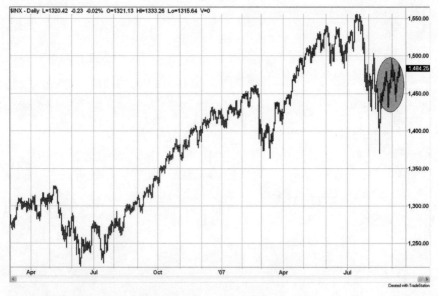

FIGURE 14.2 Getting the Big Picture, Daily S&Ps
Source: © TradeStation Technologies 1999. All rights reserved.

bottoms to buy and possible peaks to exit, while waiting for another buying opportunity. He also placed an initial stop to exit 30 minutes after the open if he was wrong and then used the low of the day as a stop for the rest of the day.

His day would have looked like Figure 14.3, where he would buy on the gap open (B) and exit as soon as the stochastics crossed to the downside (X). He then would wait for them to bottom out and would repeatedly buy when they crossed up (all the Bs), exiting as they peaked (the Xs). Using stochastics in this manner works great in this kind of environment. The problem arises when a market is strong and the indicator doesn't dip lower—then you miss half the move.

Even if your plan calls for you to take every trade, both long and short, using the same thinking as Harry, and you are making the same number of trades as John, who is chasing the market, you would be in control and not really overtrading, because you have a strategy that works for this kind of market, and you are staying disciplined with your size.

Although constantly being long or short in the market can make you money, I have found it better to pick a side and only make trades in that direction, while taking a breather instead of reversing when you decide to get out. But it all depends on the market situation. Regardless of how you

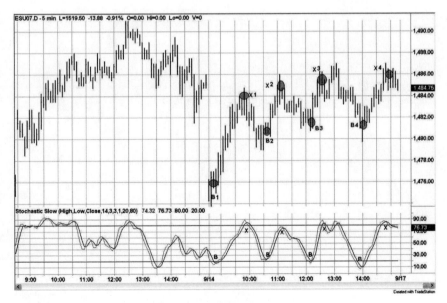

FIGURE 14.3 Trading the Choppy Market Correctly
Source: © TradeStation Technologies 1999. All rights reserved.

plan on trading, knowing in advance what you will be doing will make it easier to control yourself.

I'm just showing an example using a 5-minute chart, but you will see similar patterns on 60-minutes or daily charts. The goal in a longer term chart (Figure 14.4) is to identify the range bound area; I show this by adding support and resistance lines. You are not going to know it is range bound for a while; maybe you'll realize it at around point X, because the market didn't break the previous low. However, once you do and can establish levels, you want to be shorting near the top and buying near the bottom and not making many trades in between, and always have stops outside the boundaries. Once the market breaks the range, then you have to change your strategy. But if you put your stops in you'll be well protected.

STOP BEING IN TOO MANY POSITIONS

Being in too many positions and looking at too many markets generally results in the same thing. In both cases you have so much to do that you just can't focus properly.

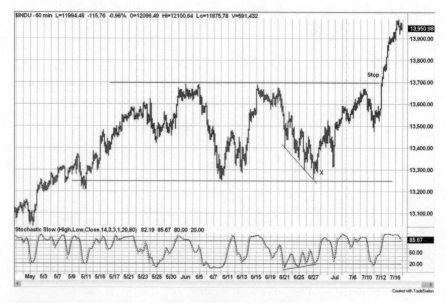

FIGURE 14.4 Longer Term Range Bound Market, 60-Minute Dow
Source: © TradeStation Technologies 1999. All rights reserved.

When you are always looking for something to trade or have to monitor 15 positions your trading will suffer and you will begin to experience diminishing returns. The only time I say that this is okay is when you have a proper computerized system that monitors different markets and gives you buy and sell signals. Your job now becomes more that of an order taker/executer rather than a trader, and it becomes easier to handle multiple positions.

Even though you may not have to look for trades in this situation, you are not off the hook. You are still responsible for monitoring the total risk level and total position size. But when you have to monitor risk, position size, and find trades, then execute them, then keep track for too many positions, you can see how you may get over your head. You will, at some point, miss something you should not have, simply because you could not concentrate properly. This is why I recommend having parameters in your trading plan that will limit what you will trade. If you don't have these parameters then you will never know what is a manageable number of positions for you.

Your game plan will help you with this because in it, you can say, "I will only trade these eight markets I'm looking at today, and I will get in only if so and so happens." Sure, there could be many trading opportunities you will pass up, but if you keep to a manageable level you should do better. Without this part of the game plan you can spend most of your day just looking for trading situations. And if you are in 12 positions overnight, it will become too much to handle when you try to manage and get out of all of them, especially if they all go bad at once.

One quick note, being in 12 random stocks overnight is a little different than being in 12 semiconductor stocks overnight. The latter is basically one big position with a little protection against any one stock having a weird move. Some people like to trade this way while others prefer picking the sector leader and having one big position. It's easier to manage one position, however, outside factor risk is better spread out when it's spread over 12 stocks that should move together. But remember, your commissions will be more when trading multiple positions.

The way the trading and game plan helps is that when you are preparing for the day, assuming you have no positions, you will have scoured the market and picked the potential markets that represent the best trading opportunities. Let's say there are 20 situations you like. However, your trading plan says you should not have more than six positions on at any time. Now you have to decide which the best ones on that list are. Out of that 20, some are going to stand out as having higher probabilities of making you money. When I traded more markets, I used to rate all the possibilities on a scale of one to five and then I'd only consider the four- and five-star trading opportunities, ignoring the weaker ones. This is what kept me from having too many positions on at once. It's not a problem for me anymore as I limit my trading to basically just one market with an occasional trade here and there if something really looks great. For the most part it's just the Dow or the S&Ps that I trade, and I consider these two markets to be pretty much the same.

USING A GAME PLAN TO HELP IF YOU TRADE TOO MANY POSITIONS

Now if on the other hand you are the overtrader who goes home with a slew of positions and then has to monitor them, as well as get out of them while looking for new trades, you are looking for trouble. I'm not going to recommend doing it, but if you have a well prepared game plan you will at least make your life easier if this is you. Hopefully, in time, you will realize it's best to keep things simpler by not being in too much stuff, but let's assume you do tend to trade too many markets.

First of all, when making a plan give yourself some sort of limit, whether it be a monetary amount or a position amount. When I used to day-trade stocks at a day-trading firm everyone had computer-imposed company limits. It didn't matter if you were a seasoned trader or there two weeks, everyone had a limit and once you reached it you were locked out from making any new trades. The new people could trade up to $100,000 at once and no more than 200 shares of any stock while the super traders may have had limits of $10,000,000 and 100,000 shares. Though these limits didn't explicitly say, "Don't trade more than 10 stocks at once," they restricted you from doing it in a roundabout way.

I prefer to have a combination of a monetary limit and a total positions limit. I have a clause in my trading plan that limits me to having up to $50,000 at risk and no more than three unrelated positions. If I traded the S&Ps, Nasdaq, and the Dow I would consider them as one position as they are pretty much the same, most of the time, but for the most part I only trade one at a time.

Back when I used to trade more markets, I looked at the stock indices, the bonds, the Euro, the grains, energies, livestock, and a few others like coffee, sugar, cocoa, and cotton. With too many positions on at once, I would be one busy beaver all day long. So in my trading plan I limited it to my best six or eight picks. Then, when making my game plan the night before and in the morning, I'd scour the markets looking for the best trades. I wasn't looking for intraday moves, but rather three- to five-day swings, so I didn't have to spend time trading them all day, but it was still overwhelming if I had a lot on. As I limited my trades to fewer markets I began doing much better. If, as you make a game plan, you know in advance which markets you are going to or want to trade that day, you will be a much more focused trader.

So let's say you decided in your trading plan that you can handle 20 positions. Some people can do this successfully and some can trade 50 stocks at once. Once you have established your limit, it then becomes your game plan's duty to be able to handle them. Your homework will be a lot harder as you will need to monitor and make notes on all your markets and positions. You should make a list of all your targets and what-ifs for all your positions and trades you are thinking of making. Even though you will spend a lot of time preparing for the day, it will save you hours of work and distractions during the day.

You will have a lot to monitor throughout the day, but without a game plan, you can forget about even having a chance. It's easy to get caught up in studying your positions or looking for exit points or get distracted by a bad trade and then let everything else fall apart because you are not focused anymore. It's too much to handle without solid guidance. I know when I used to trade everything under the sun, I would let a few things totally get away from me at times because they weren't as important as others. For example, say I was long cotton and crude and they were slightly against me. And say I was making a little bit in hogs and corn. And say I was short coffee and it was really killing me. I probably had another eight positions on, but I'll just focus on these for the example. All my attention now is on that freaking coffee trade, which is just getting worse and worse. It went through my mental stop and now I was panicking trying to figure out what to do. And while it kept me distracted, all my other small losers and winners started to get a little worse as well. Individually these trades didn't amount to much, so I didn't pay much attention to them. However, all my focus was on the coffee debacle because I was down $2,000 in it. Little did I realize I'm down about the same cumulatively in my other positions and before long panic mode hits. I then start exiting the best positions because I want to lock in a little profit and hold the losers hoping they turn around. Hopefully you know by now that this is one of the worst trading strategies you can adopt. Anyway, you get the point.

However, if I had traded a bit differently and still made all of those trades, I could have fared much better. Assume I still had the same trades on but this time I had plans for all of them. I took the time to study them, and to make proper what-if assumptions for all of them. I had set my targets and exits and I knew what I wanted out of them. Then I actually put real stops into the market. That last sentence is oh so important as mental stops are easily forgotten or missed. If you place a real stop in you can focus so much better and be so much more successful and efficient. Had I decided earlier that a proper stop in my coffee trade was about $1,200 and I was okay if I lost that amount, I would have had a mental advantage. Once I placed that stop, I could have spent more time dealing with and thinking of other markets. Maybe I could have had time to review all my trades and realized that a few of the small losers weren't acting like I had intended them to, so I should just get out of them. Maybe some of the winners hit their targets and were now retracing. It's hard to realized all these things if I was too preoccupied with the coffee trade.

Here is a case where if you trade one way, you have horrendous day, while if you are prepared you may only have a slightly bad day. I'd rather have the slightly bad day. So no matter how much you decide to trade, make and stick to a game plan and its limits. Whether it's 2 markets a day or 20, make sure your game plan keeps you in check. If you do like to trade too many positions, keep asking yourself, is this trade in my game plan? If the answer is yes, go for it. If the answer is no then ask yourself why am I making it? You better have a damn good reason for making it. Having one will help you avoid excess whim trades that catch your attention for no reason other than it was in the news or a buddy told you about it.

KEEPING TO RISK MANAGEMENT LIMITS

Another part of overtrading comes when you risk more than you can afford to lose. Sometimes this is a result of a combination of some of the above factors. But there are three main factors that could get you into trouble: trading positions that are too expensive for you, trading a size you cannot afford, or failing to have or follow risk parameters. These are all good ways to hurt yourself in worst-case scenarios. I'll go through each of those in the next sections.

Trading Rich Markets

One thing that can kill you is falling in love with fast-moving expensive markets. These include commodities like coffee or crude oil and stocks like Google or any Internet stock back in the wild days. This is especially true for traders with small bankrolls. If you have a nice sized account then you can limit the size on the wild movers to fewer contracts than you would normally trade. But if your account is limited and you normally trade 100 shares or 1 contract, you have nothing to scale back to (what are you going to do, buy 10 shares of something?) so you will be risking a lot on these markets compared with others. Sure, it's great catching a $12 move in a stock, but don't forget you can also catch it the wrong way. The moves in a fast-moving stock can be so fast and violent that even if you are trading a small quantity of it, it can blow through your limits so quickly that you stand there dumbfounded, watching it as it gets worse. These markets are dangerous and should be traded with caution and a decent sized trading account.

I gave my son $4,000 last year when he was about a year–and-a-half old and told him to invest in any stock he liked. I think he said Google. So we bought 10 shares as that was all he had money for. He has since almost doubled his money, but that is a dangerous high-flying stock for someone with a small account and a weak stomach to handle and should be avoided, unless you can put it under your baby crib mattress and forget about it for a few years.

By the way, that almost $8,000 dollars he now has covers about a month worth of preschool in New York City. That's a lot of money to play with blocks and have nap time. Can't wait to see what college will cost.

POKER ANALOGY

Here's another poker example. You walk into a casino with $300 in your pocket and want to play poker. No matter how good you are, you need to know which stake game you can play. If you sit down at the $1 to $2 table you will be well capitalized and can play, win or lose for two days straight with the little old ladies. However, if you go to a $20 to $40 table you could be heading to that ATM machine after one hand. Sure, it's great getting a killer hand and raking in $600 on it, if a few people stay in, but this game is too rich for your bankroll and the odds will be against you. Instead you should stick to slower moving steady games like a $1 to $2, or $3 to $6 limit, but even at $3 to $6 you will need to be somewhat conservative, and you still stand a good chance of hitting three or four bad hands that could leave you with a short stack of money. This poker analogy is also true for the next two points I'm going to discus. All these points fall under risk management so even though they differ, they still have the same fundamental root. And that is trading (playing) with what you can afford.

Having Too Much Size

When I say too much size, I'm referring to position size as in when you should be trading 100 shares of a stock but instead you are trading 500 shares of it. By now, it should be obvious why it is not good to do it or how it can hurt you. But sometimes you can get caught up in this scenario without ever realizing it. I remember a friend of mine was trading wheat futures back in 1992 (Figure 14.5) and he was going long and it kept going up. He started with $2,000 in his account and put on a two-contract trade and then kept adding to it as his available margin and profit went up with the trade. It was a long time ago so I don't remember the exact numbers but roughly, he added two contracts when he was up $1,000 and then three more as he made another $2,000. Then he quickly made another $5,000 and added five more contracts, this went on for about two months and he was up over $50,000 on the trade with something like 30 contracts. The more contracts he had on the faster he made money and was starting to get moves of over $5,000 to $8,000 a day toward the end. I've added numbers to the chart indicating his position size. Well, the inevitable finally happened and the great rally died out fast with no warning. He lost about $30,000 the first day, was forced to liquate a large chunk of his position, then lost $12,000 the next, then another $6,000 three days later. So he had lost more than half of his of his two months worth of profits on the first day and all his profits were wiped out within a week.

He was dead-on with his prediction of the market for over two months and got out higher than where his original trade was made, yet lost money. One thing to his credit was that he did have a plan for this trade, however, it was a really bad plan and he deviated from it a little. He got caught up in

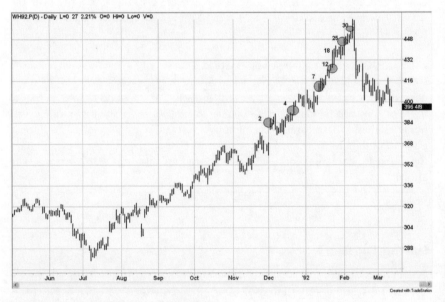

FIGURE 14.5 Wheat Futures 1992
Source: © TradeStation Technologies 1999. All rights reserved.

the excitement of the trade and though his increments were planned, they were poorly planned, plus he added more than expected, and put himself at even greater risk, considering the amount of capital he had.

His first mistake was thinking he was correct in putting on a two-lot trade with only $2,000 in his account. In my opinion, that was too risky to start with and he should have maybe had $5,000 to trade two contracts. His next mistake was adding too much too fast. Once he started seeing profits, he got a bit lackadaisical on risk parameters and got carried away with seeing dollar signs. He started adding on trades at a risky ratio. I know he had done his homework in analyzing his risk before he made the trade, and he felt that one contract every $1,000 was a fair amount to risk, but once the trade was on he changed that plan and bought whatever his margin allowed. Once he started losing, his first losses were huge due to the top heaviness of the trade. This trade was an emotional trip and took a toll on him. But at least I learned from it.

This was an example of how you can have too much size when pyramiding. But some people just have too big of a position other times as well. Not having a trading plan is the macro reason for it, which I'll go into later, but not having a proper game plan is the everyday reason for it. If you do not spend the time to prepare for a trade and know what the average move of the stock is or what you can expect to lose on a trade, then there is no way you can compare it to other trades. In one market you can risk 1,000 shares while in another 100 shares may put you in danger. This doesn't only vary from market to market but can be in the same market from trade to trade. There are times when you have to put your stops much further away to be safe and other times when the risk is so small because a proper stop area is quite close. In one case you may trade 1,000 shares safely, but in the other, 200 shares may cost you a lot more if you are wrong.

Poor Risk Parameters

Poor risk parameters can come either from lack of making or lack of making a *proper* trading plan. Or if you happen to have a decent trading plan, it can be from not having a game plan to execute it properly. I won't spend time discussing the lack of making a trading plan as by now you should know better and I've already talked about fooling yourself by not having the right risk parameters in the trading plan. What I'd like to touch on here is when you failed to use your game plan to keep yourself in line. Assuming you actually have a proper trading plan, you really need to keep to the limits of the risk parameters of that trading plan, regardless of what you are feeling at the moment. Among other things, there are two emotions that can make you forget your rules and trade recklessly and they are fear and greed.

Fear comes when you are losing or are getting close to losing. Many times a person is in a position that goes the wrong way and approaches his stop area (assuming he has one). Instead of doing the right thing and getting out, a bad trader will either ignore the stop and hope for a turnaround, or, even worse, add to the bad trade confident a turnaround is coming and thinking he will only need a small turnaround to get back to even. Sure this works sometimes, but it's not a profitable long- term trading strategy and the consequences can be painful. I know I've blown up a few times by letting things go from bad to ridiculous because first I ignored my risk parameters and then I tried to overcompensate for it by increasing my trading size—all in fear of taking a loss I should have been comfortable with (you shouldn't be making any trades unless you are comfortable with the amount you can lose).

Greed can be just as dangerous. This can happen in a way like it did to my wheat friend who got a bit too overconfident and just starting seeing dollar signs everywhere. Or it can happen like it did to me once when I was just starting out, and thought I found a perfect trading scenario and loaded up on it. Though in the long run I was right about the move, one bigger-than-normal wave made me totally lose control of what I was suppose to do. Greed turned to fear as I started losing more than I could afford, which turned into me trading even more contracts and risking too much, followed by losing too much. Greed and overconfidence come hand in hand. After winning a little, a trader thinking he is better than the market and his rules, decides he can ignore them and push a little more or make wilder trades, believing he is invincible. Who knows how long the streak will last, however, when it does end, the losses could be astronomical.

A good way to avoid these emotional demons is to take a little mental break from trading every few hours and ask yourself, "Am I sticking to my plan?" Most likely if you are not you will lie to yourself, but try and keep yourself in check as best you can.

CLOSING THOUGHTS

I want to wrap up by mentioning that having trading and game plans will help keep your overtrading in check because they give you solid rules and guidelines to follow. I'll discuss making and using rules later in the book, but basically your trading and game plan is just a compilation of rules. Most good traders have rules they follow; it's what make them good traders. I have my favorites taped on the sides of my computer, and I've done much better in the past when I followed them instead of ignoring them. Though money management rules will help you the most when it comes to overtrading, all rules will lend a hand. Rules like "only trade six positions at once" are obvious, but rules like do not chase a market until it retraces 20 percent will also help you cut back on total trades. By having rules that lead you to make high probability trades you automatically cut out some weaker trades and, hence, you'll be trading less.

The game plan is important, because if done properly it can solve all your overtrading problems. It may not help you find winning trades, but it will focus you and reduce both the amount you trade and the amount you risk.

CHAPTER 15

Money Management

The new bride approached her husband on their wedding night and asked for $10 for their first love-making encounter. He was so eager, he agreed, without hesitation. She did this each time they made love for the next 30 years. He gave her the money thinking it was a cute way for her to buy new clothes and get her nails done, and so on.

Arriving home one day, she found her husband in a very depressed state. He told her he had lost everything in the market and didn't know what to do, they were ruined. Happily, she handed him a bank book showing deposits and interest for 30 years totaling nearly a million dollars. She then showed him her stock account, which was worth well over another million and told him not to worry, they would be okay. She told him she had invested all that money she had collected over the last 30 years for every time they had sex, and this was the result of her investments.

Ending 1

But instead of a look of glee, he was overcome with disappointment. She asked him, "Why the sadness at such good news?" and he replied, "If I had known what you were doing, I would have given you all of my business!"

Ending 2

But he said, "I only gave you $10 at a time and even over 30 years it couldn't have been worth more than $30,000 to $50,000. How did you did you do so well?" She replied, "Do you think everyone is as cheap as you are?"

A proper trading plan is made up of two main things. One is the trading strategies that generate the buy and sell signals. And the other is money management. Though it may be more fun playing around making systems, you cannot forget to take into consideration how important the money management part of the plan is. The best systems in the world will not do you any good without a solid money management plan. While on the other hand, a moderate system with a solid money management plan can make you money—or at least keep you around a lot longer.

Money management plans, like systems, should be custom built because people have different risk tolerances. What one person may be comfortable with may give another ulcers. When you do put together a money management plan, make sure it is something that you both feel comfortable with and that will protect your capital. Just having one of these two factors in place can lead to either wide losses or a lack of trading because you are scared to risk anything. You want to be protective of your capital, but you need to take some risk if you want to make money.

DON'T TAKE RISK LIGHTLY

I don't believe money management and risk are given a fair shake in trading books. Every now and then you'll come across the subject with some extremely advance mathematical theories and formulas that would scare off even a statistics professor. But in general, you don't see nearly as many books on the topic and in most books it only gets a chapter or two. So don't expect this book to be any different I will, however, do my best to give you the material you need to put together a risk plan and then show you how to implement it into your trading plan. Even though you don't see as much written on the topic as it deserves you should not take it lightly as it really is the difference between winning and losing.

In my opinion money management is more important than your trading decisions, and it should be considered first when actually putting a plan together. Your money management will be able to tell you what markets you can trade, how much you can trade, how often you can trade, and how much you can risk. It is the cornerstone of setting stops and tells you if you can actually afford to make a trade or just trade in general. It will help you trade what you can afford and makes sure you are properly capitalized to trade. Though stops should be set based on technical analysis and what the market tells you a good place is, it's your money management that will tell you how much you can afford to lose and whether you have the capital to risk what the market can take from you. No matter how good the trade may look, if you risk more than you can afford to lose, you will, at some point, lose it all. Try to remember that keeping your money is actually more important than what you could make.

Don't take it lightly. Most top traders agree that even though they may have different trading strategies, it's their money management skills that make them good traders. It's typical to lose money on more then half of your trades. But with a solid money management plan you can easily make money on a 50:50 win to loss ratio trading system or even on a 30:70 system, which is a more typical ratio. If a trader spent the proper time to come up with a great money management system and traded off-the-cuff, he would, in my opinion, do better than a trader who came up with a great trading system and had no money management plan.

ANOTHER GAMBLING ANALOGY

One of the things I find interesting is that when it comes to gambling there is much more on the subject of money management than on actual gambling techniques. For example, the rules of craps or blackjack or roulette can be written on the back of an envelope. You could use the front of the envelope if you want, but for some reason everyone likes to use the back. It's the money management and risk strategies that take up a good chunk of many of the gambling books I read. Like knowing when to double down or split cards in blackjack, or how to take odds in craps. There is also a lot of crap written in some books. There are many so-called gambling systems that tell you to increase your bets when losing or to bet on red after it hasn't come up four times in row. These seem like strategies that will make you money as the odds grow in your favor. But in the long run, they are of no use as each outcome is independent of the previous ones. Yet I've seen books with such strategies. However, what is valid is knowing how to use your bankroll and what you can afford to risk and when to walk away both winning or losing, and I have seen this as the basis of several gambling books.

Even poker, which is much more a game of skill, has a lot to do with risk analysis. I'm not referring to the part that tells you how to manage your money, but to the part that tells when you should make a bet or not depending on the odds. If the odds are in your favor you make the bet, if they are not you don't make it.

THE MARTINGALE SYSTEM

The most famous (I think) of these gambling systems I mentioned above is the Martingale System, which tells you to keep doubling your bet after every loss, assuming that you will eventually get it right and win back all your money. The flaw comes in that casino tables have limits on the maximum you can bet, which is usually less then eight times doubling up. For example, doubling up on a $5 bet eight times is $640, but a $5 table has a maximum bet of $500. If you bet using the Martingale System where you double after every loss the progression would look like this:

First bet: You lose $5.

Second bet: You bet $10 and lose—down $15 total.

Third bet: You bet $20 and lose—now down $35.

Fourth bet: You bet $40 and lose—now down $75.

Fifth bet: You bet $80 and lose—now down $155.

Sixth bet: You bet $160 and lose—now down $315.

Seventh bet: You bet $320 and lose—now down $635.

Eighth bet: It would be $640 but the maximum you can bet is $500.

As you can see it would only take eight losses to exceed the table maximum bet. If you haven't noticed, it doesn't matter how many times you double up your bet. You will only win five dollars if you eventually hit. If you hit on the fourth bet when betting $40 you will win back the $35 you lost plus $5 more. Yet you've risked $75 so far to win $5; those are not good odds.

Let's say you could exceed the $500 maximum bet. On the eighth bet you are risking $640 to win $5. You have already invested $635 for your previous seven bets. If you lose that one you are out $1,275, but the casino doesn't even give you the chance. They cap your bet at $500 so even if you win you are down $135. Can you imagine risking over $1,000 for a chance to win $5? The casinos know that if someone had unlimited resources they will eventually win. That is why they set maximum bets at the table.

The other flaw in the system comes in that many times you run out money faster then you expect. Say you came to the casino with only $500 on you. You would not be able to make that seventh bet as you would only have $185 left after the first six losing bets so if you did bet all you had and won you'd be down $130 anyway.

And there is one other flaw, it does happen that there are times you get a few abnormal streaks every now and then where an outcome will happen 12 to 15 times in row. The casinos love these streaks. Though not often, they do happen and most people cannot afford to keep doubling up so many times. It is also human nature to fade the streak, so people take a beating during them. Casinos love this system as well because when you win, you win $5, but when you lose you lose over $1,000.

Some people who try the Martingale System have some success for a while and swear the system is foolproof. But sooner or later the odds will kick in and they find out the hard way about the flaws in the system. I know because years ago, I thought it was the greatest system in the world until black came up 11 times in row.

THE MONEY MANAGEMENT BASICS

Though there are several aspects to money management, and I'll run through them briefly below, just keep in mind that the overall goal is to keep as much of your money as possible. This can be done by keeping your risk and losses as minimal as can be, so that you will always have another trade to make. If you play poker you know the expression "a chip and a chair." It means as long as you have even a little bit of money you have a chance; if you are wiped clean however, you can't do a thing. Getting wiped out is not fun and if you are always maxed out there is always a chance it could happen to you.

Before I go into what is needed in a money management plan, I want to emphasize that the best risk management will not help much unless you are trading a system with positive expectancy. That is a proven trading strategy. If you have a strategy that is not going to make you money over the long run, then money management will keep you in the game longer, but you stand little chance of making money.

How Much to Risk

In General First of all, you need to determine how much you can afford to risk in general. This is money you have dedicated just to trading and is your total risk capital. You may have $400,000 available to you after selling your house. The question you need to ask yourself is how much do you want to trade with and ultimately risk—$10,000, $50,000, $100,000, or the whole $400,000? Whatever you decide on you must know that there is a chance that money will be lost if you are trading actively. If you are investing in stocks, your risk of losing it all is small compared to trading futures, but it is still there. If you cannot stomach losing X amount, lower your total risk capital. Some people are comfortable putting all their money into one stock and holding it for a while. While others may only want to trade with $10,000 for kicks.

At Any Given Time Once you've established your total risk capital, next you have to find a percent of your total capital that you are willing to risk at any given moment in time. This will be the at-risk capital. If you are trading with $100,000, you should not have it all at risk at once, and I'm not talking about just in one position but even spread out over all your positions. You are better off trading a lesser amount, so that you always have something to fall back on. I think a good amount is 50 percent of total risk capital, but this could vary based on the correlation of the positions or whatever you think is best for you. By keeping half your money safe, you'll always ensure that you'll be around for another trade, and another and another. The problem comes that when losing, people may not cut back on their positions as they are supposed to. Instead, they may even increase their risk in hopes of recouping the losses. So, if they lose half of their total money, they may risk the whole other 50 percent on the next trade trying to make it back. This is not a great management strategy and should be dealt with in your trading plan. The reason this is not a good strategy is that if you start with a $100,000 and lose half, you have lost 50 percent of your total, but if you take the remaining 50 percent and try to get it back to $100,000 on one trade, well then you need to make a 100 percent return to get back to even. Returns of 100 percent are not easily done on one trade. Plus you should never ever max out your capital at any given time; always leave something to fight your way back with. Try not to put yourself in a situation where you have lost half of your money in the first place, but if you do, the proper thing to do is to forget how much you lost and only risk half of your remaining capital.

If you choose 50 percent of your total risk capital as the amount you are comfortable risking, take the other 50 percent and earn some interest on it. Next you should take the 50 percent you are risking and break it down further. If you risk all of the 50 percent all at once, you may just lose it, so you don't want to do that. What you should do is break that up into increments that you will have at risk at once. This could be 20 percent or 33 percent or whatever you choose of the at-risk capital, and we'll call it the *at-risk-at-one-time capital*. If you are a new trader who doesn't have a clue what he is doing, you should maybe only risk 10 percent of your total risk capital at once. You are most likely going to lose it anyway, so this will force you to trade small as you learn. When you've lost that 10 percent, then risk another 10 percent, and so on. Hopefully each time it takes longer to lose it. Then as you get better, you can start increasing your total amount risked. By doing it this way you will not have a huge uphill battle.

On Any Given Trade   After you have established how much you can risk at any given time, next you have to figure out how much you are willing to risk per trade. Say you decided that $20,000 would be your maximum exposure at any given time (This is out of a $100,000 total risk capital.) An acceptable amount of your capital to risk per trade is 2 percent to 10 percent with 2 percent to 5 percent being the best ratio. The smaller your trading account, the bigger the ratio will be, but it's always best to make it as small as possible. For the sake of this example we'll assume you are willing to risk 5 percent of your risk capital on any given trade ($1,000). You may be thinking that's not a lot of money, and its not, but it's the proper amount you should risk with that size account. Most people get screwed because they risk much more than they should.

Risking $1,000 per trade also means if you really want to, you can put on 20 positions at once, but we saw in the last chapter that this isn't a great idea. This $1,000 doesn't mean you can only trade $1,000 worth of one stock at once. It means you are risking this amount, and this is where your homework and technical analysis come into play. So if you want to trade a stock that's trading at $50 a share, you have to first determine the risk of the trade and the amount you could lose per share. If you are confident you will not lose more than $3 per share you can then trade 300 shares. I know this comes out to $15,000 and some people will be confused thinking that's 75 percent of your total $20,000 leaving you little else to trade with, but depending on the account you have you may have a 4 to 1 day-trading margin and a 2 to 1 overnight margin. This means you only need to put up as little as $4,000 for the trade and you may think you can make five other trades like this. But the $20,000 only represents how much you are risking at any given time; you actually have $50,000 at risk in your account. So you have plenty of room to play with. As long as you can keep to your stop losses and control the risk to the $1,000 you established, it's okay to use your total at-risk capital to make a trade. For example, assuming you have no margin at all and you see a great opportunity in a $50 stock where you are risking 80 cents a share, it's okay to buy 1,000 shares and tie up all your capital. However, you must adhere to a stop, and you have to remember that something dramatic may happen that can cost you a lot more money, such as a drug company getting a major recall.

If you are trading commodities, the margins can really screw your plans up as they give you too much leverage. They allow you to control a huge position with little money. For example, the margin on an E-mini contract is $4,000 and only $2,000 to day-trade it. If the S&P moves 10 points in a day one contract will have a $500 move, which is a.12.5 percent move versus your outlay. To compare, look at a $50 stock like Merrill Lynch that will move about 2 points in a day the S&P moves 10 points. Assuming you are using 50 percent margin, you can trade up to $8,000 worth of the stock (to correlate with the amount you need to trade an E-mini) this means you can trade 160 shares. If you do get that $2 move, that's worth $320, this in turns equates to 8 percent of the $4,000 you needed to make the trade. So the bottom line is that you risk 50 percent more with futures when trading the same amount of money and using basically the same trading idea. And it is because of this added leverage/risk that you really need to be careful. Don't think because you have the margin available, you need to use it all. If you are overmargined and something bad happens it can destroy you. Always leave yourself a cushion for a worst-case scenario.

There was a lot to think about in last few pages, you may want to re-read them. If it didn't all make perfect sense, the main point of the section is about knowing how much money you will be risking per trade. It's important and it is the foundation of forming a solid risk plan, so make sure it is clear.

How Many Positions at Once

Another aspect of a money management plan is to decide how many positions you can trade at once. This is not as easy as just saying I'll trade a max of five positions. There are a lot of different scenarios you could take into account that will influence how much you will have on at any one time. You can, for instance, base it on a ratio of how much available money you have versus the risk levels you assumed. For example, if you already have four positions on but are only risking 25 percent of your at-risk-at-one-time capital, you may give yourself a clause that says you can trade up to seven positions as long as you are under 40 percent of your at-risk-at-one-time capital. But if you are already at 40 percent of your equity then you can only trade five positions. This way of doing it is a bit complicated and you will never have concrete rules. But it allows you to expand a bit if you are not risking as much as you would normally risk.

You can also have different limits depending on whether you are day-trading or holding trades overnight. For example, you may limit your day-trading positions to 4 at any one time, but you may allow yourself to take 10 overnight. It's easier to monitor overnight trades as you can do all your homework once the market is closed and then have all your plans, stops, and targets in place for the next day or whenever it is you get out of them. Now this brings you to another option, which is how many positions you can day-trade if you have positions you are taking overnight. If the overnight trades are long term you may want to give yourself more freedom during the day. However, if you plan to actively monitor and trade these the next day, then you may want to limit the number of new trades you put on and may not be able to trade anything new until you get out of at least some of the current positions.

And finally, I think, you will want to consider how you will handle trading in similar markets. Say you allow yourself to trade 20 stocks at once. The risk is a lot different if you are trading 20 semiconductor stocks, as opposed to four semis, three oil drillers, two banks stocks, a retailer, two drug companies, and so on. In the first scenario, you are exposing yourself way too much in one sector and it's almost like risking all your money in one stock. In the latter scenario you are spreading out your risk and are less likely to get hurt by a special event. So you should set limits as to how many positions or how much capital you are willing to risk in one sector.

Cutoff Levels

Here is a simple idea that can really save you a lot of money. You should have cutoff points, where you acknowledge you are not having a good day or stretch of days. Instead of continuing trading, you should throw in the towel, admit you are whipped, and more importantly limit a potentially disastrous situation while giving yourself time to regroup. You cannot lose all your money if you cut yourself off, so as you make a money management and trading plan give yourself limits where you will take a break from trading. Even if it is not a reasonable limit, at the very least you should have one that will prevent you from getting wiped out completely. When I first started out trading, I lost $12,000 in a day with a $25,000 account, which is not very smart. I've also blown $70,000 in a week's trading, with a $50,000 account, with the help of commodity margins. That one was really not smart. If I had had reasonable loss limits, like $2,000 a day or $10,000 in a week, and developed my game plan around those limits, I probably would have fared much better, though then I wouldn't have had enough material to write a book or two.

I know it's hard to cut yourself off when losing because first your ego doesn't want to admit you are wrong and second you always believe that you will turn it around on the next trade. And yes it does happen where the market turns around and makes a sharp move in the other direction and turns a huge losing day into a massive winning day, but these days tend to happen less than the days where your losing escalates beyond control. In the long run, you will be better off learning to walk away and recouping your senses.

The most straightforward method to come up with a cutoff level is to just use a fixed dollar amount. And once you hit it, you need to cut yourself off. It could be $2,000 a day or $10,000 a week or whatever you like. Here are some methods for coming up with those levels.

By Percent of Capital   The first one is a straight percentage of your capital. The more capital you have, the lower this percentage will probably be, but keep in mind that the less capital you have the more you will put yourself at risk. If a professional trader cuts himself off with a 2 percent loss that could mean $2 million to him. If you give yourself a 2 percent cutoff, it may mean $200 is the proper amount you should consider losing before walking away. However, this means you may not be able to trade close to anything you want to trade and it's also hard for people to keep to such a small loss. So small traders will end up having to raise up their limits to between 10 percent and 20 percent, which puts them more at risk in general compared with deep-pocketed traders. The one little hassle with this method is you have to calculate the level every day as it changes with your total capital.

By Dollar Value Based off a Percent Based off a Range   You may also set a dollar value that is based off of a percent, which is based on a range of your trading capital. Let me clear that up a bit. You can say,"I will make my cutoff point 5 percent of my capital and set it as a fixed dollar amount for every $5,000 in equity." To clear that up further, if you have between $25,000 and $30,000, you will risk $600 in a day. I set the range at the higher end of the spread because I assumed I started trading with $30,000 and use 5 percent of that ($600) until I drop below $25,000. Once you drop below $25,000 you then drop your maximum loss to $500. This is a little easier than calculating it every day and still has the same basic effect.

By a Ratio of a Good Day   You can also set your limit by first setting what you believe to be the average of what your best good days could be. Exclude any exceptional days as they will skew your results. Just take an average of your better-than-normal good days—maybe an average of your best 10 percent of days. Then come up with a ratio that gives you a number you are willing to lose based on that. I think a 3:1 win:loss ratio is acceptable. So if after substantial back testing or a year's worth of results you believe that a reasonable average of your best days is $6,000, then set your maximum loss level to $2,000. Make sure you recalculate this amount as your equity changes.

Don't Give Away Your Profits

Another cutoff you may want to have is one where instead of just protecting yourself from a bad day, you protect your profits. If you start off with some good trades or had trades overnight that really opened in your favor and you are up a good amount, you do not want to give it back. It's your money, it doesn't matter if it's paper money and you haven't realized it or if you had it to start with. Hold on to it, and preserve your precious capital (a term I used a lot in *High Probability Trading*). In the long run, every dollar counts when you figure out how much money you made or lost at the end of the year. Don't get too cocky and think it's okay to give up a bit or take chances and make marginal trades just because you are doing okay. Each trading decision you make should be made regardless of your previous trades and not on how well or poorly you have done.

To get back to the topic, if your maximum cutoff point for a day is $2,000, then you may want to have that as the most you are willing to give back during a good day. You could set this cutoff point anyway you want, just have one in your money management plan, because the worst feeling in trading are the days you were up $4,000 at lunch and walked away up $34 at the end of the day. I find those days more demoralizing than the days where I actual lose $5,000 in a steady manner. The emotional high to low swing of these days can take a toll on you.

A Longer Break

So far I've only mentioned having intraday cutoffs, but you also should have a point where you acknowledge something just hasn't been working recently and you take time to reevaluate. For example, if at any given point you are down more than 20 percent in your account, you will make a provision to get out of all your positions and take a trading break until you examine what went wrong. You can also do this by saying if you have 7 consecutive losing days or 10 consecutive losing trades you will cut yourself off as well. The goal of this is to evaluate whether you have a fundamental flaw in your trading plan that needs to be fixed before you lose even more.

It serves another purpose as well and that is that it gives you time to regroup. After a losing streak people do foolish things because their minds are cluttered with negative thoughts. By taking a break, you can start from scratch and hopefully avoid the mistakes people make when they are trying to catch up.

Position Size

Position size is another factor you will have in your money management plan, which will tell you just how many contracts/shares of any given market you can trade at once.

Position size can be derived in several ways. The simple way at the beginning is to always trade the same 100 shares of a stock and one contract of a commodity. This is a good way to start, but ultimately position size should be based more on the risk of the trade and not a fixed amount. A better way is to figure out how much at worst you are willing to lose per trade and divide that by the risk of the trade. If you established that you will risk up to $2,000 on any given trade, and you have a trade where the risk will be $400 per contract, then you can trade five contracts. This is pretty straightforward and not the most advanced method of position sizing.

One thing you can have in your trading plan is a list with a range of position size ranges that you are willing to trade per market or stock, something like what is shown in Table 15.1. One way you can determine these

TABLE 15.1 Sample Position Size Range Chart	
Crude oil	2–5 shares
E-minis	3–10 shares
Dow Mini	4–10 shares
Corn	5–20 shares
SLB	300–2,000 shares
Mer	200–500 shares
Goog	10–20 shares
Yhoo	400–1,000 shares

ranges is by margin requirements, or maybe by the average true range of the market.

After you have established your position size risk range, as you are preparing your trades every day and have to determine the risk involved with the trade, you could decide how many contracts in that zone you will trade. I don't recommend maxing it out; give yourself a cushion, because hey, if you are wrong, you'll lose that whole amount. You may also want to leave room to later add to the trade if you deem it worthy.

Stops

Stops are a crucial part of successful trading as they are the best way to protect yourself from disaster. The problem many people have with stops is that they use them incorrectly. The bad way to use stops is to say, "I can afford to lose $1,000 dollars total on these two contracts, and so I'll place my stop at $500 away because it will cut my loss off at $1,000." When randomly placed, a stop could be in the normal trading range of the trade and you can easily get stopped out on a normal move. So even though you had a good trade going on, it gets needlessly stopped out.

What people who do this usually do wrong is set their position size first and then set their stops based on how much they are willing to lose, with no regard to what the market is telling them. In reality it should be the other way around. You should determine, based on the market, where a stop should be and then figure out how much it would cost you if you got stopped out. Then you figure out how many shares you can comfortably trade.

Stops will become an important part of your trading decisions as you make and adjust your daily game plan. Stops will let you know in advance how much you will most likely lose. It helps when a loss doesn't come as a surprise; you are mentally able to deal with it better if you knew the worst beforehand. By being prepared for a loss, you will reduce the urge to stay in bad trades that you should have gotten out of. Looking to see where a stop should be properly placed, will tell you if you should get into a trade, how many contracts you can safely trade, and where to get out. They will limit your losses and protect your profits as well.

The Reward-to-Risk Ratio

One thing you should do is establish a reward-to-risk ratio below which you will not enter a trade. I talked about this in detail in Chapter 10 so I just want to refresh it in your mind now, as it is a crucial step in establishing your risk parameters. If you are making a proper money management plan you need to work on establishing a level that you find acceptable to make a trade at. At the very least you need to know what the risk is and what the potential gain is and make sure the reward is greater than the risk You should also take into account the chance of the trade working. Though I look for a 3:1 ratio as a minimum, I will make a trade at a 2:1 ratio if the setup is a particularly strong.

Changing Trading Size

Knowing when to increase and decrease your trading size will be another factor that should be considered in your money management plan. You should have predetermined rules to know when you will ramp up or scale down your trading, based on your account size or performance. Having this predetermined can save you from the potential disaster of increasing your size too much like my friend did in wheat or being too aggressive on a losing streak.

You want to know when it's okay and proper to increase or decrease the amount you will trade/risk based on your account size. I prefer using the percentage based on a range of my trading capital method I discussed earlier in the chapter. Once you set that range, win or lose stick to it. Do not let winning and losing streaks, ego, fear, or stupidity cause you to change it.

Some people increase their position size as they are doing better on a trade, others increase it as they are losing hoping to make money back. Same with scaling back, some like to cut down their trades when winning and others do the opposite. The proper thing to do is add to winners and cut back on losers. It's easy to get caught up the wrong way if you let emotions control you, so it's best if you have provisions for it in your trading plan.

There is another time you need to change trading size that has nothing to do with your account size and that is when the volatility changes. If 10 contracts were proper in a small range market and then it explodes, only

2 or 3 contracts may be proper to trade. This is about changing risks and should be addressed in a proper money management plan.

INCORPORATING YOUR MONEY MANAGEMENT PLAN INTO YOUR TRADING PLAN

Now that you have a good idea of how you should be making a money management program for yourself, your next step would be to make one, and after that comes the even harder part and that is to make sure you follow it. The only way to accomplish that is to implement your risk strategy into your trading plan and game plan. I'll go through how you should do so below with a hypothetical example of implementing money management rules into a trading and game plan.

As you set up your rules in your initial trading plan it may look like this (keep in mind that you will be adjusting the numbers on a periodic basis as time goes by):

1. How much money do I have to risk?

    I have $200,000 I can afford to lose, (well I don't really want to lose it) but I do have $200,000 dedicated to trading.

2. How much I will risk at any time?

    I will never put to work more then $100,000 at any given. And of this I will not risk more than $20,000 at any given time, though I can use my excess capital to cover the cost of holding positions.

3. How much will I risk on any given trade?

    I will risk up to $5,000 on a trade in a trade in either the E–mini or Dow mini. I'll risk up to $2,000 in any other market or stock and no more than $7,500 in total in related markets.

4. How many contracts/shares will I trade per market?

    I will use this (abbreviated) list to determine my range of contracts per market:

Crude oil:	2–5 contracts
E–minis:	3–10 contracts
Dow Mini:	4–10 contracts
Corn:	5–20 contracts
SLB:	300–2,000 shares
Mer:	200–500 shares
Goog:	10–20 shares
Yhoo:	400–1,000 shares

I can trade up to the number of contracts/shares that will allow me to stay within the risk levels I established per trade per market. I will use the reward-to-risk ratio weighed with the odds of a trade working to decide how close to the max of that limit I should get.

5. How many positions will I trade at once?

I'll trade up to three commodity positions and five stocks at once. I'm also okay holding this amount overnight.

6. What's my minimum max-win to max-loss ratio?

In general, I will not take a trade where the reward-to-risk ratio is below 3:1, however, under an exceptional opportunity I will accept a 2:1 ratio.

7. What is my daily cutoff point?

If I'm down $6,000 in any position I will exit it regardless of anything else. If I'm down $9,000 in total I will liquidate all my losers and not put on any new trades unless my losses get cut to under $5,000. If I'm down $12,000 in total I'll liquidate all positions and call it a day.

8. What is my high to low cutoff level?

As soon as a trade has reached 50 percent of its target level, I will look to reposition my stops so that at worst I will break even on the trade. Once a trade has reached its target level I will position my stops so that I will not give back more than 33 percent on that profit.

This is not set in stone. If the proper place to set a stop is not within that margin, I will place it at the proper place, but in general I do not want to give back more than one third of any trade that has reached its target.

9. How will I increase size?

I will only increase a position by a third or half of its initial size, only if I'm making money on it, and I would get into it as a fresh signal and my total risk on the position hasn't changed due to moving of stops tighter.

10. When will I adjust risk parameters?

If my equity changes by 25 percent I will reevaluate risk parameters.

INCORPORATING YOUR MONEY MANAGEMENT PLAN INTO YOUR GAME PLAN

Now that you have applied your money management plan into the making of your trading plan, the important part is implementing it into an everyday game plan. I'll assume you are starting the day from scratch and have no positions on. As you go through your preopening trading opportunities and find the list of things you want to trade you should be considering risk as well. In your game plan you should address and answer the following questions:

1. How many potential trades are there that I like?

   Look through the charts or however it is you pick your trades and determine how many you may want to be involved in. If you picked eight and your limit is five, then determine your favorite five first, but keep the others as backups in case you never trade some of the others.

2. What's the maximum loss per one contract of each trade I like?

   Go through the charts and determine the proper spot to place a stop and then figure out how much money it will cost per one contract or minimum number of shares you'd trade.

   Trade 1 has a $400 risk, trade 2 has $250 risk, trade 3 has a $1,200 risk, and so forth.

3. What is the reward-to-risk ratio of each trade?

   Go through all the possible trades and determine how much you could make on them. Then determine the reward-to-risk ratio of each trade and make sure the ratio is greater than the reward-to-risk ratio you have established in your trading plan. If it is not I'd ignore the trade. Take into account the probability of the trade working as well when you determine which trades you will take.

   Trade 1 has an 80 percent ratio, trade 2 has a 60 percent ratio, and so on.

4. How many contracts of each will I trade?

   Now that you know the risk of each trade you will have to determine how many contracts of each you may want to trade. You may want to include provisions for scaling into the trade here. I will trade up to 10 contracts of trade 1. I will put on seven initially and if it meets a second criteria later I'll add the other three.

5. What is my cutoff point for day?

   Determine how much you are willing to lose for the day based on your trading plan criteria. It's good to have these numbers in front of you so you will actually adhere to them.

   My maximum loss on any position is $6,000.

   My daily maximim loss on all positions is $12,000.

6. When will I change position size?

   You may want to have a provision that will let you increase size if you are up a certain amount on the trade. Or decrease size if you want to lock in profits.

If I'm making $1,000 on this trade and it is above the 20-period moving average I'll add to the trade by 20 percent, only if I can increase my stop.

If I'm making $1,000 on trade 2, I'll get out 50 percent to lock in some profits.

7. When should I adjust risk?

If I'm down $1,000 and the trade doesn't seem like it will work, I'll cut my position in half. If the market volatility has increased to a certain level, I will lower my total number of contracts to keep my risk as it was before.

These are all suggestions of things you can do to help you manage risk. It is a great method of giving you something to rationalize before every trade and to make sure it lies within your risk parameters.

ESTABLISHING MONEY MANAGEMENT PROCEDURES FOR OPEN POSITIONS

Next you need to make provisions that will consider what happens if you are taking trades overnight. You will need to make a list of questions that will help you decide if you should take them. If you come in in the morning and you have positions on, you need to establish a game plan for both getting out of those open positions and getting into new ones.

The next thing that arises is how you review your open positions. You need to monitor trades on a regular basis and recalculate anything that can affect your positions. Market conditions change throughout the day and as such so will the risks involved. As risk changes you may need to cut back on some positions if you plan to stay within your risk parameters. I look at my risk and stop levels at least five times a day to determine my risk. One, before the open; two, after I get into any position; three, around midday; four, toward the end of the day; and last after the close. Plus, I will look at them if I sense something has changed.

CLOSING THOUGHTS

Money management will get you far in trading, as well as life. Whether it's in your long-term perspective or in your everyday planning, do not attempt to trade unless you have a solid money management plan. One of the benefits of taking time to subject each trade to being put through money management and risk parameters is that it will force to you make trades with a higher probability of doing well. You will learn to weed out the weaker ones if they don't meet your standards. You will tremendously cut back on your overtrading as well as the potential to totally wipe out.

I'll be honest and say that proper money management can get really difficult with some extravagant formulas that only a mathematician can comprehend and that is beyond the scope of this book. If you can get to that level, you will be way ahead of the game. Position sizing and proper risk to take versus capital are not straightforward equations. But even if you can't compete with PhDs hired by the top trading firms to come up with risk formulas, just having something competent will be invaluable to you when you trade.

CHAPTER 16

Trading Rules

When Albert Einstein died, he met three people at the Pearly Gates. To pass time, he asked what their IQs were. The first replied 190. "Wonderful!" Einstein exclaimed. "We can discuss Ernest Rutherford's contribution to atomic physics and my theory of general relativity." The second answered 150. "Good," he said. "I look forward to discussing the role of New Zealand's nuclear-free legislation in the quest for world peace." The third mumbled 50. Einstein paused, then asked, "So what is your forecast for the Dow?"

E veryone has trading rules, either formal or informal. They could be as simple as don't lose more than $1,000 per trade or as elaborate as don't buy unless it's after 10:30 A.M., the market is higher than the previous day's high, volume is above 500,000 shares and the 3-period moving average is above the 14-period moving average, and it's not Monday.

Regardless of what your rules are they are the foundations to a trading strategy and a trading plan. They will help keep you disciplined and they will be the backbone of your game plan.

TRADING RULES

A trading system is simply a bunch of rules pieced together. In order to be a valid system it needs to include a minimum of three things, well actually four, the first three are:

1. A rule to get in.
2. A rule to exit with a loser.
3. A rule to exit with a winner.

Once you have those three things in place you basically have a system, it's that easy. The fourth rule is a money management rule that tells you how much to trade, but you can separate that from your basic system if you like. Coming up with those rules, however, and making sure they work, well, that's the hard part.

Developing a set of trading rules takes time. As you learn more and more about trading and what kind of trader you are, you will come up with rules without even thinking about it. But even after reading one good book you may start to have developed a few rules that will make up the core of your trading decisions. The key is having them, making sure they are sound, and then making sure you follow them. I keep my favorites written out in front of me as they help me with my discipline. Though I have specific rules for entering and exiting trades, the rules I keep in front of me are more generic and do lean toward keeping me in line.

Trading rules will be the core of your trading plan, as trading plans and trading systems are basically just a set of rules to get you in and out of a trade, with consideration to risk as well. Following the rules is where the game plan comes into play. There is no point in having a trading plan if you can't follow it, so you need the game plan to act as an enforcer of your rules.

This chapter, though nestled in the latter part of the book, could be the most important in helping you to create your trading and game plan. Without trading rules you would never be able to piece together a strategy. You could, of course, use a black box system and put it on cruise control and do nothing. You wouldn't even have to place orders because software these days can generate and place your orders for you, but then you wouldn't be a trader, nor would you be reading this book.

I could never begin to touch on every rule people have, so you need to figure out yours on your own. You will do this by trial and error, by reading books and magazines, by listening to experienced traders, or by dissecting other systems. There are rules for size, buying, selling, stops, limits, pyramiding, scaling, cutting back, overtrading, timing, indicator usage, trading off news, and almost anything else you can think of. The most popular rules are probably the age-old "buy low and sell high" followed by "cut your losses and let your winners ride."

USING YOUR RULES TO MAKE A TRADING PLAN

In *High Probability Trading* I showed the list of trading and money management rules that I keep in front of me all the time. For the most part they are still the same with a few little changes. Below is my current list of rules as well as a few others and I'll show how they apply to my general trading, how they correlate to my trading and game plans, and how they help make me be a better trader by focusing on discipline. I will not get into the nitty-gritty of my actual trading and money management strategies, but you cannot make those without solid trading rules.

Before I had a formal trading plan, I had strategies based on trading rules that I thought would help me be a better trader. I later turned these into a trading plan and used those rules in my game plan to enter and monitor my trades. I'll separate them by category to make it easier to follow, though on my desktop they are in random order. As you read them you'll also see they were the basis of this book. I'll show how you can apply your rules in making a trading and game plan. This is not going to be a full formal trading plan that would include trading signals but just the beginnings of what goes in it. I have more in my trading and game plans that I don't have quick rules for, and some rules don't even make it to the plans. They are there to keep me on my toes but overall you'll get a good idea of what to do. I will write this in a kind of think-out-load manner with extra notations to make it a little clearer as to why I'm writing what I am, but which I wouldn't normally write down.

MY TRADING RULES

Money Management

PPC (preserve precious capital).

Don't need to be maxed out.

Don't trade more than six positions at once.

Don't risk more than 5 percent on any trade.

Don't double up a loser.

Entering Trades

Have a reason for every trade.

Trade in the direction of the major trend.

Look for better entry levels, look at a chart first.

Avoid rushing in if stochastics are near extremes.

Wait for pullbacks.

Buy dips and sell rallies.

Look at higher time frames.

Scale in and out.

Think exit first.

Don't trade the news.

Don't get cute.

Exiting

Exit losers 30 minutes after the open.

Dump losers first.

Take smaller losses and take them quicker.

It's okay to take a loss.

Exit bad trades within 45 minutes.

Avoid big losses.

Have predetermined stops.

Know where my stops are.

Don't overstay my welcome.

If it ain't working get out.

If the trade is done GET OUT.

Don't need to hold out for top dollar.

Discipline

Think like a pro.

When losing bad, take a small break.

Trade less and be more selective per trade.

Stay away from markets that hurt me—like gold.

Don't be a gambler.

Follow my plan.

Don't make stupid trades.

Don't chase the market.

Go over my trades.

Don't let a bad trade get to me.

Don't surf the Internet while the market is open.

Think outside myself.

APPLING THE MONEY MANAGEMENT RULES

The overall goal of my trading and game plan is to preserve my precious capital, everything I do in trading will revolve around that. I will do that by first establishing rules as to how much I am willing to lose or trade at any given point. I will never risk more than 5 percent of my capital on any given trade, but I prefer to keep it down to 2 percent. And I will never have at risk more then 50 percent of my capital at risk nor 20 percent at once. I will also not max out my capital by overmargining myself even if I haven't reached my risk limit. In order to do this, I will stay at least 20 percent below total margin requirements.

I will not trade more then six positions at any time. This will help me be more selective and trade less, which in turn will keep me from overtrading and help me stay focused. There is one exception to the rule: I will consider three related markets or stocks as one position but will reduce the amount of shares I would normally trade in that market or stock.

As a strict practice I will not add to a losing position unless it was predetermined in my game plan that I would be buying on the way down as I build a position. But if I have a trade that is not working, I will not add to it simply to get a better price. I can, however, get a new signal in an existing position that upon proper investigation, I may deem to be a reasonable new trade, in which case I would consider adding to a losing position. This can happen when you use several trading systems or are using systems in different time frames that give you different trading signals.

As I was writing this last section, I realized it's going to be hard to separate my rules into trading plan and game plan, because they are involved in both. My list of rules is what I would consider the essential start in creating a trading plan, however, I could not make a game plan or follow a trading plan if I did not use them all again in the game plan, which I don't feel like rewriting, because it's 4:30 in the morning and I'm tired. But basically everyday as you make a game plan you will do so in a manner that will apply all these rules to your trading. For example, you will make sure you don't risk more then 20 percent of your capital or trade more than six trades at once. The longer you trade the less you will need to write stuff like this down, as over time it gets imbedded in your head, but these rules will be the core of your monitoring system and if you can't follow them, then you have to write them down.

APPLYING THE ENTRY RULES

I don't have actual trading signal rules in my list of quick rules; but I do follow a couple of particular sets of signals and patterns to make my trading decisions. I'm not going to show any actual signals here, just assume they are part of my trading plan.

What I do want to show is how I take my trading rules and think out a strategy that will then be part of my trading plan and act as a way for me to monitor my plan. I definitely would not write all this out anywhere. It's a think-out-loud plan-making process. But these thoughts are overshadowing every move I make.

As I'm preparing to make a trade, I will make sure I have a reason for it. The overall reason will be that it fits one of my trading criteria and that I have examined the trade carefully. I will also know where I will exit it, whether I'm winning or losing on the trade. I will look at the charts, and not just in one time frame, but I'll look at 5 minutes, 30 minutes, 60 minutes, daily, and weekly charts to make sure it is a viable trade and not just in the middle of nowhere. Plus, I'll use the different time frames to determine stops and targets. This helps me determine the trade's reward-to-risk ratio, and if the trade does not have a reasonable reward-to-risk ratio, I will not make it. Once I fine something that I like, I will use the multiple time frames to look for better entry levels, and hold off on making the trade if my indicators make me believe I could get a better price by waiting. When a market breaks out of a level, I will resist the urge to jump into a trade as soon as it breaks. Again, I will look at it in a smaller time frame to try and get a better price by buying on a dip or selling on a rally. This strategy will also apply to trading the news. I will use the news to be alerted to something, but I will revert to my charts to actually make the trade.

As far as what I'm looking for in the market to help me evaluate making trades, it is a combination of indicators and patterns, including but not limited to stochastics, RSI, volume, MACD, and Fibonacci retracements. I will, for the most part, only trade in the direction of the major trend, looking for dips and rallies to benefit from. However, I do look at reversal patterns and systems and if I get a sound signal near a support or resistant level, I will trade looking to catch a reversal in the market.

ANOTHER RANDOM RANT

I did have one goofball criticize my first book, when I mentioned something similar. He wrote a review saying one minute I state only trade with trend and then in the next chapter I write about trading reversal strategies. Well the truth be told, you can make money either way, and I do. Some of my best trades were timing a turn in the market and riding it out for a while. Yes, trading with the trend is always your best bet and if you try to go against a strong trend for no good reason you will get eaten up. But there are times when those trends end and the market has a few clear signs that it may turn. If you are a disciplined trader and know when to get out if you are wrong, reversal systems can be very rewarding. So if for any reason that same person is reading this book as well, which I doubt given his first review, I wrote what I wrote, because it's okay to be flexible and look at things from different angles as long as you have a reason for it.

Reviews are funny, I've gotten a couple of hundred reviews either on Amazon, directly, or a few other sites, and 95 percent were great, touting it as a great, insightful trading book. Many even said out of 50 books this was the best trading book ever, it has helped their trading tremendously, and so on. Then there are people who say, don't waste your money, this book is crap and has nothing original in it. Or even better, " This book is pure crap, I only read the first couple of chapters and found nothing worthwhile in it."

So I guess you can't please everyone. I even have friends who say the Beatles and Mozart are overrated.

APPLYING YOUR EXIT RULES

Now comes the exit part of my thinking process. I as look over my rules I realized my biggest concern has been with cutting losses. Most of my rules seem to revolve around that and only a couple focus on getting out with winners. Maybe it's because when I made those rules most of my trades were losers. I have to start by reiterating a point from the entry part of my rules and that is I make sure I know where I'm getting out before I get in. Trying to come up with exit points after the fact is hard if you're blinded by a good trade or scared by a loser. So it is best to know in advance where you are getting out and write it down, so it's as clear as day. Besides, if you don't have a predetermined stop, how can you evaluate the risk and rewards of the trade?

After having a predetermined stop that acts as a safety net, and knowing where it is, I need to focus on getting out of a trade before it hits that stop. The first thing I want to do is not waste my time on a trade that is not working properly. I won't stick around for my stop if the trade is not doing what it was supposed to or if I'm day-trading and it's still negative after 45 minutes. If I'm in a situation where I need to unload trades because of margin calls or everything just seems to be going wrong, I will always exit my losers first. It's human nature sometimes to take your winners and lock in a profit and hope the losers turn around, but it's not the correct way to do it.

One thing I need to remember is that a stop is only a worst-case scenario exit and that it is okay to a take a loss if a trade is not working, and a small loss is better than a big loss anytime. Losses are part of trading so get used to them, don't hesitate if you are wrong, and don't worry about the commission; in the long run the $11 on one trade is not that important. What is important is that I don't turn a $120 loser into a $3,400 loser, trying to get back my commission.

Now if I'm making money on a trade, I need to concentrate on a few things as well. First, if the trade is done, get out. Do not get greedy or try to make more than the trade is willing to give. Overstaying my welcome is something I want to avoid, unless I get a one-time-only invite to the Playboy mansion. When you stay in a position after you should have been out, it becomes easy to give back part or all of your profits and even turn it into a loser. The other important thing to remember is that I should not expect to get out at the peak of the move or trade. I won't know where the peak is until the much later and the market has sold off. If the market hits my level and retreats, I should not insist on getting the previous best level it made. It may not get there again, and I may watch the trade go negative waiting for that best price again. So once again, if the trade is done, get out.

Like the entry, I should try and time my exit to get the best price I can. But if I miss my exit by trying to time a better exit, I need to reevaluate and come up with a new plan to exit the trade as soon as possible.

APPLYING THE DISCIPLINE RULES

Now comes the most important section of my rules, and that is those which deal with discipline. Discipline can be broken into two parts. One is to have the discipline needed to do the right thing as a trader, and the other is the discipline to follow the rules, systems, and plans you made.

First of all, I want to always think like a pro, I need to constantly ask myself am I doing the right thing or just making a stupid trading decision. As I've mentioned before, I need to have a good reason for every trade and that is the start of trading like a professional. If a trade or my trading decisions are not part of my plans, then I'm acting amateurish and I shouldn't expect to do well. Making stupid, low probability trades is the same as gambling and should be avoided. The best way to do this is to constantly think like a pro. For example, chasing the market when a trend line is broken and getting filled at a high level during the next three hours because it sold off, is a novice's mistake. I also need to have the discipline to make fewer and more selective trades, just like a pro would.

Discipline is also key when it comes to taking losers. Losers should be small before they get out of hand and once they are taken, they should be considered history. I shouldn't keep looking at the market trying to get back in again to remake my loss. Once the trade is over, I need the discipline to walk away from it. In the same way, I need to walk away from the market when everything is going wrong. It's okay to lose a little, but sometimes it gets so nerve rattling it's time to take a short break to regroup.

One rule that affects my trading plan is to not trade markets that normally hurt me. I have never made money trading gold and silver, and there are a couple of stocks that seem to have the better of me. So I don't trade them anymore, no matter how tempting they may look, I need the discipline to avoid them. I don't have this in my trading plan, but when I'm making my game plan I do limit it to the few things I do trade and I rarely even consider trading anything else.

Finally, until the next chapter, I need to have the discipline to follow my game plan and rules every day, every trade. Because if I cannot keep to them, they will be not be worth a lick.

THE TOP 25 RULES

After writing everything above, I decided to go through my giant stack of trading magazines I've accumulated over the last 21 years, as well as do a search on the Internet looking for "trading rules." For the most part, I found that the rules tended to be same regardless of where I looked and I looked at a lot of sites. Some places had the six most important rules, others had the top 50 rules of trading and others everything in between, but what I found was that most tend to agree with my rules. I'll condense what I found as best as possible giving you the top 25 rules (with a little commentary) I found and hope you can use some of them to your advantage. Though simple, these rules will make you money if followed, with little extravagance needed. What I found interesting was that many appear throughout this book already. So I hope I do not get repetitive. By the way, these are not necessarily my rules but a compilation of what I found. I personally don't agree with every single thing below and some things may not be how I would say them, but I'm open to hearing other points of view.

Rule 1: Trade with the Trend

Out of all the rules everywhere I looked, the most popular and what I think is the most important money-making rule is to trade with the major trend. Though the most obvious of rules, it is too easy to try and sell rallies in bull markets, thinking the market has moved too far, too fast. I have lost lots of money doing this. Hell, I thought crude was overpriced at $40 a barrel a couple of years ago and starting shorting it. Well, it's close to $100 a barrel now. Same with Google, many people thought the trade was overpriced at $400 ($702 today). By getting caught on the wrong side of these major moves you not only lose money, but you do not make the money you could have if you followed the rule. In a bull market, try to be long or on the sidelines. Remember, not having a position is a position.

Rule 2: Buy Strength and Sell Weakness

Similar to trading with the trend, you need to trade where the money is and not against it. Many people want to buy when prices have fallen hoping for a new rally. But professionals buy because prices have rallied. They don't follow the adage "buy low, sell high," but prefer to "buy high and sell even higher." Don't try and change the trend by yourself; instead, go with what's strong. It's strong for a reason. Don't buy simply because a stock is low or sell because it's high.

You can think of it this way. If you were a pro baseball player you'd prefer to get traded to a strong team on its way to playoffs instead of a last place team in hopes that they turn it around. The same holds true when looking at different stocks within a sector: You should buy the strongest or sell the weakest.

Rule 3: Have a Plan for Your Trade

This one I obviously like. When putting on a trade, think of it as if it has the potential to be the biggest trade of the year. Don't enter a trade until it has been well planned out, you have a strategy for adding to the trade, and plans set for exiting the trade. Before you enter a trade you need to have done your homework and decided where you will be looking to get in and out of the market, regardless of if you are losing or winning on the trade. Do not formulate a new opinion during market hours. Once you have decided to follow a certain strategy, stick to it. If the strategy is sound then over time, you will make money.

Rule 4: Predetermine Maximum Losses in Every Potential Trade

As part of planning your trade, you should determine the worst possible thing that could happen on that trade. By doing this you will not be surprised when it happens and you can still concentrate on trading normally, as opposed to freaking out and panicking should it get to that point. If you do get to that point and you are freaking out then you know your potential maximum loss is too big and should be lowered for the future. Knowing your potential max loss, will help you establish how many contracts to trade, as well as be able to determine if the risk is worth the trade.

Rule 5: Don't Chase the Market

Patience is a virtue traders must have. When you get the urge to jump into a trade that is moving or that you've missed, you should give it some thought before rushing in. You should wait for a correction to occur or a solid entry level before putting that trade on. The market rarely just takes off without a breather or retesting of a level. I've seen it happen too often when rushing into a trade, that 15 minutes later it goes against you and you have to sit on it for quite a while as it gets back to the level you entered. Be patient and don't worry if you miss a trade, there will be more.

Rule 6: Give a Trade Time to Work

Patience also is involved once you are in a trade. After you have entered, give the trade time to develop and create the profits you expected it to when you planned it. Taking profits too soon is extremely costly in the long run. The real money in trading will come from the couple of really big moves you capture, not all the nickels and dimes you make along away. I'm sure you've heard the adage "let your profits ride," well, this is where it is key. If you are too fidgety and exit too early, you will lose a lot of potential money.

Rule 7: Keep Losses Small

On the opposite side of let your winners ride, you have cut your losses, and when you combine them you get one of the oldest expressions in trading. You need to be able to take small losses instead of big ones. Small, quick losses when you know you are beat are better than giant losses that beat you. A small monetary loss is not as important as the mental capital that is used up when you sit with a losing trade. Losses are a cost of doing business and you should accept them easily, or you will never be a successful trader. Don't try to justify a bad trade by convincing yourself that it will sooner or later turn into a good trade. Successful traders are able to ride through downturn periods as they know they will hit a string of losses at some point. The goal of trading, however is make a net profit after a sequence of trades, so don't worry about an individual loss, just try to do the right thing every time.

Rule 8: Do Not Add to Losses

Most top traders swear by this one. Never, ever, under any condition, add to a losing trade, or average into a losing position. If you are buying, then each new buy price must be higher than the previous buy price. If you are selling, then each new selling price must be lower. (I mentioned earlier an instance where you can break this rule. Large traders putting on a big position will try to do so little by little and welcome a drop in prices so they can slowly build a position without notice, but to them this is part of their big trade, they are not adding to a losing trade.)

When you do add to a winning trade correctly, you should do so in smaller increments than your original trade, as this will prevent you from losing the whole thing fast in a downturn. Between 25 percent and 50 percent is considered acceptable.

Rule 9: When the Reason for the Trade Is No Longer There, Get Out

When you plan a trade, you should get in for a reason; if that reason changes, your trade is no longer valid, so you should get out. You may get back in if you have a new reason to do so. But if not, winning or losing, it's time to exit the trade or at least reevaluate it.

Rule 10: Use Volume to Help You Trade

Volume is an often overlooked indicator, but it can tell you a lot about what is happening with price movement. Strong volume can confirm a continuation in price or a reversal, whereas weak volume can tell you a move may be ending or a reversal signal is probably not a great one. You should take time to learn how to read and use volume, as it can help your trading immensely.

Rule 11: Make Sure the Technicals Confirm the Fundamentals

Don't trade until the technicals and the fundamentals both agree. This one I differ with a little, though it can be sound advice and when they do agree, you have a hell of a trade on your hands. However, I prefer to use the technicals to confirm if the news is having any input or not. Remember that a great trade is one where the market does not react the way you'd expect it to on news and you fade the news. This coincides with another age-old adage: "buy the rumor; sell the news." The charts are reality and factor in all news and can tell you a lot about what the market is doing, so have faith in them.

Rule 12: Don't Trade Illiquid Markets

There is a reason some stocks and markets are thinly traded (it's because nobody wants to trade them). Don't question that reason just avoid them as well. Thin, illiquid markets can do funny things fast, so stay away and only trade active stocks or markets. They don't need to be the most active markets out there, but big enough that they won't spike on a decent size order or if one player makes a move.

Rule 13: Take a Break When Losing Big

When sharp losses in equity are experienced, you should consider taking some time off. Close all your trades and stop trading for the day or longer. The mind can play games with itself following sharp, quick losses. The urge to get the money back is extreme and should not be given in to as it can lead you to blow out.

Rule 14: When Trading Well Push It a Little

When trading well, you should increase your aggressiveness a little. Things tend to happen in streaks, both winning and losing, and everybody will go through great streaks every now and then. Try to cash in on a good streak, but know that every streak must end and don't get too cocky and aggressive or you could wipe out all your earnings in one trade. They key word in this header is "little." Yes, it's okay to step it up a notch, but keep it controllable and never get overly greedy.

Rule 15: Never Risk More than 5 Percent of Your Account Equity on a Trade

This seems to be the most quoted amount I have found. I've seen 1 and 2 percent as well but 5 percent is acceptable for a regular trader's account size. By sticking to this rule you will protect yourself from losing all your money at any given time. You will also be able to figure how many contracts to trade and whether or not a trade is too risky.

Rule 16: Trade Your Personality

As a general rule, your trading style should match your personality. You will have trouble trading someone else's style if it doesn't fit how you think. I wrote a whole chapter on this so you know how I feel about it.

Rule 17: Prices Have Memory

Here's one I like, that I really didn't talk about. Prices do tend to remember levels. They will tend to revert back to a support or resistance level that is clearly visible on a chart. Actually it's not the prices that have memories but it's the traders who make notes of certain prices and then move the market toward that level, as they keep trading in one direction until a traget is hit and then they exit.

Rule 18: Trade What You Trade Best

Trade more in the stocks or markets that are working for you, and less in those that are not. If you are a great crude oil trader, just trade crude oil, you do not need to be involved in everything. If you are trading several positions, look at those various positions and try to add to the trade that has the most profit while subtracting from the trade that is either unprofitable or is showing the smallest profit. This also helps you with "let your profits run."

Rule 19: Monitor Yourself

The best way to learn about how you are doing as a trader is to keep track of what you have done. Keeping a diary with all your trades, reasons for putting them on, and how you acted on them, will help reveal a lot about your trading. If done correctly you will begin to see patterns that could help you eliminate some of your bad trades, while concentrating on winning ones. You will also learn about yourself and your strengths and weaknesses.

Rule 20: Know Your Markets

The best traders specialize in only a small number of indices, futures, or stocks, and get to know them intimately. Spread yourself out too much and you won't know the markets nearly as well. As I mentioned early in the book, you can get to really know how a market reacts by studying and trading it every day, and this will give you an edge in trading. Stretching yourself too thin will make you start to lose your edge. If the pros trade one or two markets, then why do you think you are better than them?

Rule 21: Don't Be Greedy

Greed is one of the emotions that can hurt you in trading; once your trade is done, get out. You do not need to squeeze every last penny out of a trade, more likely than not you will end up giving some money back. Greed will also kill you if you try and make too much money by trading a larger position than you can afford. Instead, go for steady, consistent results.

Rule 22: Don't Trade Scared

Like greed, fear is another deadly trait one can have. People who trade scared make bad trading decisions. They exit trades at the wrong time if they are ahead hoping to lock in a profit. Some people are scared to pull the trigger. They see a trade and then just watch it, or worse they are in and cannot pull the trigger to get out. They may be scared to take a small loss and let it grow into a huge one. Or they are scared that they just took a big loss and now need to make it up. If you are scared, take a break from trading until you figure out how to calm those fears, because most likely you will lose more money if you don't.

Rule 23: Hope Is Not a Trading Strategy

Another favorite of mine. Nowhere in a proper trading plan, will you find the word hope. Once the word starts popping into your trading decisions and thoughts, most likely your trade has gone awry, and you are now stuck in a bad position looking to get out. Once you start hoping, get out and move on.

Rule 24: Keep It Simple

I've learned that the simplest methods work best. When you start to rely upon multiple and complex indicators, you may end up having so much going on that you may not be able to make a rational decision. Or you may have different indicators pointing different ways not giving you any clear signals. It's like having too many cooks in the kitchen trying to make a stew, they just get in each others' way. Some of the best traders only use a chart and a trend line. They do not need any fancy schmancy things to clutter their brains.

Rule 25: Take a Part of the Profit to Reward Yourself

And last, when you make money, take a part of that profit and give yourself a reward, it will make you feel better about yourself and your trading. There is nothing nicer then giving yourself a treat, like a $4,000 Martin acoustic guitar, with trading money.

CLOSING THOUGHTS

Trading rules will make up the cornerstone of your basic trading methodology. All your buy and sell and risk scenarios will come from them. And you need to develop and implement a set if you want to make money in this business. Not only will they guide your trading if used and followed, but they act as a method of monitoring your trading as well. They are what will help you distinguish between doing the right thing versus the wrong thing. Once you have solid trading rules, all you have to do is go over your trades and make notes as to whether you followed them or not and how you did when you followed them or not. Without these basic rules you will have nothing to measure yourself with and will only be adding one more hurdle on your way to becoming a great trader.

CHAPTER 17

Focus and Discipline

A school teacher hurt his back and had to wear a plaster cast around the upper part of his body. It fit under his shirt and was not noticeable at all. On the first day of the term, still with the cast under his shirt, he found himself assigned to the toughest students in school.

Walking confidently into the rowdy classroom, he opened the window as wide as possible and then busied himself with desk work. The classroom was a bit unruly and he tried to get them to quiet down several times, but to little avail.

As he was trying to work, a strong breeze made his tie flap annoyingly, he kept rearranging and rearranging the tie, but nothing worked. As he was asking the kids to quiet down one more time, he also became disgusted with the wayward tie and he stood up and took a stapler off his desk and stapled the tie to his chest in several places. Discipline was not a problem from that moment on.

Having a great trading and game plan and the best trading rules in the world is fine and dandy, but it won't help you a bit if you cannot stay focused on them and have the discipline to follow them. If you are a person who gets easily distracted you will have problems trading, no matter how good your trading and game plans are. As you know, the game plan is supposed to help keep you focused on the trading plan, but you need to stay focused on it if it is to work.

STAYING FOCUSED

Staying focused encompasses many things from developing your plans, to following them, to reviewing them, to keeping from overtrading and staying within your money management rules. As soon as you begin slipping up in any aspect of trading, your bottom line will begin to suffer.

One of the reasons professional traders do well, is because trading is their sole business and they have fewer outside concerns. I'm referring to traders who work for firms. They'll get a salary and a nice one, too, and do not have to worry about where their day-to-day money is coming from. Sure, they are concerned about their fat bonuses, but it's more of a dangling carrot than a distraction. The everyday guy trying to trade has so much on his mind that it can be hard to stay focused. For starters, some people try to day-trade while having full-time jobs. I've known quite a few lawyers, doctors, accountants, receptionists, drummers, firefighters, and so on, who try to day-trade while doing their other job as well. It's impossible to stay on top of things when you cannot devote your full attention to trading. There are thousands of housewives who have tried trading in between dropping the kids off at school and going about their regular business. They, too, have little chance of success because they cannot focus just on trading. If you are in a position and a baby cries, or a client calls, or you have to perform a root canal, you cannot stay focused on your trade. Sure they were great traders when the market went straight up in the late 1990s and all they had to do was buy and sell higher, than buy even higher and sell even higher. But put them in a normal trading environment and they will most likely not be able to focus enough to make money.

Another reason the pros do well is because unlike some new traders they do not need to make money in order to survive. They may need to make money in order to keep their jobs, but they can trade without the stress of having to make enough money to cover their mortgage. Someone who is putting up a good chunk of their own money to become a day trader and has no other source of income, is constantly concerned about his financial well being. His concerns will distract him from being focused on trading and will cause him to slip up more frequently. Not to mention he will be more likely to lose discipline if he tries to make more money than he should and trades beyond his means if money becomes an issue for him.

DISTRACTIONS

I recently opened a bar (Tequila Jack's) in New York City. The week before I did I cashed out of a lot of money. Then I tried to make one last big trade on February 27, 2008, to give myself some extra money to play with. I put on a nice size option trade in the S&Ps, and the next day the market plummeted (see Figure 17.1) due to problems in Asia and I blew, pretty much, the whole premium in a day. I wasn't even able to watch the trade as I had to go to the Department of Health and the Department of Consumer Affairs to get permits for the bar and outdoor seating area. So instead of having an extra $50,000 to $100,000 cushion, I lost about $20,000 in two days, all due to me losing my discipline and making a trade I normally wouldn't simply because I wanted more money. I also ignored my money management parameters by risking more than I normally would.

Buying the bar has been a huge distraction, which has caused me to stop trading for a period of time. I'm a pretty hands-on kind of guy and I oversaw the whole renovation, staffing, setting of policies, creating the menu (we have great Mexican food if you are in the area), and quite a few other things. As such, I devoted most of my time to the bar, then I had to write this book and was not able to concentrate on trading as well. I tried to for a couple of weeks, but I wasn't able to spend the time I needed on game plans every day so I wasn't as effective. Nor did I have time to make a new trading plan that would let me trade on a longer term basis. So for a few months I stopped altogether to concentrate on my bar and occasionally the book. The place began to run itself and, much to my editor's chagrin, I

FIGURE 17.1 One Last Trade
Source: © TradeStation Technologies 1999. All rights reserved.

ignored the book and was able to get back to trading. However, now I have to finish the book because I already asked for two extensions and I believe my editors are beginning to lose patience. So I will have to cut back on trading if I don't want to trade half-assed. I still look at the markets every day, but unless I see something extraordinary that I think can be a long-term move (by long-term I mean at least a week or two) I just look at the market to help with the book. I do know I didn't do great during the period in which I wrote *High Probability Trading*, so I'd rather be safe this time.

JUST TWO MORE DAYS

As I'm reviewing the book just before handing it in, I just want to say this is one of those chapters I wrote out of order—all of the trades I talked about in the middle part of the book came a few months after writing this chapter. But now I have two more days before I hand it in and that makes me a happy camper. I didn't make a lot of trades in the last few months. But I did okay and now I'm eager to get back into it full tilt. Until I buy another bar or restaurant, of course. The market has been insane lately. Today the Fed had to bail out Bear Stearns, and the market plummeted after being up 400 points the last two days.

It doesn't matter what is distracting you, it could be illness, depression, financial woes, kids, trying to buy a house, a bad marriage, or even the opposite, you could have just met someone and fallen in lust and are giddy with joy, constantly daydreaming about the person, getting nothing done. And worse, you can be going through both a bad marriage and a fantastic new lover at same time. Regardless of the reason, if you aren't focused you will not trade well. Making and keeping to a game plan are time–consuming, and if you cannot spend the proper time doing it, your trading will suffer.

HAVE A ROUTINE TO HELP YOU WRITE A GAME PLAN

Not only do you have to be disciplined in trading but you also have to have the discipline to write your game plan, make your scenarios, and review your trading every day. When I traded full-time I had a routine that helped me do this. Every day after the markets close, I got up and went for a walk around the block, I would buy a candy bar and grab a can of Coke. After sitting for most of the day, my lower back compressed and I also needed to stretch my legs out. That walk really helped loosen me up and allowed me to stay focused on trading for another hour after the market closed so I could start on my game plan for the next day. Then when I was all done I'd take a nap.

Besides the bar and the book I've also became a stay-at-home dad for the last three years. As part of my routine now instead of taking that walk, I'll take the kids to the park for an hour as soon as the market closes. Just for the record, there is nothing as amazing as being able to watch two babies grow into little people. It's hard work but definitely puts a smile on your face. It's one of the main reasons I stopped day-trading and started trading longer term. I wanted to be able to spend time with them. I do have a nanny come in every morning to help out if I'm trading, otherwise, I'd have no time for anything. But I know for sure I will not have the time to get back to serious trading until my daughter heads off to preschool in a few months.

My problem has always come in the morning because I'm a late-night person. My normal bedtime has always been, even as a teen, between two and three in the morning, and I can function fine on five hours of sleep, so long as I take my nap every afternoon. I only need an hour in the morning preparing and my commute is from the bedroom to the den/office, so I don't need to wake up super early, though I'd prefer to sleep in till 10. My routine is the same every morning. I go to the bathroom at 7:58 A.M.; unfortunately, I wake up at 8:00 A.M. But seriously, after using the bathroom I sit in front of my computer and go through any news and charts that will help me and start writing my game plan and coming up with scenarios for what I'm looking at. I usually finish this by about 9:00 A.M. and take a shower. And I'm ready to go by 9:20. I do not like to initiate any trades in the first 30 minutes of trading so I eat breakfast during this time while I look at the markets and see how they feel. Maybe my morning trading has suffered because I don't get a full eight hours of sleep, but I refuse to believe that.

Having a routine as you prepare to trade will definitely be an asset as it gets you in the habit of doing what you need to do. Unless you do the same thing day in and day out, it's hard to stay focused on creating a game plan.

FOLLOWING YOUR PLAN

Not only must you be disciplined to write your game plan every day, but you have to follow it. By making the game plan you are giving yourself a clear direction in which to trade and a huge advantage over traders who lack one. What's the point in taking the time to write it all down if you are not going to use it or stick to it? But it's not always easy to do so. You can get distracted or change your mind, or completely ignore things and your game plan is worthless. However, if you are one of those who can stay disciplined and follow his plan then you will have a good chance of being a great trader. If you are undisciplined and cannot follow a strategy, I don't believe you have a chance of being successful no matter what you may think.

HOW TO STAY FOCUSED IF YOU HAVE TROUBLE STAYING FOCUSED

Now, I do not know if discipline is something you either have or you don't. Can an undisciplined person learn to become disciplined? Maybe, but it's going to take discipline to learn to become disciplined. And if you don't have it to begin with you, you will have trouble learning it. But there are some things I think you can do to hopefully help you get there. First of all you have to have that trading plan and game plan. They are the most important steps in being disciplined, as you can't be disciplined if you have nothing to be disciplined about. The discipline factor comes into play when you can follow those plans without second guessing yourself. If you are having problems with discipline here are a couple of things I think can help you develop it.

Trading Rules

Make a set of simple trading rules and make sure you follow them. If you start by making rules as simple as you can it will be easier to follow those rules. Keep track of how you do when you break those rules and how you do when you follow them. If you do this you may see a pattern of how you do when you stick to the rules and this may cause you to become stricter in following them. If your rules or strategies tell you to exit a trade once it reaches a certain area, get out and don't question it. Once you can do this repeatedly you will start being disciplined.

Keep and Analyze a Journal

Very often overlooked or thought of as beneath people, a journal is one of the most helpful tools a trader can have in recognizing patterns in his behavior, which can lead to better discipline. It's not just keeping a journal that's important; you need to review it to analyze your trading. Just by taking the time to keep a journal every day and for every trade you will gain discipline. But the real discipline will come as you learn to analyze how you did versus your trading rules and game plan. Look for the number of times you followed your rules or not. It doesn't matter if you made money or not, the goal is to get that ratio of following your rules to not following them higher.

Trade Your Style

You will never be disciplined if you cannot follow your strategies. It gets harder and harder to follow strategies if they are against your style of trading. So if you want to work on discipline only trade with strategies you are comfortable with.

Monitor the Markets

Set aside a time to monitor and review the markets every day. Do it like clockwork, whether or not you traded them, and not only will you gain discipline, you will learn more about what makes the market tick. Discipline means doing the same thing over and over again and this is just one method of learning it.

Be Consistent

Concentrate as hard as you can at being consistent, whether it's in every day things like going to the gym or in the way you trade. People who go to the gym on a regular basis, eat right all the time, and never smoke are disciplined people. If you want to improve your discipline join a gym, set an hour to go, and just do it every day.

When it comes to trading try to make the same trade in the same situation everytime. If you vary your trading for no reason and buy one morning on a gap lower open and sell the next on a similar gap lower open, you have no consistency and therefore no discipline.

Don't Trade over Your Head

It is easier to stay disciplined when you are trading and risking the proper amount for your account size. Once you start trading beyond what your account can really handle, you may make foolish decisions if a trade goes awry. Keeping to the right risk will mean you have a better chance of sticking to your game plan as panic and fear will become less of a factor.

Learning the Expensive Way

Some people think they are disciplined as they paper trade and follow all their rules to a T. But once they step up to real-time trading, everything goes out the window. Paper trading is good to a degree but it cannot get you the experience you ultimately need. One way to gain that experience, and it's not free, is to actually practice trading with real money. This is going to sound a bit unorthodox, but find the cheapest market or stock you can, by that I mean one with small range and lots of volume like corn or SIRI. Make yourself a simple strategy with several trades a day. Trade just one contract or 100 shares and practice. After a couple of weeks you'll probably be up or down $1,000 at most. That's not important, what is important is that you learn to follow your rules to the letter and get real-time experience. If you get an exit signal, sell without a thought. If you get a buy signal, buy without hesitation. Once you are doing this correctly and consistently, you will have gained some discipline. If you can't do this, go into real estate or something else, because you won't make money trading. It's like when I wanted to become a better poker player. I started playing at low-stakes tables and practiced my discipline. That meant only playing the hands that had a high chance of winning. It was boring but effective. Learning and practicing at a low-stakes game is much more effective than doing so playing online with no money (paper trading), or playing with stakes too high where you cannot concentrate on doing it right, instead of how much money you are making or losing. Money can be a distraction, but if you make the money minimal and you lose, as you are very likely to do at the beginning, take it as a lesson or tuition for a class on discipline. If the stakes are too high then that lesson will be quite expensive, plus your emotions may just get in the way.

MENTAL SIDE OF DISCIPLINE

Above I mentioned several ways to learn discipline using the market to help, but discipline comes from inside you and you need to train your mind, to get it. Here are a few ideas on how you can possibly learn discipline from within.

Get Help from a Shrink

Probably the best way an undisciplined person can turn it around is to get help from a psychiatrist. Through some counseling and maybe hypnosis you may be able to become disciplined. There are many therapists who work with traders to make them better traders. I have no proof it works, so don't get upset with me after spending $12,000 in therapy if you still can't trade.

Keep Your Mind Clear

Besides the therapy approach I think you can be more disciplined if you trade with a clear mind. If you cannot focus all your energy on trading, you will have trouble being as disciplined as you could be. I knew I wasn't able to focus entirely on trading the last year so I had to change the way I trade so that I could stay focused on what I was doing. I have the discipline to trade the way I'm currently doing it, but if I were to be more active, my trading would suffer as I couldn't keep my mind clear enough to concentrate and be disciplined on the market and doing everything I had to to succeed. Maybe going to therapy will help you with this one, as well as a few of the points below.

Keep Your Emotions at Bay

Try to stay in control of yourself and not let your emotions take over when entering, monitoring, or exiting a trade. Panic and euphoria cloud your judgment when trades go haywire or better than you had hoped. Your emotional state of mind should be the same on great days or days when nothing is going right. This is where you need to take a cue from a good poker player, who shows no emotion regardless of winning or losing. Don't gloat when winning or smash a keyboard when losing. If you cannot keep your emotions at bay, you will have trouble staying disciplined on doing the right things.

Don't Get Overconfident

Though you need confidence to make it as a trader, you'll get into trouble if you get overconfident. Once you get overconfident, which usually comes after a winning streak or a big win, you think you are invincible and may let your guard down. Once you do this you may no longer follow your plans and leave more to chance. You may also ignore your money management rules and that can hurt you fast. Overconfidence also affects you by letting you get lazy. You may not make a game plan, or may not back test a system, because you think everything you do will work. At this point, your discipline is shot as your mind leads you to think you do not need to follow every single rule.

Think Points, Not Money

If you noticed, I rarely mentioned how much money I've made or lost on the trades I've made throughout this book. I only mentioned how many points it was. Once you start thinking money, it can sway your thinking as a big dollar loss or win can get your emotions going. But if you were to only think about how many points you made or lost, you can keep those emotional highs and lows curbed and concentrate more easily on trading correctly.

Imagine and Feel the Loss Before It Happens

One way I have found to be able to keep my discipline while trading is to be prepared for the worst-case scenario. I try to imagine how I would feel if I got stopped out and lost the amount I was risking. You need to be honest with yourself beforehand; could you handle the loss without an emotional change in your attitude? If the loss is too great you may have trouble keeping your discipline as it nears the stop area and you cannot handle taking the loss. But if you were to feel the pain beforehand, prepare yourself for it, and know you could handle it, then you have a better shot of sticking to your plan, when the time comes.

Picture Yourself as a Professional

With every move you make, think like a pro. Keep asking yourself would a pro do this? Am I making an amateurish move? Is Marcel going to be proud of me? As you apply this simple task to more and more situations your mind will start to think in a more professional manner, making better, more disciplined trading decisions.

Learn to Say "So What?"

If you are good, you will lose money and be wrong at best half the time. You will get out of winning trades too soon and you will exit losers only to see them turn around big, and you'll completely miss a trade here and there. And that's if you're good, forget it about if you are a mediocre to bad trader. Well, you need to brush off all the negative things when they happen and not take it personally. As long as you make the high probability trades and stick to your plans it does not matter if you are wrong or miss something. So learn to get over the negativity associated with losing and just say, "So what?" Don't be disappointed if something does not work out. Your job is to move on to the next trade with a clear mind and start from scratch. You can't be a perfectionist and expect to be a great trader. The best home run hitters in baseball are also the guys who strike out the most. It's part of the game, and they learn to take a strikeout in stride and try to learn from the experience so they react better the next time. Cy Young, the all-time winningest pitcher in baseball, is also the all-time leader in losses. He learned to shrug off a loss and figure out why he lost and then come back to pitch two winning games after each loss. This is a much better strategy than pressing or trading all riled because something didn't go your way. Just let it go or you could easily lose discipline on the next trade.

Don't Be Afraid

Fear can kill you in many ways. There's the fear of losing money, the fear of being wrong, the fear of missing out, or leaving money on the table, and the fear of letting go and taking a loser. Any trader who trades scared, will have trouble controlling his emotions, and hence will not have the discipline to trade properly. You need to overcome your fears in order to be a good trader. Trading is not for the weak or the scared, and if you are one of those you will have trouble keeping to your plans. One method you can try is to find something you are scared of in real life and just face it. I'm scared of talking in public, but as soon as I finish this book, I'm going to work on it, joining Toastmasters and taking some workshops and then going out and doing it.

KEEPING TABS

Besides working on discipline from the mental aspect of it, you can also try to develop discipline by keeping tabs on yourself. There are several ways I can think of that you can achieve this. The most effective is keeping a journal, others include having someone to answer to, or looking over your own shoulder.

Keep a Journal

A journal can be helpful in several ways, the first method reminds me of when my father tried to quit smoking. One method he used was to have a piece of paper rubber banded around his pack of Benson & Hedges 100's. Everytime he smoked or had the urge to smoke he would write the time and the reason down on the paper. Keeping this little journal was supposed to help him realize he was smoking too often and for no good reason, and by being an annoying task it would get him to go longer and longer between cigarettes. He was able to see that he was smoking more than he thought and tried to cut back. Unfortunately, he tried too late and got lung cancer and died at the ripe old age of 46. (So I recommend you quit smoking if you do.) Before this he only knew he was smoking about two packs a day; he didn't realize he was lighting up every 15 to 20 minutes at times, for the majority of the day. He then realized it was a bit too much. Just taking the time to write down why you are making a trade in a journal and what your thoughts about that trade are will help you get disciplined into making better trades.

A journal will help you see things in your trading that you just will not see otherwise. It can help you see how you did when you followed your rules and how you did when you ignored them or how you did when you held for less than two days as compared with when you held two for more days. Many traders tend to ignore the journal-keeping part of trading, but it really helps. Top poker players do it all the time as well. They make notes of how they played and what they did right or wrong; they also keep notes on their money management and on opponents. As they review it they learn how to handle different situations better and how to take the gamble out of their gambling. It's an invaluable tool to have that does not take long to do, and I strongly recommend keeping and reviewing one.

Have Someone to Answer To

This is something that his been extremely helpful for me. At times when I got a little reckless, I told friends, coworkers, or girlfriends, to go over my trading every day. I gave them my rules and parameters and told them to really get on my case if I was breaking them. I even gave them permission to exit my trade if I missed a stop. When you have no one for a boss to answer to, you can do whatever you want. But if you are in fear of getting fired or having a friend chastise you, you may try a little harder to do the right thing. For me, I sometimes needed help keeping my overtrading and total risk-taking in check. When I began to feel embarrassed if I did overextend myself, I stopped doing it.

Step Outside Yourself to Keep Yourself in Check

I wrote about this in that other book I wrote, but one thing that has helped me, especially when I'm in a bad position, is to make believe I'm looking over my shoulder and analyzing the trade from a fresh point of view. I make believe I am giving someone else an opinion. When you are in a position you start to think with that position. And it's only when you can look at it without attachments that you can make a rational decision. Try it sometime, clear your mind of your established ideas on a trade, and think of it from scratch, as if you were looking to put on a new position. You may be surprised by what you find.

Reviewing

It's not easy to always stay focused. There will be many times when your emotions will get the best of you, and it could be when you are winning or losing. You may decide not to follow your game plan for whatever reason, it doesn't matter. What matters is you have to do the best you can to keep on track. This is where constant reviewing comes into play. If you have a plan for your reviewing and have to answer for every trade you can keep yourself in check when you start to stray. At the end of the day you should go over all your actions to see if they fit what you had in your game plan for them. If you strayed and you made trades that weren't in there or exited at levels that you improvised, or traded too many shares, then you are not staying disciplined. Reviewing your own performance is a great way to see how well you stick to your rules. I have found it to be one of the most helpful tools I have at my disposal.

UNWINDING AFTER THE DAY

Trading is definitely a stressful day-in day-out job and it's important to learn to unwind after looking at computers all day and making split-second decisions that could cost you a lot of money. For me, my walk around the block and then later my nap, work great at helping me to unwind, as does playing with my kids. I also find at least an hour a day to play piano and/or guitar, though I tend to play "The Wheels on the Bus" and "Twinkle, Twinkle Little Star" now more than the Beatles and Stones I'd prefer, but it's still a great method of relaxing. But different people have different ways to unwind. I know several guys who go to the gym everyday after they are done trading. I know a few who go out and have a drink or six, hopefully at my bar. I know more than a handful who like to smoke a joint everyday to unwind. They are all good traders and this is their routine that helps them unwind after the day. I'm actually amazed at the number of incredibly successful people I know who now in their late 30s and 40s smoke pot pretty much every single day. I have friends who are surgeons, pediatricians, lawyers, traders, bond salesmen, stockbrokers, accountants, real estate brokers, investment bankers, credit analysts, owners of successful companies, professors, and grade school teachers, just to name a few who smoke all the time. And all the time I was growing up I never smoked, thinking it would screw up my mind and I'd never be successful. I feel like I'm not normal. I own a bar and I don't drink, maybe I have one drink a month. I smoked pot three times in my life (and yes, I inhaled), yet many of the people I know smoke it all the time. But I guess it's not as bad as Donald Trump who recently launched a high-end vodka called Trump and he claims to not drink at all.

The bottom line is to take some stress off and enjoy yourself a little. If you are too wound up and uptight all the time, you may have trouble staying focused and when that happens you can lose your discipline. Learn to find ways to take the stress off—go to the gym, play tennis, do puzzles, play guitar, just find something that you enjoy doing. You should also learn to reward yourself when you do good, go out to a nice dinner, a fun concert, or plan a great vacation. And last is that once those markets are closed and you've done your homework, relax. If you cannot relax because you hold positions overnight, then only day trade. But whatever it takes it is important you learn to enjoy yourself.

CLOSING THOUGHTS

If you want any hope of succeeding as a trader you will need to be disciplined. Sure, you need to have all the trading tools, plans, and strategies you need to be disciplined about established already. But they alone will not make you a good trader. Only once you can follow those plans and rules can you have hope of making continuous money. The lackadaisical trader, who leaves some things to chance and takes too much risk, is going to have trouble making it in the long run. I've shared a few things that have help me in gaining discipline, and maybe you can come up with some others that could help.

Reviewing my trading has been one of the most helpful things for me when it comes to staying focused. I was able to see how I stuck to or deviated from my plan. The more I did it, the more I was able to learn to stick to the rules. You may not even know that you are straying from your plan until you review your trading. Reviewing also helps me in that it keeps the idea of why I put on a trade fresh in my mind, which, in turn, lets me stay focused on it more, the further it gets from when I put it on. This and playing cards is what help me the most. There may be something else that you find that helps you, but whatever it is work on your discipline—you will need it.

CHAPTER 18

Learning How to Win

A trader moved to Texas and bought a donkey from an old farmer for $100. The farmer took the cash and agreed to deliver the donkey the next day. The next day, the farmer drove up and said, "Sorry, but I have some bad news. The donkey died." "Well," replied the trader "then, just give me the money back." "Can't do that," replied the farmer, "I went and spent it already." "Okay, then. Just give me the donkey." "What ya going to do with a dead donkey?" asked the farmer. "I'm going to raffle him off," said the trader. "You can't raffle off a dead donkey!" the farmer said. "Sure can," said the trader. "Watch me. I just won't tell anyone he's dead."

A month later the farmer met up with the trader and asked, "What happened with that dead donkey?" The trader said, "I raffled him off, I did. I sold 500 tickets at two dollars a piece and made a profit of $898," he said.

"Didn't anyone complain?" inquired the farmer. "Just the guy who won. So I gave him his two dollars back."

This could be seen as a continuation of the previous chapter, as everything in there is leading you to become a better trader, but there are so many more things you can do to achieve success that I needed one last chapter to wrap things up. I will repeat a few of the important things from throughout the book that I deem will make you a winning trader. Plus, there will be a few new thoughts as well. Unlike the rest of the book, where I had outlined all the chapters before I wrote them, I'm winging this one, and so it will be random advice as I think of it. I'm sure I will miss a lot of great advice, so keep doing your homework and learn as much as you can on your own.

I believe people can become wining traders if they try hard enough. It's not something that you will get overnight, but with enough time, patience, money, and guidance it can be done. I'll give you ways to trade that I think can help you or that have helped me. Some of these are just simple things that, when you add them all up, will make you a much better trader. Not all are my ideas; I have gotten many through reading books and magazines over the years. Unfortunately, I cannot recall which issue of what magazine I read something in maybe 20 years ago, so I hope nobody gets offended if I stole their idea and incorporated into my trading. I will, however, give you a list of reading materials that have helped me. Even writing my books has been a tremendous help in my trading. If you think keeping a journal may help, imagine how much you can learn after writing close to 800 pages of material.

CLEAN OUT YOUR CLOSET

I read this one somewhere, a long time ago, and it applies to people who have trouble letting go of losing and marginal trades. There are many, many people out there who have way too many clothes and shoes in their closets. Some people have suits from the eighties that they have not worn in 17 years, hoping they come back in style, others have shoes that haven't been worn in three years, or sweaters in two years, or underwear whose elastic doesn't hold it up anymore. Just get rid of them already, there are people out there who could use them. Though what a homeless person will do with a three-inch stiletto and a three-piece power suit is beyond me, you get the point. It's these people who cannot let go of old clothes and junk that are the ones who have the most trouble letting go of trades. But if you are one of these people who cannot exit a loser, go into your closet and if you haven't worn something in two years—give it away. It may sound like an ungodly thing to do to a woman, but if you cannot do it, you may have trouble when it comes to letting go of a loser or a trade that is not working. Many traders end up marrying a stock and cannot let go no matter how bad it gets. This is one way to help you kick that habit.

DON'T BLAME OTHERS FOR LOSSES

If you lost money trading, it's your fault and no one else's. It's not the Fed's fault, nor the economy's, nor the weather's. It's not the market makers who drove a market down who lost your money, nor is it the floor traders or brokers, nor someone who gave you a bad tip or idea. If you lost money it's your fault and your fault alone. Learning to take the blame and the burden of the mistakes will make you a better trader or at the very least a less annoying one to your friends, family, and coworkers.

THINK OF IT AS AN EXPENSE AND NOT A LOSS

Every business has expenses it must incur in order to operate. At the bar I have liquor, food, payroll, advertising, paper goods, spoiled meat, utilities, and so forth. Traders have expenses as well, and a major part of those expenses will be your losses. Do not think of a loss that occurred in a properly planned out trade as a loss, but think of it as a cost of doing business. You are going to have losses and there is no way around that. Never beat yourself up over them or take them personally. They are just a way of getting you closer to that big winning trade that is coming around the corner.

SELF-DESTRUCTIVE BEHAVIOR

I can't help you with this one, but you need to take a real evaluation and ask yourself if you suffer from self-destructive behavior. It's quite common. There are many people who subconsciously believe they do not deserve to succeed. Maybe they grew up poor, or were always put down by parents. I don't know all the reasons nor have the answers, but if you are one of these people either work it out yourself, seek help, or quit trading, because you will always do something to sabotage yourself.

LEARN FROM MISTAKES

You are going to make a lot of mistakes as you trade. Even if you have been trading for a decade you will still make a few here and there. Hey, not every pitcher who throws a hanging curve is in the minors, there are a lot of seasoned veterans who still do it every now and then; it happens. They just do it less because they have learned to learn from their mistakes. As a trader you need to as well. Every time you do something stupid make sure you know why and try not to do it again. A journal is invaluable in helping you do this, which is why almost all trading books mention you should have one.

If you do not know how to handle mistakes and start cursing and smashing keyboards you won't learn a thing; instead take that energy and use it to understand what you did wrong.

TRADE, TRADE, TRADE

Like practice, practice, practice is how you get to Carnegie Hall, the only true way you will become a better trader is to trade. The more you trade, the more you will learn, the better you will see the markets, the better you will understand money management, and so on. A million books cannot teach you what real life experience can. Nor, in my opinion, can paper trading make you feel the emotional highs or lows of making and losing money. Only the real thing can. There is a lot to get as a trader, so if you understand there is a learning curve and trade accordingly at the beginning, you will stand a chance of succeeding. If you come flying out of the shoots at full pace, it is extremely likely you'll be taking a break soon to gather more capital to try it again.

CURB YOUR EMOTIONS

Here is something I find critical that others may not. If you want to be a great trader you cannot let your emotions run amok. You need to think and feel the same way when you are winning and when you are losing. Greed and fear are the two most talked about emotions, but there is also euphoria and depression that can affect the way you trade. I've seen so many people completely lose control after a bad loss that it gets to them and they start trading worse both because they are not thinking straight and because they are trying to recoup losses. In poker it's called going on tilt, and it comes after taking a bad loss you think you should have won. You then start betting more aggressively out of anger to get that money back. What happens soon is that you end up going home after losing all your money. It will happen in trading as well if you cannot keep a steady composure.

LOSSES ARE IN THE PAST

Here is a great tip to remember that will help you tremendously. A loss is something that happened in the past, forget about it. You are not getting that money back no matter what you do, it's gone forever regardless of how upset you get. You have to not let it influence your next trade or adjust your money management because of it. Trade the next trade with no memory if you want to succeed.

MONEY MANAGEMENT IS MORE IMPORTANT THAN TRADE SELECTION

You will never go broke if you use proper money management, even if you make 12 bad trades in row. You can, however, go broke on one trade with horrendous money management skills. I wrote about it in my other book, how one customer lost his whole account on his first day of trading by overtrading crude futures. It can happen, and it only takes one uncontrolled trade to do it.

It doesn't matter the size of the account. If you have a solid money management plan you can be around for quite a while and this is one major step into making it as a good trader.

TREAT YOURSELF

Don't let trading rule your world, you need to enjoy life as well and you need to get rewarded for what you do. If you are able to buy yourself something nice every now and then, subconsciously your trading may improve, just for these bonuses. Even if it's something simple at least you know you bought that six-pack of tube socks from the street vendor with a trading win. This is more for the struggling new trader than the old pro. But even if you work at Bear Stearns and you had a good string of trades, take some of your own money and buy yourself something.

PRESERVE PRECIOUS CAPITAL

Similar to the money management idea, you need to preserve your precious capital. Always trade from the point of view of, "How much can I lose and what can I do to limit that loss?" It's more important to not lose big then it is to win big. So keep doing the appropriate things to let you hold on to your money. Because once you have no money, you can't trade anymore.

HAVE A CUTOFF POINT

One simple way to preserve your capital is to have a cutoff point. As part of your trading and money management make sure you have a dollar amount and/or number of consecutive bad trades that you will cut off yourself at. Doing this ensures you will not suffer a devastating loss or massive losing streak. You need to do whatever it takes to not let losers get out of hand, and this is just one way.

JUMPING IN TOO SOON OR GETTING IN TOO LATE

If you want to make the most out of a trade, then you need to have timing. Timing will get you in and out of trades at much better levels than if you rushed or missed a trade. It will also keep you from making some bad trades. If you miss a move and now it's too late to get in, you need to wait for a safe place to enter it instead of chasing it, otherwise your stop may become too far away. Timing also applies to getting in before a move happens. Trying to guess a turnaround in the market can be quite costly if you are wrong in a strong trend.

You can actually jump in too soon and get in too late with the same trade. This happens when you rush to get into a trade because of a news item or break of a technical level; in the minute it takes you to get in, the market may spike, you buy and then it reverses. So you got the peak. If you had gotten in a little sooner you'd be fine. And if you had waited you would have either not taken the trade or got in at a better price. So by rushing in you end up missing the move.

Working on timing is all about discipline, following rules, and a game plan. It definitely is something that should be worked on as it will both save and make you money.

DO NOT LET BIG WINNERS TURN TO LOSERS

Here's another little tidbit of information that can make you a great trader. Once you have a trade that is working and has neared your expectations, make sure you do not let that trade turn into a loser. If you do this you have made a really bad mistake. You need to learn to lock it in as a winner as it nears your target—not necessarily at its peak level, but you should never let it go all the way back. Once a trade has reached its target, you need to think of it as a new trade. And if you are letting it go all the way back to breakeven then your risk/reward ratio in general is a bit screwy.

MAKE A LIST OF RULES

I'm sure by now you have either traded long enough or read enough to have enough knowledge to make a set of rules you can trade by. Getting your thoughts on paper and keeping them in front of you will help drive them into your brain. If you can't think of them, do a search on the Internet for trading rules and you'll find quite a few, or use the ones I laid out in Chapter 16. I'm sure you can apply a few of those and use them. The bottom line though is to have them. Oh, and try to pick the ones that fit your style the best.

TRADE YOUR STYLE

Reread Chapter 4. You will never make money in the long run if you do not trade a style that suits you, as you will not be able to stick to it.

USE A PROVEN STRATEGY

I'll be very straightforward. Do not trade with a strategy you have not back tested and know works. If you do then you are asking to lose. No matter how sound you think your strategy or system is, make sure it works before throwing away money trading it. If you do use a proven strategy and know how to manage your money, there is a fantastic chance you will be make money trading.

TIPS ARE FOR BARTENDERS

I've gotten many hot tips over the years and only two have come to fruition in a timely matter. If someone gives you a hot tip or idea, research it yourself before you risk money. Unless you are having lunch with Warren Buffett who gives you a surefire stock to invest in, I would take all tips with a grain of salt (at the very least you know where that expression arises from now) and not trade them. What normally happens is you have a friend whose sister's husband works at a company and he tells you that her company is *maybe* going to be bought out at $50 a share and you'd be wise to buy it. Three years later they finally get bought out at $37 a share.

I have found most tips will not come through, so you'd be wise not to follow them.

LEARN AS MUCH AS YOU CAN ABOUT WHAT YOU ARE TRADING

If you want to be a great trader make sure you are on top of your markets. Learning what makes a stock or market tick can only help you. Keep in mind that the best traders in the world usually focus on one market. They know it inside and out and they get rewarded for that. Try not to get too diverse in your trading or you will spread yourself too thin and will not be able to stay on top of everything as well as you should.

KEEP LEARNING

Never stop learning. No matter how long you've been trading, you can always learn something new. Keep reading books that could help and keep learning from yourself. Try and take a lesson out of every bad trade you make. Do not ignore the great trades as well, as they can teach you something that may just make you a better trader. If you know good traders, try and pick their brains and actually listen when they tell you something. Don't just yes them if they want to impart some advice. If they are making money they must know something.

READ AND LEARN

Though I have read quite a few books over the years below are the ones that have made a lasting impression or impact on me. I'll list them in order of when I read them. I have read other books over the years, some of which I cannot recall their full titles or their authors, so I guess they didn't leave much of an impression on me. Many books out there in my opinion just plain suck and do not teach you anything; it's just someone who wanted to get a little ego boost and wrote a book with nothing really helpful or practical inside. Publishing firms (like movie studios) know this as well, as they make 80 percent of their money on 20 percent of their books. But having the publishing house's name on the shelf at the bookstore is free advertising, plus they do not always know which books will succeed. Hey, I was a totally unknown person who was given a chance and a very small advance and five years later *High Probability Trading* is still ranked high on Amazon's list of top finance and stock books. What I'm getting at is don't just buy a book by its cover, take a look at Amazon and read the reviews first and make sure that, on average, people have gotten something out of it. Anyway, I did manage to take something out of the following books and I do recommend them.

Technical Analysis of the Futures Markets by John Murphy

Market Wizards by Jack D. Schwager

Reminiscences of a Stock Operator by Edwin Lefèvre

Option Volatility & Pricing by Sheldon Natenberg

Trade Your Way to Financial Freedom by Van K. Tharp

Trading for a Living by Alexander Elder

The New Market Wizards by Jack D. Schwager

The Complete Day Trader by Jake Bernstein

The Trading Systems Toolkit by Joe Krutsinger

Trading With the Odds by Cynthia Kase

Extraordinary Popular Delusions & the Madness of Crowds by Charles Mackay

The Disciplined Trader by Mark Douglas

Come Into My Trading Room by Alexander Elder

High Probability Trading by me (I reread it last year and it reminded me to do a few things I had gotten lazy about), and if I write another book after this one buy it as well.

The Three Musketeers by Alexandre Dumas—this doesn't have a thing to do with trading, but I read it at 13 on my father's suggestion and I've been an avid reader since. Thirty years later and a ton of books since, it and its sequels are far and away my favorite books ever. I enjoyed the book so much when I was a kid, that I never stopped reading or learning everything I could, especially about history, since.

I have also subscribed to *Technical Analysis of Stocks and Commodities* and *Futures Magazine* since the early nineties, more recently I started liking *Active Trader*. I have found them to hold a wealth of helpful information. I've taken away a lot from them over the years, especially when I began writing systems. I also found a lot of insight from the trader's interviews *in Technical Analysis of Stocks and Commodities*.

TRADE WITH A PLAN

And finally, do not forget the main reason I wrote this book (after the advance and royalties), which is to get you to trade with a game plan. If you have your trades all planned out and have a reason for every trade and follow that plan, you will be a better trader than most. The key is doing it and doing it consistently.

FILL IN YOUR OWN

Wait, there is one more I just thought of to finish the book with. But you have to do a little homework assignment. Take 10 minutes to jot down in the space below any idea I did not present that will help make you a better trader.

_____

_____

_____

_____

_____

_____

_____

_____

FINAL THOUGHTS

That's it. I'm done. Now I can go back to having a little time for me and trading full-time again. I hand in the book tomorrow and as luck would have it my girlfriend was lucky enough to get new job that starts in two days. It's good because I did need that extra time that she provided with the kids while she was off work, and I finished writing this book.

I'm concerned about getting back to trading full-time because the markets have been insane. It's about 2:30 in the morning on Sunday night March 17, 2008, and earlier today it was announced that JPMorgan would buy out Bear Sterns for $2 a share; it was $80 a share about two weeks ago. The Dow futures are down 225 points after closing Friday down 200 points. This puts it at its lowest level since October 2006 and just below the day when I took that nap while my daughter decorated my apartment with her yellow crayon.

Hope you got something out of the book. If you did, buy copies for all your friends and family. Even if you didn't learn a thing about trading, I hope I at least made you smile or laugh at some point.

Feel free to e-mail me at Marcel_Link@yahoo.com or visit MarcelLink. com, and if I get over that fear of speaking in public, look for me at a seminar.

About the Author

Marcel Link has been trading since 1988, when he first lost a then-staggering $600 in S&P index options. Since then he has fared better.

Over the past 20 years he has traded futures on the floor of the New York Financial Exchange and Cotton Exchange, has had his own commodities brokerage firm (Link Futures), has been a commodity pool operator, has day traded equities for several large day trading firms, and has become a well-respected author.

He currently is an independent trader trading mostly index futures. He is available for consultation and will begin giving seminars in 2008. For more information and to contact Marcel Link, visit MarcelLink.com.

Index